# THE AMERICAN INDIAN CRAFT BOOK

Marz and Nono Minor

*Illustrations and photographs by the authors*

UNIVERSITY OF NEBRASKA PRESS
LINCOLN AND LONDON

First Bison Book printing: 1978


**Library of Congress Cataloging in Publication Data**

Minor, Marz.
  The American Indian craft book.

  Includes index.
  1. Indian craft.  2. Indians of North America—Industries.  3.
Indians of North America—Social life and customs.  I.  Minor,
Nono, joint author.  II.  Title.
TT22.M56    1978        745        77–14075
ISBN 0–8032–0974–6
ISBN 0–8032–5891–7 pbk.


Bison Book edition published by arrangement with the authors.

☙

Manufactured in the United States of America

In memory of
KODA BU
whose name in the Santee Sioux dialect
roughly translates to
"Noisy Friend"

*FOREWORD*

The story of the American Indian is more than warpaint and feathers, though that is part of it. There is another side, just as important, which is apparent in the creativeness of their daily living. Contemplative, gentle, and metaphysical, the American Indian lived a love affair with nature. Their ancient wisdom shows in what they wore, how they made their clothing, in what they ate and how it was prepared, in the disciplining of their children and the warmth of their home life, in their methods of adapting to the environment and, especially, in their philosophy of life.

This is a book not only for reading, but for doing. Try making some of the things the Indians lived with, by following the diagrams and patterns given here. See how creative you can be, and in so doing come to better understand these first Americans.

Apology is made to the specialists who might disagree with the groupings of tribes and customs, or with some other aspect of this book. The Indians have called the white man's books "talking leaves," and this book is only one small leaf of the many that would be needed to tell the complete story of the American Indian.

To know a road, one must travel it. To know the taste of meat, one must chew it. To know a people, one must get acquainted. Perhaps this book will help you to do that, so that you will know the American Indian a little more truly.

M.M. and N.M.

## ACKNOWLEDGMENTS

The photographs in this book, unless otherwise noted, are from the Indian collection of the Kansas City Museum of History and Science, Kansas City, Missouri.

Grateful thanks are extended to the museum board, the director, and the staff for their helpfulness.

Many of the articles shown are from the famous Colonel Daniel B. Dyer collection of Indian artifacts now on display at the museum. The first showing of this collection was in 1887 at Kansas City's old Crystal Palace. In 1910 this remarkable collection was given to the Kansas City Board of Education for use by the people of the city, and as a nucleus for a public museum.

It is fitting that this collection came finally to be displayed in what was originally a seventy-two-room mansion situated high above the Missouri River, within sight of the Kansas City skyline. Built as a home by lumberman R. A. Long, it occupies a city block enclosed by stone columns and an ornamental iron fence. Deeded to the city in 1939, it became the Kansas City Museum of History and Science.

Along with the Indian collection, there is a costume wing, a natural history building, the Hall of Minerals, various rotating exhibits, a planetarium, a library for both reference and archival material, and daily classes in the museum rooms where schoolchildren not only see but also learn of the background of exhibits.

Guided by the museum association, this museum has evolved into an important educational and cultural landmark of the city.

MARZ AND NONO MINOR
Kansas City, Missouri

# CONTENTS

## LIST OF PHOTOGRAPHS

(Photographs by the authors; 35-mm. cameras, Panatomic-x and Tri-x film)

# INTRODUCTION

## *ABOUT A PEOPLE*

The general basic philosophy of the American Indian embraced all of nature. No man owns the land, it belongs to the Great Spirit and his children. Those who use the land must keep it clean and beautiful for those who will come after. No man owns the woods or the forest, the waters and the rivers, the soil or the earth. It belongs to all. Wild plants, trees, flowers, all belong to the Great Spirit and man must take care of them for him. No man owns the game and the animals, the fish in the waters, and he must take only what is needed. All who are old and sick or helpless have the right of protection of the tribe. All children, regardless of birth, have a place in the tribe.

There were no misfits, because everyone had work delegated to them, according to his skills. Children were generally loved, but were given duties which they had to learn, and which would be of help to them in later life. All had their place, no forgotten elders, no destitute widows or unloved orphan children. Every being, even the animals, were believed to be a part of the Great Spirit, and therefore important.

The Indians had no written language, so even the spelling of their names was not always the same. They were not only given names by other Indian tribes, but by the white settlers as well, and these were often very different from the names they gave themselves.

# ORIGINS

There is some dispute as to where these first Americans came from, but the most accepted theory as to their origin is that some fifteen thousand years ago these people came to this continent via the Bering Strait following the great herds of migrating animals. By the time Columbus had arrived at this new world, the natives of the country were living in scattered villages in all parts of the North and South America. There were an estimated 800,000 people, misnamed Indian, but they were as different and individual as the Europeans who settled here, or as the Asians, whose land they had left. Some of the Indians were lean with hawk-like features, others were heavy with broad, round features. Skin tones differed from light ivory to dark brown or bronze. Their hair was usually coarse and straight, but a few tribes had soft brown hair.

There were basic tribal or group characteristics as well as individual differences. Two things seemed general among the Indians: they were seldom bald and rarely left-handed. Most Indians had very little facial hair, and what they did have was plucked out by means of shells or wooden tweezers. This was often painful, but a smooth-faced man was attractive to the ladies. A few Indians living on the Northwest Coast might have a sparse beard or small moustache.

When the Indians migrated to this continent it is unlikely they brought seeds, as none of the plants cultivated here were known in the Old World except the gourd which is native to both America and Asia. The Indian gave the Old World, among many things, the potato, tobacco, corn, chocolate, and tomatoes. All these were cultivated in the Americas before 1492 and it is estimated that farming in this hemisphere began about 7000–5500 B.C.

The language or dialect spoken by these early people has been separated into language groups by historians, and the people classified into cultural areas according to the part of the country they lived in.

The Woodland people of the Northeast were mainly forest

16

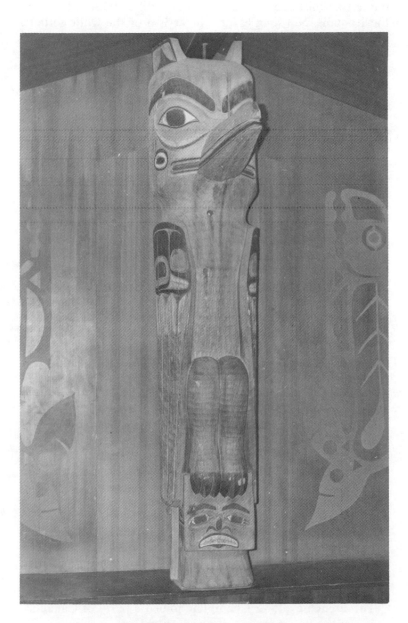

Carved totem pole from the Northwest Coast people.

hunters and fishermen. The most powerful of these tribes were the Iroquois. Not long before the arrival of the white settlers, the Indians of the Iroquoian tribe, in 1570, formed a League of the Iroquois. This was done by an Indian known as Deganawidah, a Huron living with the Iroquois, and by a Mohawk chief named Hiawatha.

Legend says that Deganawidah was born of a virgin mother and that he had a vision or inspired dream in which a huge evergreen tree was trying to reach the sky toward the Master of Life. This represented both the women and the men, or the sisterhood and the brotherhood, as this tribe was a matriarchal society. The roots were the five Iroquois tribes. It is also told how Deganawidah's mother and grandmother tried to drown the newborn baby by thrusting him through a hole in the ice. Three times this was attempted, but each morning the astonished mother found the baby in her arms. The name of Deganawidah had been spelled various ways, among them Dekanawida and Deganawida.

It is also told how Hiawatha paddled his canoe down all the lakes and rivers, visiting the tribes and preaching peace. He advocated many reforms and united the tribes for peace, as well as for war. According to the League of the Iroquois, each tribe was to maintain its own independence, but was to act for all the tribes for their common good. There could be no war until it was voted upon by the League. There was no written constitution within the League, but it had such fine rules that it was greatly admired even by the early colonists, and it is said that the Constitution of the United States was based upon this League of the Iroquois.

The Iroquois Confederacy was made up of the tribes of the Cayuga, Mohawk, Oneida, Onondaga, Seneca, and in 1722 was joined by the Tuscarora from the south, making it the Six Nations. The Iroquois was the name given the powerful confederation of these tribes.

The Iroquois fought their relatives, the Huron and Erie, but were stopped in the west by the Chippewas. They were driven back by the Cherokee in the south, and the French drove them back in the north, or they would have gained all the lands in their surrounding territory and become supreme rulers.

The French explorer Champlain joined a party of Canadian

Indians in battle against the Iroquois, and because of this during the French and Indian Wars the Iroquois joined the English. During the American Revolution the Iroquois League agreed to let each tribe decide if it wished to fight with the English or not. Only the Oneida and a few of the Tuscarora did not join the English.

The Woodland Indians first used the wampum beads or belt. Wampum is made up of *wamp*, meaning "white," and *umpe* or *ompe*, meaning "a string of white beads." Some of the shells, however, were made from the clams the Iroquois called *quayhon* or *qyayhen* which had a purple lip and a white inner part. Wampum was made from both the white and purple beads, and some were even striped. The white wampum was the most common and had less value.

The early wampum beads were made from shells shaped into beads with crude stone tools, the holes drilled in them with stone drills, then polished by rubbing them in the sand. When the Dutch arrived in Manhattan, they started using wampum beads as trade and made them in great quantities. Now they were made with hammer and chisel. Conch shells and other seashells were cut out and holes drilled in them. The beads were then strung on a wire, and the wire strings of shells put through a grindstone until the rough edges were ground away and the whole string of beads was rounded. They were polished and placed on a string about a foot long, usually fifteen to twenty beads on a string. Purple beads would be worth fifteen to twenty cents, the white about half that much. As the early Dutch and English had no small copper or silver coins, they used the wampum in trade with the Indians.

The Indians had first made the wampum into necklaces, armlets, headbands, pendants, and wrist bands, to be worn at religious ceremonies. They used only the white wampum, as white meant peace, good health, and all things good. The purple had the meaning of sorrow or anger, and a red bead, or the color red, signified war.

In the League of the Iroquois, every treaty or official act was accompanied by a strand of wampum beads or a wampum belt. The belt told, in picture, the story of the agreement entered into. These were woven by the women of the tribe and strung together on strings of vegetable fiber or leather. Both ends of the string were fastened to the ends of a bow to keep them tight. They were then woven into and around on the strand with a bone needle. After the design was woven, fringe from one to several feet long was added to the ends and the belt was completed. Sometimes colored beads were added to the ends of the belt and these also had special meaning.

No message from a council or tribe was considered binding unless accompanied by a wampum belt or a string of wampum beads. This was considered proof of good faith on the part of the tribe who sent the belt. The belt was handed over to the keeper of the records who put it in a special leather container for that purpose only.

In the League, all six tribes had their special duties. The Onondagas, or People of the Hills, were the Keepers of the Wampum, and the First Nation or tribe. The Mohawks, or Possessors of the Flint, were the Second Nation. The Oneidas, or People of the Stone, were the Third Nation. The Cayugas, or People of the Murkey Land, were clever hunters and were the Fourth Nation. The Seneca, or People of the Great Hills, were the Door Keepers and the Fifth Nation; and the Tuscaroras were the Sixth Nation.

Children followed the mother's clan, or family group, and in many cases a boy could not follow his father as chief, or even inherit a war club, and it was the women of the tribe who made the arrangement for marriages. Usually a girl was married to an older man who could provide for her, and a young man to an older woman, possibly a widow who had a corn field. The boy went into the wife's home.

In principle the League was for peace, prosperity, power, and equality for all, with the most important being peace. All matters of great importance had to be voted upon by the League and required a unanimous vote to pass.

The Indians of the Southeast were very unlike the northern tribes. Some tribes had their bodies heavily decorated. This was a form of tattooing done with a garfish jaw and soot of the camp fire. Each design was an official insignia and was started in boyhood, with each design telling of the man's exploits as he grew. A warrior might give the impression of wearing figured tights if seen from a distance, especially if he had accomplished great deeds or been in many battles. The women usually did not tattoo themselves, as they had no war honors. However, if a woman had done some great deed within the tribe she would be allowed a marking or scratching, as it was called.

The arrival of the white man in Florida and the Southwest spelled disaster to the tribes living there. Many were completely wiped out. The Natchez were met by De Soto when he marched through their land in 1542. The people of this tribe were sun worshippers and called their leader the Great Sun. De Soto claimed to be the younger brother of the sun, but when the Indians wanted him to use his power and dry up the Mississippi and he was unable to, he had to flee with his men down the Mississippi and into Mexico. Their leader, the Great Sun, was supreme, and only a few select elders and his wife and children could enter his cabin. He was carried about on a litter, at a fast pace, by relays of eight men, who without breaking step, passed the litter from one team of runners to another.

These tribes were mainly farming people who lived near their farmlands in houses grouped into larger settlements, somewhat like towns, with a council house in the public square.

It was from this section that the first Indian alphabet was developed. Sequoyah, the son of a white father and a Cherokee mother, developed the written alphabet and submitted it to the Cherokee nation in 1821. Within a few months after it had been accepted, thousands of Cherokee could read, and they soon had their own newspaper.

The Cherokee, Choctaws, Chicasaws, Creeks, and Seminoles were put down in government records as the Five Civilized Tribes. The Seminoles were not really a tribe, but an offshoot of the Creeks. The word *seminolay* in the Creek language means an outcast or runaway and was applied to any Indian, regardless of his tribe, when he had left the tribe for any reason. It was the runaway Creeks, Apalachees, and a few other members of now extinct tribes like the Caloosas of southern Florida, who gathered together to form a band known as the Seminoles. They speak the Creek tongue, but strangely the Creeks were their most bitter enemies.

The road to fame for every Creek boy was the warpath, and

a boy was called a baby name until he had gone on his first warpath or had his first scratching. There were some boys of gentle nature who did not like war; in this case they were permitted to wear women's clothing and work with the women. They could never gain fame, but neither were they reproached for their choice.

The Five Civilized Tribes were formed as a federation in 1859 and given territory west of the Mississippi. Their combined population at that time was 84,507 and they were given acreage of about 230 acres for each man, woman, and child.

The ever expanding spread of the settlers forced these people back, and in 1820 to 1839 the United States government forced the remaining tribes to a new home west of the Mississippi into what is now Oklahoma. This lasted from 1838 to 1839 and the long bitter trek made by many old and very young was known as the "Trail of Tears." Over half of the tribes died on this bitter march.

The most common conception of the Indian is that of the Plains Indian with his spreading eagle headdress, his buckskin and tipi, the buffalo hunters of the prairie. However, not all of these plains people lived in skin tipis; some tribes had permanent homes made of earth.

The Pawnee lived in earth lodges and believed that the sun was the giver of life and gave blessing to Mother Corn. However, after the arrival of the horse their life changed, as it did for other tribes who obtained horses.

In 1832 mule trains carried trade goods over the Santa Fe Trail, and the Kiowa and Comanche, who had been enemies, joined forces and made a game of raiding the wagon trains. Soon silver was added to the decoration on their costumes and their horses. Bright kerchiefs and mirrors became a part of their dress. The mirrors were also found to be useful in signaling.

In 1851 the Indians around Fort Laramie, Wyoming, were offered a promise of annuities of $50,000 a year for the next fifteen years if they would allow roads and military posts within their country. Then boundaries were set for each tribe and they were to stay within them. Two years later a similar arrangement was made with the southern tribes, but they were offered only $18,000 yearly.

To the white man this was a step toward peace, or so he felt, but to the Indian it meant a struggle to the end. Each fort meant more soldiers, more traders, and more hunters. Soon hunting became a pastime and the great herds of buffalo were killed in alarming numbers by the white hunters who killed for sport. Soon the livelihood of the Plains Indians began to vanish.

The Indians petitioned Washington not to allow liquor to be brought into their country, as it was being used unscrupulously in trading. A law was passed to this effect, but traders and others had visions of getting rich through the sale of liquor to the Indians, and the law was disregarded. Next came the settlers seeking land, and after the Civil War hundreds of soldiers who were discharged came looking for a new life in the western lands. Some men joined the army because they were fighting men, and it wasn't uncommon that when the Indians gathered for their own tribal ceremonies, the soldiers would stop and scatter them, creating confusion and ill-will.

The Basin–Plateau tribes represent many different racial groups, with many of these not found in any part of the country. For example, Kutenay, which included the Flatheads, were a race by themselves. The people of this area had the fish-hook and net over 4,000 years ago, and also a type of duck decoy. Agriculture was not generally practiced in this area, and small bands roamed about the territory. They were organized into family units of twenty-five to thirty people, guided by an elder of the tribe who was known as the "talker." During the winter two or fifteen groups might share a valley, where they had put a store of food the previous year. Some families returned to the same place each year, others moved to new locations each winter.

It was practical to take two wives and a woman often had two husbands. The Basin people rarely saw a white man until the mid-1840's when trappers and explorers passed through their land. In 1843 Frémont opened the route from the Oregon Trail through the Basin to upper California. The passage of the wagon trains offered the Indian access to coffee, flour, and sugar.

Among these tribes a woman could have a vision dream and become a medicine woman. Vision quests were not important to a girl, however; all she really had to do was to be a good wife. If she did have a strong dream, in which she could heal those attacked by a witch, she was considered to have special powers.

When gold was discovered in California, the traffic through the territory was constant, and in 1847 when deposits of silver were discovered in Nevada, people poured into the territory overnight. Ironically in a country where the Indian had almost starved, millionaires were made almost instantly.

The tribes of the Northwest Coast raised little, other than tobacco. Food was from the sea, with a few roots and berries. The people of this area made excellent homes of massive fitted timbers and boards split from cedar logs. There were a number of language groups in this area, and these were the people of the totems.

The totem poles were carved cedar posts which showed animals and the family coat of arms of the tribe, all brilliantly painted. Their early blankets were of otter fur, and later of wool. They had obtained copper from the Canadian Indians and iron. The men wore a type of armor and a helmet; they also wore basket hats. These people were imaginative and skilled woodworkers and their work was very functional.

Between the years 1774 and 1794 hundreds of ships reached the Northwest Coast bringing tools of iron, and the carving of the totems became a real art. Ships trading along the coast in 1785 and 1795 had crews of Chinese, Hawaiian, and others who jumped ship and lived among the Indians. Some of the adventurous Indians would join the crew and return with tales of the lands beyond.

The Salish Indians living on Puget Sound wove blankets on a loom, which was not used by any other tribe in this area. It was very simple, with roller top and bottom, but made differently from the looms of the Southwest. The warp was of goat wool and the weft of white fluff as thick as a finger. This was made from mountain goat and dog wool. Herds of small white dogs were owned by the women who kept them separate from the other dogs and drove them about like sheep.

Among the Yuroks of California, the chief did not gain his position by bravery in war or even by reason of inheritance or election; he was simply the richest man in the tribe. He owned the biggest dwelling, in which most of his relatives lived. Should his wealth be lost, his position was also lost. Wealth consisted of blankets, baskets, shells, skins, and dried fish, also a peculiarly shaped copper plate. The prize object was the skin of an albino deer.

The Indians of Southern California had a total of 104 dialects. The early Spanish told of how they could not travel more than a couple of hours without running into a tribe speaking another new language. The tribes were small, the largest number being about 1,000 people, and some as little as one hundred. Many of these Indians later became known as Mission Indians, having been brought together under the Franciscan Fathers, when missions were established in 1769. When the missions were disbanded after California became a part of the United States, many of these Indians were left destitute. They no longer knew their old ways and could not live on their own. Some of these tribes died from starvation, others joined other Indian tribes. The California Indians were a peaceful people, but could be fierce fighters when their land was invaded. The pottery of these people was rather crude, but they made a small, brilliantly colored basket of feathers and shells which was a work of art. When the Spanish first contacted these tribes in the seventeenth century, they said the women were very beautiful, with many of the children fair and almost blond.

The Southwest tribes still live today much as they always have, particularly the Pueblos. Their way of life has changed little in the 400 years since the Spanish passed through looking for Cibola, the seven cities of gold. This is an ancient civilization, over 1,350 years old. These people are skilled potters and excellent weavers, as they were before the Spanish came.

In 1540 when the Spanish came seeking the seven cities of gold, it was the first contact the Indians of this area had with the horse. At first they believed the horse and rider were one. This, plus the fact that the men wore a shiny cloth through which no arrow could pass, made the Indians very fearful, until the Spanish began to sicken and die, soon becoming too ill to travel, so that they had to turn back the way they had come. But other Spanish came, this time not for gold but for land. They took the best land, leaving the Indian the poorest land on which he was barely able to raise enough food to survive.

The Pueblos had learned how to irrigate their dry land and raised corn, pumpkins, melons, gourds, and cotton. In this area the men took care of the fields and did most of the weaving. They would twist the cotton into thread and weave it into clothing in underground ceremonial rooms called kivas, from which women and children were barred. It was believed that it was in the kiva that the first man entered into the world from the undeground.

Dry land farming was done among the Hopi and Zuñi. Their gardens were located at the mouths of washes to take advantage of the rains. Among the Hopi and Zuñi there was little to marriage, and divorce was simple. The wife would set her husband's things outside the house and the man knew this was no longer his home. The Hopi father was sent away from the home at the time of childbirth, and after twenty days the child was presented to the father and at that time given a name.

The Navaho and the Apache were newcomers to the desert land; these tribes broke away from their own family group in the northwest of the United States, perhaps because of food shortages or wars. Some reached this land of the desert around A. D. 1000 and surely by 1550. The Pueblo taught the Navaho weaving, but much of their history is obscure until 1600 when the Navaho hogans were found scattered near streams and on the ledges above them. These were called *Dinetkah*, or "Home of the People." The Navaho believed that if a person died inside a hogan or Navaho home the home must be destroyed to rid it of evil spirits. Ill people are taken outside the hogan, so their spirit can be in the free air, and the hogan will not be entered by bad spirits. There were a vast number of spirits in the legends of the Navaho, and the desire of the Navaho was to keep his life in harmony with the universe and the higher powers.

The Apache name is derived from Zuñi meaning "enemy," for the Apache were fierce warriors. Both the Navaho and Apache had the mother-in-law taboo, and no son-in-law could look at, or speak to, his mother-in-law. Because of this, the mothers-in-law wore small silver bells in their ears to warn of their approach.

26

The leader of the Apache, Geronimo, was captured and his people sent first to Florida, then to Alabama, and finally to Oklahoma. This was the Chiracahua band.

The Spanish offered bounty for the scalp of the Apache, and would steal their children to sell in Mexico.

The Pimas living in this area were farmers; after the arrival of the Spanish they added wheat and alfalfa to their crops. In their battles with the Apache, they never took a man prisoner but spared the women and children by adopting them into their tribe. Also they never scalped their enemies, as they felt all enemies, and especially the Apache, possessed an evil spirit and they would not touch one after death. The Pima women were expert basket makers.

From this varied ancestral background came the people called Indian. Even though this single name applies to all, they are as different and individual as any other group of people, with different racial characteristics, languages, and customs. When one can look beyond the name to the individual, and not accept the stereotypes as truth, then one can begin to learn about a people.

# PART I

# CLOTHING AND
# PERSONAL ADORNMENT

*(Crafts begin on page 49)*

Fashions among the American Indians varied throughout the tribes, but basically Indian clothing was divided into three types; everyday clothing, which was practical and plain; war attire with special decorations; and ceremonial dress, usually heavily ornamented and symbolic. Their clothing came from nature—plants woven into fabric, wool from goats and sheep, feathers from birds, and the hide of animals. The Indians, although superb hunters and fishermen, did not waste nature's bounty. Nothing was taken that was not needed for food, shelter, or clothing. An Indian woman was not only an artist in the dressing of the skins, but in how the skin was worked and cut to prevent waste. Every bit of hide was used, and everything left over from the cutting of large garments, such as dresses and shirts, was utilized for moccasins, pouches, bags, small items, and fringe, with the very small strips saved for lacings.

Sewing was done by both men and women, although it was usually the woman's task. However, men did the sewing on certain types of war and ceremonial items, which it was sometimes considered unlucky for women to touch. Sinew from the tendons of large animals served as thread, as did the fiber of small plants, especially the agave. Bone awls, which punched holes for the thread or thongs to be pushed through, were used in fine sewing, as bone needles were often too large.

CREE CHILD JACKET (Back view)
The buckskin jacket is made in the Woodland floral design and has the American flag beaded on each shoulder. The colors are red, blue, yellow, green, and black. There is fringe down the back of the sleeves and around the bottom. Note the eagle feather and a turkey feather attached to the shoulder.

# MOCCASINS

Moccasins, in some form, were worn by almost all tribes, with the style the same for men, women, and children. However, there were tribal differences in decorating which was done with dye, beads, quills, fur, and fringe. It was believed that moccasins must be made beautiful, because the foot should be as lovely as the flowers and grasses it walked upon. The earth must see that the Indian was not unmindful of her.

Although generally similar in appearance, the moccasins of each tribe were cut or sewed in slightly different ways and these small differences were a clue to the wearer's tribe. The northern Athapascan moccasin track revealed a T-shaped seam at the toe and heel. The Plains Indian made a hard, flat-soled track, and the Woodland Indian left a more soft, rounded sole track. The moccasins of the Nez Perce had seams along the side from the big toe to the heel. The Cheyenne Indian might leave a tattletale mark—a little tail or fringe added in the back seam of the moccasin—because a man who had won many honors might add the tail of a small animal to his footgear.

To deceive an enemy, or when going on the warpath, an Omaha Plains Indian would wear the moccasins of another tribe. Usually, though, Indians did not wear the footgear of another tribe, as it was felt that to wear the moccasins of another tribe was to accept its laws and customs and give up one's own tribe with its personal ties. This was especially true among the Iroquois nation. Prisoners intended for adoption were given the moccasins of their captors to wear so that their feet might tread the new path.

As moccasins quickly took up moisture, in wet weather or when traveling across boggy ground it was necessary to wear an over-moccasin. This was to protect the moccasins and keep them clean. These over-moccasins served as a kind of over-shoe and were at times soaked in oil and filled with buffalo skin to keep the feet dry and warm. In the winter, moccasins were often made of buffalo or bear pelt, and fashioned with the fur side inside. Among the Woodland Indians boots of moosehide with the hair on the outside were worn over the moccasins in winter. These were made from a section of skin of the animal's hind leg, where the hock bends so that the boot came with an almost readymade heel. In this area, moccasins were stuffed with deer hair or cattail fluff, to add warmth for winter.

The Apache people designed their moccasins with long legs, stiff rawhide soles, and turned-up toes. The turned-up toe protected the foot from being pierced by cactus thorns, and the long legging-like uppers kept out the sand and also protected the legs from the bite of the rattlesnake.

In ancient times the Hopi wove and wore sandals of yucca fiber, but when they found moccasins were better for running, they adopted them. The woman's moccasins required a whole deerhide, cut in half diagonally. Actually these were moccasins plus leggings, the hide being wrapped around the leg until it looked thick, which was a mark of beauty among the Hopi women. Every young Hopi bride had to have a pair of these, and the thicker the wrapping of hide the better.

The moccasin was one of the first items of Indian dress copied by the white man. The early French explorers found their stiff-soled boots unsuited for woodland traveling by canoe and snowshoe. Frontiersmen, trappers, and scouts found moccasins to be the most suitable footgear for life on the plains and in the woods. At times, they too, like the Indians, found it advantageous to add heavy fringe around their moccasins in order to obliterate their tracks as they walked.

Among some tribes, children's moccasins, even new ones, would be found to have holes in the soles. This was done so that evil spirits, seeing the moccasins were unfit for travel, would not harm or kidnap the children.

Sometimes moccasins are seen with heavily beaded soles. These were generally burial moccasins. Dolls sometimes have the soles of their costume moccasins beaded; this indicates that the doll belonged to a child who had died very young, and would never walk the beautiful earth.

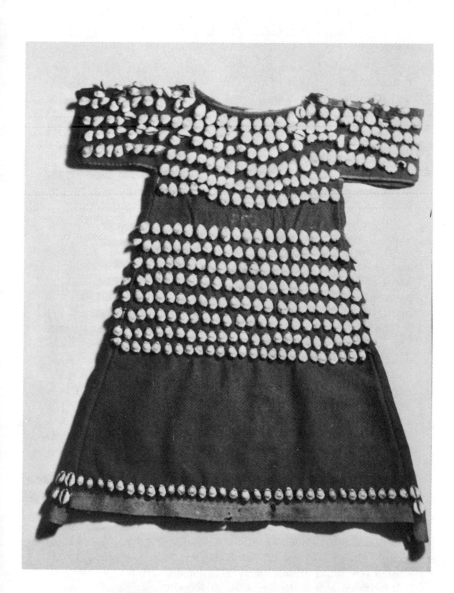

**CHEYENNE BLANKET DRESS**
A child's red dress decorated with cowrie shells.

# DRESSES AND SHIRTS

The most widely copied and perhaps the best known of all Indian dress was that of the Great Plains: the heavily beaded and ornamented buckskin dress of the women, and the great sweeping feathered headdress of the men, with their fringed and beaded buckskin shirts and leggings. This costume still typifies the Indian to some people, yet many Plains Indians never dressed like this. Perhaps a woman could not bead well enough to decorate her dress in this way and so used fringe or other trimmings, or a man might never win enough honors to be allowed to wear the great eagle-feather headdress.

Preparation of the buffalo hide for making clothing was done in groups, somewhat like our old-fashioned quilting bees or sewing circles. As the women tanned the hide they chatted and gossiped about camp life and the antics of the children. Most of the dresses were made from soft-tanned elk or buffalo hide and extended from the shoulder to the ankles. Later the dresses were made shorter, to the calf and even the knee.

The Woodland women wore a skirt and blouse type of dress, and also a dress much like the one the Plains Indians wore. These were of skin and later of trade goods fabrics. Their daily clothes were for cover-up with little sewing done on the garment. Excess ends and edges were merely cut into fringe and this was the only decoration on their working clothes. The ancient one-piece dress, tied at the shoulders and held in with a belt, barely overlapped at the sides, especially on the left side. This allowed the thigh to be readily bared for rolling fibers against it to make twine.

When broadcloth and velvet became available to these Woodland tribes during the latter part of the seventeenth century, the women started making clothing from these rich fabrics. They favored colors of dark red or wine, dark blue and black. These new clothes were beautifully decorated with ribbon and beadwork of floral design, and were usually intended for social or ceremonial occasions.

The later Seminole dress is perhaps the most colorful of

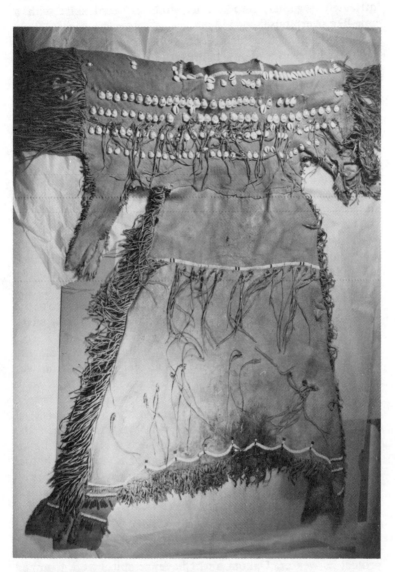

**OLD-TYPE DRESS—tribe unknown**
A buckskin Plains dress showing the old-style use of the skins. The dress is decorated with cowrie shells and beads, as well as fringe and tin cone jinglers at the hemline.

all, being made up of bits and pieces of colored cotton stitched intricately together, into a long, full, gathered skirt with a cape-like overblouse.

The women of the Pueblo tribes wove cotton and from this they made their one-shoulder dresses held with a sash wrapped many times around the waist. Much of the cloth was dyed blue from dye extracted from the sunflower seed.

The Apache woman quickly changed her work dress, which was a long, plain deerskin dress made much like the Plains dress, into a formal costume by adding a sort of shawl collar. This was a horizontal cape collar longer over the arms than in the front and back. The ends over the hands were often fringed, and as these people were skilled in the art of painting, these cape collars were beautifully painted. A silver belt was added to hold the dress tight.

The Navaho women, after contact with the settlers, and possibly because animal skin became scarce, changed from their old buckskin dresses to the cotton skirt and velveteen top still worn today.

The shirt of the Navaho man was made similar to the woman's, but while hers might be tucked into her skirt, the Navaho man wore his as an overblouse, belted with a silver belt.

Generally the shirt of the Indian was of two types: the everyday shirt worn for cover-up and warmth, and the war or ceremonial shirt worn only on occasion. The shirts were different not in style, but in decoration.

The war shirt was one of the most important items of Indian dress. Actually it was not worn in battle, when the wearing of any shirt could be a hindrance to a man in hand-to-hand combat. It was usually worn after a victorious battle, and then only by those who had the authority and honors to wear this sacred bit of apparel; generally they were the chiefs and older warriors. These shirts were heavily fringed, beaded, embroidered, or painted, and the symbols told of the heroic deeds of the owner. Trimmed with hair or weasel skin, the shirt was considered to have great medicine, or to be able to protect its wearer. Dakota and Cheyenne shirts were trimmed with hair, while the Blackfoot and Crow Indians preferred white weasel skin in place of hair fringe. These were some times mistakenly called "scalp shirts" by the white men, because of the belief that the hair on the shirt was that of enemy scalps. More often the hair was from the man's own head, or a bit of his wife's hair. Each lock meant a coup, or act of bravery, won by capturing a horse, taking a prisoner, getting wounded, or saving a life in battle, much like our Purple Heart and other medals.

In winter the Iroquois wore knee-length shirts usually made of two hides sewn over the shoulders and up the sides, somewhat like the woman's dress. The sides were fringed, with the fringe carried over the shoulders. The bottom of the shirt was also fringed and simply decorated with quill or beads. Later the Woodland Indians adapted this shirt to the new fabric, velvet, and embroidered or beaded it in place of fringe.

The Apache war shirt was somewhat like a poncho. It was made by folding a large skin in half and cutting an opening in the center of the fold for the head. This was draped over the shoulder like a cape, forming wide sleeves. Fringe was added for decoration along the bottom and across the chest.

In early days, the Seminole tattooed their bodies so elaborately they hardly needed a cover-up shirt. When a boy was given his first name, a small mark called a scratching was made on his body. When he first accompanied the warriors to learn the art of warfare he was given a second name and more tattoos. By the time he reached middle age, he was decorated from his ears to his toes. With the coming of trade cloth, the tattooing disappeared, and a jacket blouse was used instead.

The Northwest Coast Indian shirts were sleeveless and were outstanding because of the typical designs used. (See Part V, Arts, Decorations, and Symbolism.)

## LEGGINGS AND BREECHCLOTHS

Leggings were an article of clothing worn by both men and women, and usually the design matched the moccasins. The man's reached from the ankle to the hip, while those of the woman came only to her knees. Among the tribes in the West, the cloth or skin of the leggings projected beyond the seams on the outer side and was cut either into a triangular flap or fringed. The eastern tribes had the seam up the front with no flaps or fringe which might catch on bushes while traveling through the woods. Old-style leggings were made of skin and reached above the knee. The lower portion was heavily decorated with beads or quill, and fit the legs as tightly as possible. These leggings were split above the knee and were tied onto the breechcloth belt, or were tied about the legs.

Among Indian men the universal garb was the breechcloth, also spelled breechclout, and a belt or sash. When a boy was a few days old a belt or soft tie was placed about his waist or hips to accustom him to the later wearing of a breechcloth. While at home usually only a breechcloth and moccasins were worn. The shirt and leggings were added for warmth when away from home, or for ceremony. At times a robe was added. The breechcloth was a length of soft buckskin or fabric about a foot wide and six feet long. The early settlers called this "Indian breeches." The breechcloth passed between the legs and was tucked under a belt in the front and back. The ends hung down from the belt like narrow aprons and these ends were often heavily decorated.

The Woodland Indians wore a smaller type of leather breechcloth under aprons which were about eighteen to twenty inches square and tied together at the hips. These were usually made to match the leggings and moccasins with floral designs in beads or embroidery. The aprons were later made of the dark shades of velvet so favored by the Woodland people.

## VESTS, CAPES, AND ROBES

The vest was one item of Indian clothing believed to be adopted from the white man. These were made from hide and decorated with quill, beads, or paint. Later cloth was used for making the vest. Since they were elaborately decorated, they generally were worn as a bit of ornamental costume.

Another article worn sometimes for warmth but as often for

SIOUX MAN'S VEST
The vest is beaded on buckskin in the Lazy Stitch and has fringe around the bottom. The beads are white, dark blue, and yellow. The inside shows rows where stitching is caught between the buckskin.

ornament or decoration was the cape or blanket robe. In winter, many of the Plains Indians wore fur capes made from the pelt of the coyote, otter, or badger. A painted buffalo robe was highly prized; in winter it was worn with the fur inside, and in warmer weather it was worn tied about the waist or over one shoulder. Both men and women wore blanket robes, and in the case of the men, these were often painted with the deeds of the wearer. The way a man wore his robe could also tell a story. In many tribes the robe was a status symbol, as well as a means of keeping warm. The robe could be worn with the neck section of the hide under the wearer's arm, or it could be worn loose. When stopping for a chat, if the wearer changed the position of his robe it could indicate he was getting impatient. A young man might wear his robe over his head to hide from a girl, or he might sit outside her home wrapped in his robe, in hopes she would come join him. If she too slipped under the robe, it was a sign his love was returned and they were considered engaged. Young children had robes and these also were painted to tell of the small deeds of the child. When traveling, an Indian might roll the robe and carry it on his shoulder. Another use for the robe, aside from serving as wearing apparel, was to send signals from one Indian to another.

Some of the western tribes had robes of woven rabbit hair. Among the desert tribes rabbit skin blankets were worn against the desert chill.

The Basin–Plateau people made capes of the feathers and skin of ducks; the hide of the woodchuck with its long fur also made a warm robe. The men wore their cape of skins as a tunic, belted at the waist or wrapped around as a form of kilt.

The Northwest Indians, especially the Chilkat, made a blanket robe of woven bark and mountain sheep wool which was coveted by all the coast tribes. These robes were usually kept for ceremonial wear. They were decorated with black, blue, or green and yellow designs of totem motifs, very geometric and formal in style, with a long, shimmery fringe of goat hair.

Indians were very wise in using what was at hand. To rid their clothing of troublesome insects, they simply left it on an ant hill for a day or two. To mothproof their pelts and furs they dried the body of a bird, usually the martin or kingfisher, then pounded it into a fine powder, and sprinkled it over and among the furs.

## HAIR STYLES

Like all people of the world, Indians were very proud of their hair, probably because it was luxuriant. They believed that somehow the hair was connected with the great mystery of life, and they were always careful not to let any of their hair fall into enemy hands. Should someone get another's hair, even a small bit of it, the person could be harmed, so all combings were carefully burned.

Few Indians suffered from baldness, and both men and women took great care of their hair. Bear grease or fat was a favorite dressing, and the men would at times mix soot with the grease to make the hair seem blacker. Their hair had a glossy, bluish or brownish black look, but it would become bleached by the sun, taking on a rusty hue.

The tribes of the East Coast cut their hair close on the sides leaving a ridge from the forehead to the back of the neck. The top was then trimmed like a pompadour. The scalp lock was allowed to grow long and was braided down the back, then decorated with shells or other ornaments. At times the ridge on the top was decorated with a roach of deer bristles which had been dyed red.

The men of the Woodland Indians wore their hair in several ways, depending upon the tribe and personal taste. Some wore their hair full length in braids, others wore it unbraided and bound into two bunches on each side of the head. Still others cut their hair into a roach. In this style, most of the hair was cut and the head was plucked bare with only a strip of hair about two inches wide left from front to back. The scalp lock was left long at the crown of the head in the middle of the roach. At times the scalp lock hung loose, at other times it was braided, and sometimes it stood up on top of the head.

Seminole women wore their hair long, but the men had several styles. One favorite style was to cut the hair short around the crown, then comb the rest of the long hair upward,

43

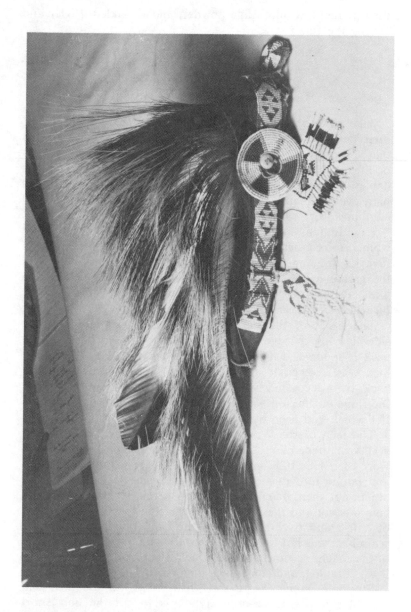

**SIOUX ROACH HEADDRESS**
A dyed red horsehair and feather attached to an elaborately beaded
headband.

and tie it together at the top of the head. A bird feather or animal tail was then added to this. Some men shaved their heads or plucked the hair out in different patterns.

The Pawnee had a ridge from forehead to crown, the scalp lock separated in a small circle. The hair was parted and stiffened with grease and paint, making it stand up like a horn.

The Dakota wore his hair in two braids, often painting the center part red, and adding horsehair to lengthen the braids.

The Nez Perce and others of the far western tribes wore their hair long and unbraided.

The Pueblo Hopi men cut their hair straight across the forehead, in a form of bang. For ceremonies they wore wigs of black wool and bangs of dyed horsehair. Before marriage, Hopi girls dressed their hair in two big circles on each side of the head in the form of a squash flower, putting it in a single braid after they were married.

In some tribes, when mourning for the dead, the hair was worn loose, and in others it was cut off. Many tribes wore false hair at times.

## HEADDRESSES

Before the arrival of the white man, many Indian tribes could be identified by their headgear, as each tribe had its own distinct type. The best-known headdress is the spreading eagle feathered headdress of the Sioux, which is seen on pictures of Indians from the Seminoles to the Apache. The headdress could be made from feathers, cloth, animal horns, or pelts, and the way it was made, the number of feathers, or what was used often told of a man's bravery and the honors he had won. The Omaha wore a roach made of deer's tail dyed red to designate honors won. A winter fur hat that was a ring of fur decorated with a feather was worn by some of the Plains tribes. The Cheyenne wore a buffalo horn bonnet during some of their ceremonies.

Many braves wore a single eagle feather. One way to wear it was to stand it upright from the back of the head, another was to place it straight at the side of the face, the tip of the

PLAINS GARTERS

**CHILD'S BELT—Plains tribe unknown (Side view)**
Little leather, studded belt about 8 inches in diameter with dangles
of strike-a-light bag fetish, chain, key and piece of metal, and
amulet holding umbilical cord. The small bags are decorated with
tin cone jinglers and are elaborately beaded.

quill sticking into the braiding of the hair. A feather often hung from the man's right braid, and if more than one was worn it indicated honors. Sometimes a fan-shaped cluster of feathers was placed at the back of the head pointing downward and to the right. Headbands of quill work or beadwork were also worn. These passed around the back of the head from ear to ear and were held in place by a narrow buckskin thong across the forehead. At the point where the beadwork joined the thong a beaded rosette held the band.

The Woodland men wore a unique cover-up cap or hat. It was a type of skullcap which was made on a frame and entirely covered with rows of small overlapping feathers. Variations were made by covering the frame with feathers and embroidery or beading, or with feathers and fur, or all fur. Standing erect on the crown of the cap was a short tube of bone, holding a feather which rotated as the wearer walked.

Most of the eastern tribes didn't wear the feathers that the Plains tribes did, but a man might wear a feather of acknowledgment for bravery. This could be worn at whatever angle he pleased.

Both the Woodland and Plains Indians had a form of winter cap or hood. Made of skin or cloth, it covered the neck and extended over the face, protecting the wearer from rain and snow. This was usually decorated with feathers or beading and embroidery.

The people of the Northwest Coast wove a broad-brimmed basketry hat which shed rain.

## JEWELRY AND DECORATIONS

Most of the tribes had some kind of personal adornment in the form of jewelry and, in some cases, tattooing of the skin. With the Indians as with everyone else, vanity played a part in their life, and in many cases this seemed more pronounced among the men.

Where the people had to wear more clothing for warmth and were quite bundled up, they had little room for jewelry other than nose or ear ornaments.

Beads made from small shells were common. These have been carelessly called "wampum," but the real wampum were small cylindrical beads made of the white and purple part of clam shells by the Iroquois, and later translated into the European term for money. Beads could be made from bone, stone, animal or bird claws, pine nuts, seeds, parts of hoof, fish vertebrae, quills of the porcupine, and pieces of gold, silver, or copper in the form of coins and spent gun shells. With the arrival of the white man came trade beads of glass, which were then used in place of quill.

The most widely known of Indian jewelry is that of the Southwest Indian with their silver and turquoise necklaces and silver belts. Bracelets and knee bands of beads and quill were common items. Indian women had small pouches or make-up kits for their face paint. These were a proud and independent people of great inventive- and creativeness, and their clothing and personal adornment reflected it.

## INDIAN MOCCASINS (Soft-Soled Type)

This moccasin, worn by the Woodland Indians, and sometimes by the Plains Indians, is easily constructed. It can be made from suede, buckskin, leather, leather-look, or suede-look materials, as well as from felt or heavy wool. However, it is best to make a pattern before cutting into leather.

A paper pattern can be made, but it might be easier to fit a pattern made of an old piece of material such as an old sheet or pillow case, or any muslin-type material that can be marked on. This pattern can be quickly stitched together and tried for fit, then the stitches pulled out, the material pressed flat, and your pattern is ready to be used.

The material should be large enough to fold over in the middle lengthwise, as shown in Diagram 1, and the bare foot placed as in Diagram 2. Mark a line ½ inch from the fold line and 1 inch from the bottom, and place your bare foot against this as shown in Diagram 2, then draw a curved line ½ inch from the big toe tip and ½ inch from the widest part of the foot, which is at the base of the toes or the ball of the foot. Continue the curved line from the wide part of the foot

# INDIAN MOCCASINS (Soft-Soled Type)
Pattern for right foot—reverse it for the left foot

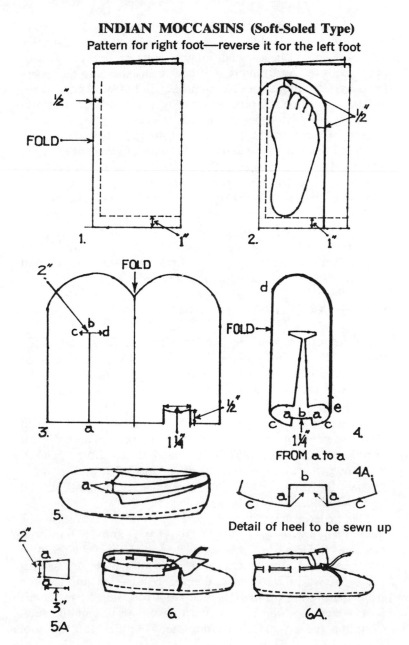

FROM a to a

Detail of heel to be sewn up

straight down to the bottom of the material. Unfold the material and lay it flat as in Diagram 3. On the right side, place your foot on the center of the right fold ½ to ¾ inch in from the bottom. Mark this and draw a curved line around the back of your heel about 1¼ inches. On the left side mark where your instep comes at approximately $b$ on Diagram 3. This is how far up your foot the moccasin will come and where the tongue (5A) will be placed. Make a line here ($c$–$d$), 2 inches long; this will be approximately 4 to 5 inches from the toe-tip of the material. Draw a line from the center of $c$–$d$ to the heel, as shown on Diagram 3 as $b$–$a$. Now turn this material wrong-side out, so the lines you have just drawn are on the outside and sew the material together around the toe and straight down to the heel. When sewing, use a darning needle and strong linen thread which can be waxed. Your neighborhood shoemaker may have shoemaker linen and wax that you can buy for this. For some leather it may be necessary to get an awl and punch holes around the edges and then sew through these. After the edge is sewn together, turn right-side out and cut the line $a$–$b$, slipping your right foot inside as you cut. In this way you can be sure as to how far you are cutting. Next cut the line $c$–$d$ across the instep. Your moccasin will now look like the one in Diagram 4. Now in the same manner, sew up the heel. See Diagram 4A. Each side of the heel marked $a$ should be sewn to $b$ from the corner to the center, then sew the back of the heel marked $c$ from the bottom of the heel up toward the ankle. Be sure you have again turned the moccasin wrong-side out so the stitching will be on the inside. At this point some adjustments can be made, if necessary. Before turning the moccasin wrong-side out and stitching it, slip your foot into it and pull the heel together. If the moccasin seems large you can pinch the material together, marking it with a sharp pencil, and cut off the extra, following the original outline, then sew it up.

Your moccasin should now look like the one in Diagram 5. Cut a piece of material for a tongue, approximately 2 inches by 3 inches; see Diagram 5A. Sew this to your moccasin from $a$–$a$ in Diagram 5. Next cut slits in the upper flap part of the moccasin so a thong or lace can be pulled through this and tied under the tongue. (See Diagram 6A.) This pulls the moccasin tight to the foot and holds it on. Your moccasin is now finished for the right foot. To make the left one, reverse the pattern. To see how the left foot pattern will look, hold this pattern for the right foot up to the mirror and you will see it in reverse, or for the left foot.

## INDIAN MOCCASINS (Puckered Type)

This type of moccasin was a favorite of the Woodland Indians; in fact the Chippewa's name is derived from these mocassins—it means "People of the puckered moccasin." Your foot serves as the pattern for these—either foot, as there is no right or left. One pattern fits both. Put your bare foot on the material as in Diagram 1 and draw an outline. Measure 2 inches from the toe and each side of the wide part, or ball of the foot. Draw a circle around the upper part of the foot halfway down the material from *a* to *a,* then measure out another 2 inches from *a* to *b* and straight down to *c*. Next clip ½ inch from the bottom and 1¼ inches apart where the back of the heel would come at *d* on Diagram 1. Cut another half circle, see Diagram 2, one half the length of the other piece, or the length of the toe end around to *a* on Diagram 1. To get the correct width of this piece, measure around the ball of the foot, or the widest part. Use a tape measure, a ribbon, or a piece of string. Stand on it and bring it up around your foot. The width of Diagram 2 should then be a little less than one third of this measure. Place the large and small pieces edge to edge, as in Diagram 3, and sew them together. The distance around the larger or bottom piece is almost twice as long as that of the small top, so the bottom piece must be puckered every quarter inch. Take a stitch through the bottom piece twice the length of the corresponding stitch in the small top. This will cause the larger piece to pucker, and if done correctly the two sides will have the same number of stitches when finished. When the stitching is pulled tight the bottom will pucker up over the side of the foot, forming the toe of the moccasin as in Diagram 3A.

Cut small slits in the wide part of the bottom piece (see *e* in Diagram 1). These will later be used to lace a thong through and for the moccasin tie. Sew up the heel now (Dia-

# INDIAN MOCCASINS (Puckered Type)

**One pattern fits either foot**

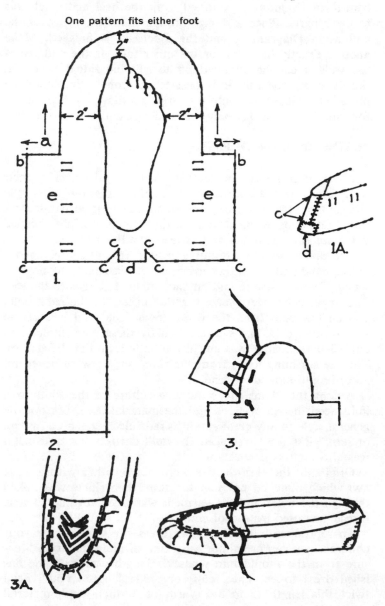

1.

1A.

2.

3.

3A.

4.

gram 1A) by stitching the *c* or bottom part together, then trim *d,* of Diagram 1, rounded to fit the heel and stitch this to the *c* parts. Place a thong through the slits, turn over the cuff as in Diagram 4, and the moccasin is finished. Make another exactly like this for the other foot. If the cuff seems too wide it cán be trimmed off to suit individual taste. On this type of moccasin it is best to embroider the small toe piece before it is sewn onto the larger bottom part. See Part V for samples of various patterns, and instructions for beading.

## PLAINS INDIAN DRESSES

These dresses were made from soft tanned elk skin, their style following the natural shape of the skins and with little change from tribe to tribe, other than individual tribal decorations. Some of these dresses with their beautifully beaded yokes weighed as much as fourteen or fifteen pounds.

The dress was cut without a pattern to suit individual requirements, and in cutting every effort was made to prevent waste. Two skins were laid on each other, tail ends to the top. The upper edges were sewn together except at the neck hole; and on the sides from the waist down. The hind legs of the skin formed cape-like sleeves. Usually these were midcalf to ankle length. Fringe was cut at the bottom and at the sleeves. The dresses hung loose from the shoulder, or were belted in, according to individual taste.

Among the Plains tribes the new culture of the white man influenced the decorations and the material used, but not the general style to any great extent. Trade cloth was used instead of skin, glass beads replaced the quill decorations, and metal was also used as decoration.

Originally the skin dresses were put together with a bone awl which punched holes in the skin; then sinew was poked through the holes and the garment was laced together. Later, thread was used instead of sinew.

To reproduce a Plains Indian dress for yourself, or your children, you can use almost any kind of plain material. Measure from the shoulder to whatever length you want the finished dress to be, knee, calf, or ankle length. You'll need twice this length: 3 to 3½ yards of 36-inch-width material

# PLAINS INDIAN DRESSES

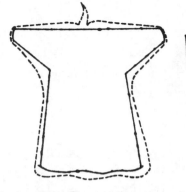

1. How dress is cut from outline of skin    2. Finished and beaded dress

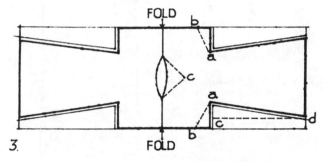

3.

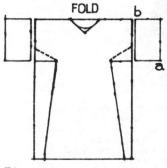

3A.

Pattern for making
modern adaptation
Double lines are to be
sewn up the sides
and under the arms.
Variation can be made
by cutting from *a* to *b*
for slanted sleeves
and a V neck at *c*.

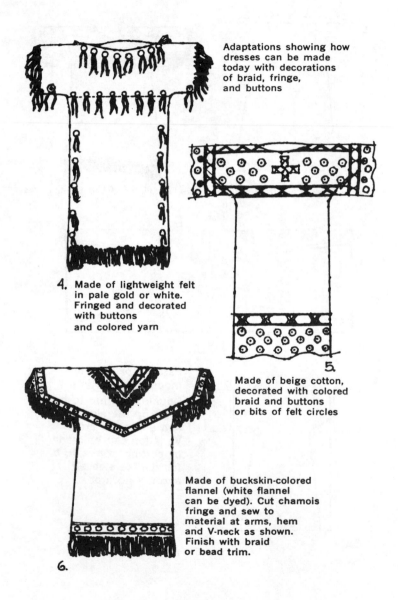

Adaptations showing how
dresses can be made
today with decorations
of braid, fringe,
and buttons

4. Made of lightweight felt
   in pale gold or white.
   Fringed and decorated
   with buttons
   and colored yarn

5.

Made of beige cotton,
decorated with colored
braid and buttons
or bits of felt circles

Made of buckskin-colored
flannel (white flannel
can be dyed). Cut chamois
fringe and sew to
material at arms, hem
and V-neck as shown.
Finish with braid
or bead trim.

6.

should be plenty for a woman's dress. Measure around your hips and then add 2 or 3 inches, as the dress should hang freely from the shoulders and not be tight around the hips. See Diagram 3 for laying out of material. Fold the material at the shoulders as in Diagram 3A and cut so that both sides are even.

If you want longer sleeves, add a band of fringe or an additional piece of material (see Diagram 3A-*a*) sewn to dress at *b*. Cover the sewing line with a decorative band or a small line of fringe or beads. The dress can be cut with a slight flare at the bottom (see Diagram 3, double line from *a* to *d*), or the side seam can be cut straight from under the arms to the hem (see dotted line *c* to *d*).

Diagrams 4, 5 and 6 show adaptations of this pattern with decorations of braid, fringe, and buttons. Indian women decorated their dresses to suit themselves, and according to how artistic they were. Not all Indian designs had symbolic meanings; many were merely adapted to whatever was being worked on. Shells, buttons, small bells, yarn, ribbon, thongs, claws, bits of metal, all were utilized for decorating.

Children's dresses were made exactly like the adult dresses, but in miniature.

## WOODLAND INDIAN DRESSES

Women of the Woodland tribes wore dresses made of soft deerskin, much like the Plains Indian dresses. Later, when trade blankets were available, these were used for making dresses, along with velveteen of black, dark blue, and wine color.

At one time Woodland women wore a simple sheath of two skins fastened at each shoulder and tied with a belt. Today this could be copied to be worn as a sheath over a body suit (see Diagram 3).

Diagram 1 is cut like the pattern for the Plains Indian dresses. Make it of dark blue or black velvet or velveteen. Decorate the armholes, neck, and three rows around the bottom of the dress with flowered braid. From this hang small tin cone jinglers (see Part V for instructions on how to make the cones).

# WOODLAND INDIAN DRESS

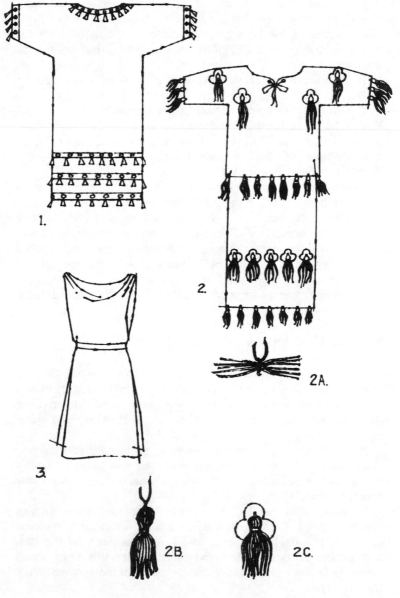

1.

2.

2A.

3.

2B.

2C.

# SEMINOLE INDIAN DRESS

1.

*(See page 60)*

The dress in Diagram 2 is made in two pieces. Measure your length from waist to hemline, depending on whether you want it knee, calf, or ankle length. Add 3 inches to the measurement of your hips and cut the material in a rectangle: the length, your measurement from waist to hem, and the width, your hip measurement plus 3 inches. Put an elastic band through a hem at one end for the waistline. Around the hemline put wool tassels (see 2A/2B for directions for making them). Put several strands of yarn together, tie in the middle, then fold this over and tie below the fold. About a foot above the hem, appliqué flower designs and in the center sew yarn tassels (2C). Make the blouse part like the upper portion of the dress in Diagram 1. Cut the blouse about hip-bone length or a bit longer, depending upon the length of the skirt and your proportions. Decorate the bottom of the blouse, the sleeve edges, and around the neck with appliqué and yarn tassels as shown.

## SEMINOLE INDIAN DRESS

The colorful Seminole dress can be copied using rickrack and braid. Actually it is a patchwork design of many little pieces of various colored cottons sewn together to make a full gathered skirt. An easier version is to start with a gathered skirt of plain cotton and then sew strips of braid, rickrack, or multicolored bands around the skirt as in *a* Diagram 1. (See instructions for making the Navaho dress.) Use colors of pink, red, green, blue, yellow, and white.

The top is a circle like cape (*b*). Material is gathered on a wide neck band, much as the skirt is gathered. Braid borders are sewn around the bottom and it is just pulled on over the head. The cape is usually wrist length and can be a contrasting color to the skirt. The more colorful, the better. Wear a simple white blouse under the cape.

## PUEBLO INDIAN DRESS

The women of the Pueblo tribes of Arizona and New Mexico have a basic costume consisting of a rectangle of cloth. In pre-Spanish times this was cotton, but later it was made of black wool. The rectangle is folded in half across the width and wrapped around the body so that the fold is on the left side of the body, from the left armpit down to below the knee. The upper corners are fastened over the right shoulder with the edges of the rectangle falling along the right side of the body and held together by a cloth belt. Later a cotton dress was worn under the folded rectangle; however, elderly Hopi women still wear only the rectangle, as in the ancient way. Sometimes a white cotton blouse is worn under the folded garment, with a white petticoat peeking from the hemline. The Pueblo rectangle black dress was made formal by the addition of an embroidered shawl of white cotton, high white puttee boots, and lots of jewelry.

This Pueblo dress can easily be copied. See Diagrams 1, 1A, and 1B (the sash). The rectangle can be of black or

# PUEBLO INDIAN DRESS

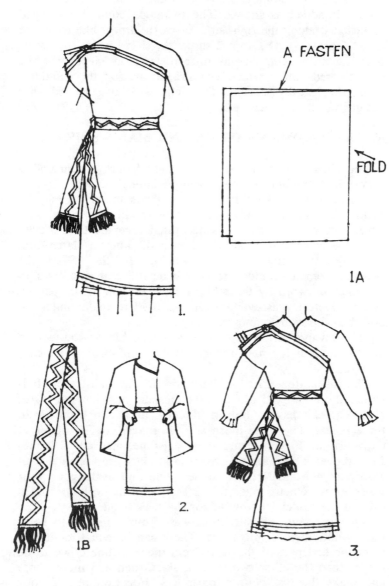

A FASTEN

FOLD

1A

1.

1B

2.

3.

dark blue—the latter is more common today. Sometimes a border is added as shown. The rectangle could be snapped or fastened along the right side, or worn almost like a jumper (see Diagram 3). Diagram 2 shows the shawl which was worn over the dress. This was another rectangular piece of white embroidered cotton which was draped around the shoulders along the lengthwise side. The belts were usually red with designs in black, green, and white.

## NAVAHO WOMAN'S DRESS AND MAN'S SHIRT

The Navaho woman's skirt is made of dark cotton and is very full. Sometimes borders or decorations are sewn around the lower part of the skirt, at other times the skirts may be plain. These are worn with velvet tops usually decorated with silver buttons or beads and a decorated silver belt. In ancient times the Navaho wore simple dresses of skin, and later wool blanket-dresses much like the Pueblo. In the 1870's the Navaho women adopted the very wide full cotton skirts similar to those worn by the white female settlers of the period. After velveteen was available it was used to make shirts for both Navaho women and men.

The Navaho cotton skirt and velveteen blouse for women and the blouse for men are colorful, comfortable, and easy to make.

The full cotton skirt can be made in any plain color. It is gathered onto a band which is the measurement of your waist. The skirt can have a bottom flounce, or it can be made in three pieces. The three-piece skirt is fuller, yet fits better at the waistline. First measure your waistline, then add 2 inches for lap-over where the waistband and skirt are fastened. Cut a strip of skirt material 4 inches wide and as long as your waist measurement, plus the 2 inches. This will be folded over in the center lengthwise for the waistband.

Whatever your measurement was, from waistline to hemline, is now divided into three. These can be equal, or if you want the first part of the skirt from the waistline down to be longer than the other two tiers of skirt, then add inches here and make the two bottom parts less. For example, if your skirt length is 30 inches you might make the upper tier,

# NAVAHO WOMAN'S DRESS AND MAN'S SHIRT

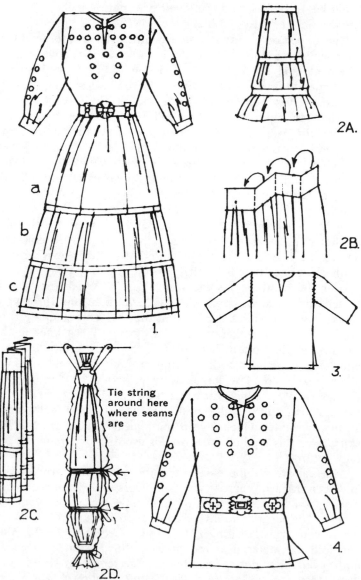

Tie string around here where seams are

marked *a* in Diagram 1, 12 inches, the next lower, or *b,* could be 10 inches, and the lower or *c* part 9 inches. Or they could be cut equally, 10 inches.

The upper or *a* part is cut two times the measurement of your waist, the next section (*b*) is three times the waist measurement, and the lower or *c* portion is cut four times the waist measurement. For example, if your waist measures 25 inches, the first section will be 50 inches, the second 75, and the third or lower skirt section will be 100 inches. Gather the upper skirt piece to the waistband, the next to this one, and the lower to the middle section. Braid or binding can then be sewn over the seams where the skirt pieces are gathered together, and around the bottom as shown in Diagram 1. To give the skirt the pleated-gathered look of the Navaho, wash your skirt after it is finished; don't wring it out, but, holding it by the waistband, fold the waistband in about 3-inch folds as shown in Diagram 2B. When it is folded it will look similar to the one in Diagram 2C. Pull the skirt down straight to the hemline. It will be dripping during this time, so hold it over the bathtub or some sort of drain. When the skirt is folded and straight, pull it, waistband first, up through a stocking which has been cut off at the toe. This stocking tube holds the skirt together while it is drying. Tie a knot in the stocking at the bottom hem part of the skirt and at the top, and hang it up to dry. Tie string around skirt and stocking where seams are. Use large safety pins or clips for hanging (Diagram 2D). When the skirt is dry and you take it from the stocking tube, you'll find that it has dried with small vertical wrinkles which give it the appearance of the Navaho skirts. For this type of skirt, *do not* use drip-dry material; use only cotton.

The velveteen blouse is made the same way for women and men. Measure across your shoulders and beyond on each side 3 to 4 inches, depending upon how loose you want the blouse. The length should be from shoulder to 5 or 6 inches below your waist, or longer if you like (see Diagram 3). You can fold the material at the shoulder line, or cut two pieces and have a shoulder seam. Measure the length of sleeves you want; they can be loose or with a cuff as shown. The width of sleeves should be 9 to 10 inches for the front and the same for the back. Leave 9 or 10 inches loose from the shoulder down when sewing the underarm seam; this is where the sleeves are sewn to the blouse. Cut a round neckline and a front slit, leaving enough room to pull it on over your head. When sewing the underarm seam, leave about 4 inches at the bottom loose for smooth fitting over hips. Hem the bottom. Finish the neckline with a cord or band which can tie in front or loop over two silver buttons for closing. The sleeves can be finished with cuffs as shown or with elastic run through a band at the wrist, or left loose and held with silver bracelets. Decorate the blouse with silver buttons on the front and along the sleeve edge as shown, or across the shoulders, or anyplace you like. A silver and leather belt, and lots of silver, turquoise, and coral beads will add to the Navaho look.

You might find a shirt or blouse pattern in some of the commercial pattern books. Look in the costume section, or adapt a shirt pattern. As long as the blouse is of velveteen or velvet, loose-fitting, long-sleeved, and decorated with silver or tin, it will have the right look.

### SHIRTS

Almost all Indian tribes wore some type of shirt. What was called a war shirt was actually a ceremonial shirt worn after the war party returned to camp. (The description of the war shirt decorations is given in Part VI.) Most of the shirts were similar to the Plains type shirt. Originally made of soft buckskin, a shirt could be made from two skins (see Diagram 1). The skin is cut so that the middle portion and hind legs make the shirt front and the other skin, the back. The forepart of the skin and the front legs are folded along the dotted line and make a sleeve; this part from the other skin makes the other sleeve. The skin of the underhead makes a neck tab (Diagram 1C). Attach the sleeve portion (Diagram 1B) to the body portion (Diagram 1A) as shown in Diagram 1. Cut the neck lower as shown by the dotted line, large enough to pull on over the head. A slit can be made a few inches down the front, which will be covered by the neck tab. The sides under the sleeves are caught by thongs in two or three places and the sleeves are caught together near the wrist. See Dia-

65

# SHIRTS

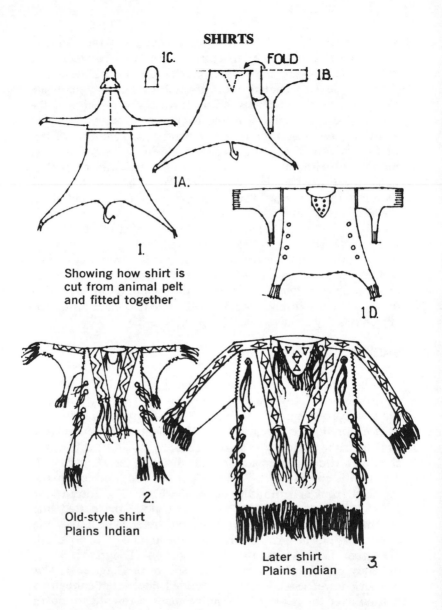

1C.

FOLD

1B.

1A.

1.

Showing how shirt is
cut from animal pelt
and fitted together

1 D.

2.

Old-style shirt
Plains Indian

Later shirt
Plains Indian

3

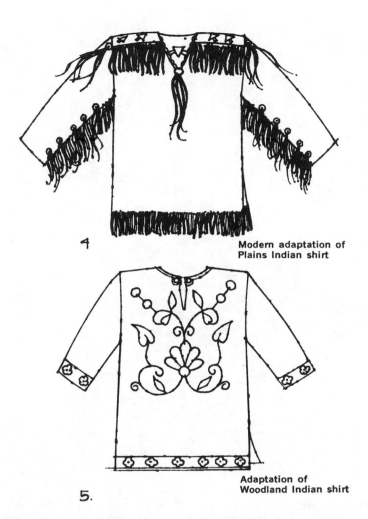

**4**

**Modern adaptation of Plains Indian shirt**

**5.**

**Adaptation of Woodland Indian shirt**

gram 1D; the dark lines are where the skins are caught together, the dots along the side are for the thong lacing to hold the sides together. Fringe the leg portions which hang down, then add bands of beading and strands of horsehair as shown in Diagram 2.

Later the shirts were given more form in that the long leg

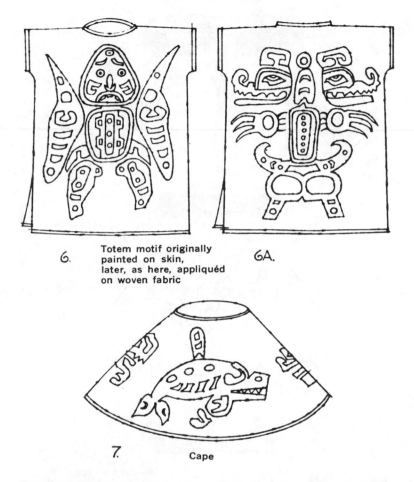

6. Totem motif originally painted on skin, later, as here, appliquéd on woven fabric   6A.

7. Cape

portions were trimmed off, and they were more carefully fitted. This shirt is simple to copy. Use your own shirt for size, but cut it a little larger, as the shirt should fit loosely. You can use the basic pattern of the Navaho shirt as described previously. To make this shirt, use buckskin, wool, flannel, suede-look cloth, or heavy cottton. For the Plains Indian type use a pale shade of gray, beige, or gold. Chamois fringe can be cut and added at the bottom and at the sleeves and neck tab. Sew bead bands or embroidered bands, as shown, with horsehair or yarn strands sewn at the ends of the bands (see Diagram 3). Tie under the arms with leather thongs as was done in the older type shirt. Tin cone jinglers can be tied on with the horsehair or yarn at the end of the bands and at the shoulder. (See Part V for description of how to make the tin jinglers.)

Diagram 4 shows another type of shirt, made from the basic pattern but with less decoration. The shirts should reach somewhere between the hip and knee, so make your shirt the length that suits you. Use decorations from Part V, or make up your own.

Diagram 5 is an example of a Woodland Indian shirt. This is made on the basic pattern, of black, dark blue, or wine colored velveteen or some other heavy dark material, and then embroidered in the floral designs of the Woodland tribes. Bind the neck, sleeves, and bottom with red, and a floral border, as shown.

The Northwest Coast shirts are made of dark woven material with the designs appliquéd on. Diagram 6 shows the front and Diagram 6A is the back of the same shirt. This is the basic pattern without sleeves. The armholes, neck, and bottom of the shirt are bound in contrasting material. These can be made of cotton cloth with the designs painted on instead of being appliquéd, which is time-consuming.

Diagram 7 is a cape made of woven material cut in a circle and pulled on over the head. It is about 24 inches in length, and trimmed around the neck and bottom with an appliquéd design.

## INDIAN LEGGINGS

Leggings were worn by both men and women. Men's leggings reached from ankle to crotch and were attached to a waist belt, or tied about the upper leg, while the women's leggings came only to the knee and were tied above the calf with thong or beaded garter bands. Those of the women usually were beaded to match their dress and were close fitting, being either wrapped, buttoned, or made so that the

# INDIAN LEGGINGS

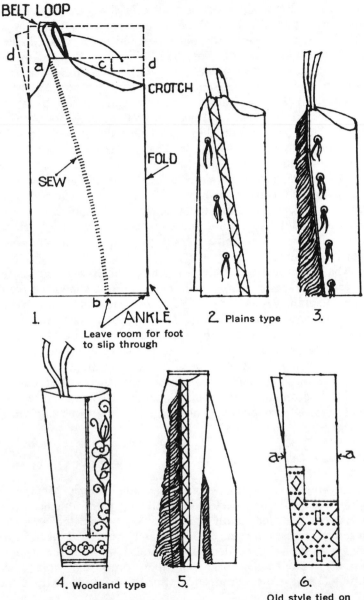

**BELT LOOP**

d a c d

CROTCH

FOLD

SEW

b ANKLE

1.

Leave room for foot
to slip through

2. Plains type

3.

4. Woodland type

5.

6.

Old style tied on
at belt line with
thong or above knees

foot could barely slip through, and the legging was almost as close-fitting as a stocking. Some women's leggings were fastened to the moccasins and became a part of them, like boots.

The leggings of the men were loose, much like the cowboy "chaps." Men's leggings were open both in front and back and were fastened by thongs to a belt which held the breechcloth, which was always worn with leggings. The leggings of western tribes, whether made of cloth or skin, extended beyond the outer side seam and were cut into a triangle flap or fringed. The leggings of the eastern tribes usually had the seam up the front and had no flap or fringe, being more like tight-fitting trouser legs. These were decorated up the front, while the western tribes decorated their leggings up the outer side.

Generally 2 yards of material, 24 to 26 inches wide, will be more than enough material to make a pair of leggings. If you are using leather or some other expensive material, it would be best to make a paper or muslin pattern; then when you have fitted it to your satisfaction, use this to cut your leggings and there will be no waste of expensive fabric or leather. Fold the material in the middle lengthwise as shown in Diagram 1. Measure from the crotch to the ankle for inside length, and from the waist to the ankle along the outside of the leg, where the belt loop is cut. Measure the belt loop about 2 or 3 inches and then angle the material toward the front or fold of the material (see c in Diagram 1). Do the same at a. The dotted line shows the outline of the material when it is folded. To save material, you can use material in length from the ankle to d of Diagram 1. Then the belt loop can be cut from the fabric left above the crotch line, or thongs can be sewn on to loop over the belt as shown in Diagram 3.

Stitch a diagonal line from a to b (see Diagram 1), leaving just enough room at the bottom for the foot to slip through. The material at the back can then be fringed or left loose. Decorate over the diagonal sewing with beading, shells, or loops of thong, as in Diagrams 2 and 3, Plains Indian leggings.

# BREECHCLOTH AND APRONS

(Plains Indians)                    (Woodland Indians)

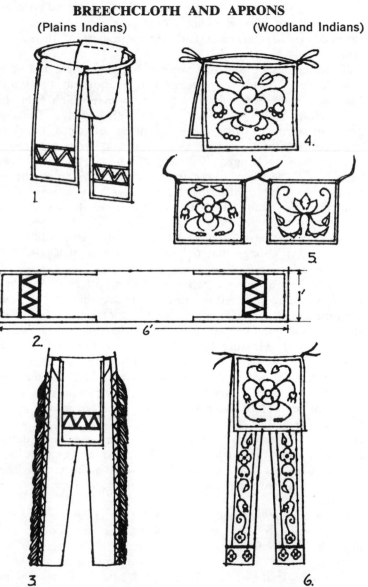

Diagram 4 is a Woodland legging, which is made straight, more like a trouser leg, with the decoration up the front and around the bottom. Belt loops or ties are placed at the side as in the Plains legging.

A very modern adaptation of leggings can be made by sewing braid or beading along the outer leg seam of tight leg slacks to cover wide fringe which is cut wider at the bottom to give the look of the triangle flap of the Plains Indian legging (Diagram 5).

Diagram 6 shows the old-style leggings which were tied at the waist or around the upper leg with thongs.

Women's leggings are made like those in Diagram 6 but are cut off at a–a just below the knee and tied with thong or a beaded band. The women's leggings were usually heavily beaded to match their dress.

## BREECHCLOTH AND APRONS

With Indian leggings, a breechcloth or apron is always worn. The breechcloth is simply a piece of cloth or soft buckskin about 1 foot wide and 6 feet long, depending upon how the wearer wanted the breechcloth to hang. Generally they were a little longer in the back. The ends are drawn between the legs and over the belt in front and behind. The ends, and sometimes the edges, are decorated with beading, or strips of contrasting color. The breechcloth, leggings, and moccasins were often decorated to match. In cold weather, or for ceremony, a decorated shirt was added to the outfit. For breechcloth measurements and directions, see Diagrams 1, 2, and 3.

See Diagrams 4, 5, and 6 for apron patterns. These are worn instead of breechcloths, by Woodland Indians. The aprons are generally made of dark cloth, blue, black or wine velveteen, embroidered or beaded in the floral Woodland patterns. The aprons are square and about 18 or 20 inches, depending upon the size of the wearer. The back apron and the front apron are usually decorated with different patterns, and each is bound in narrow contrasting color and is tied at the hips. Aprons, leggings, and moccasins usually match.

# VESTS

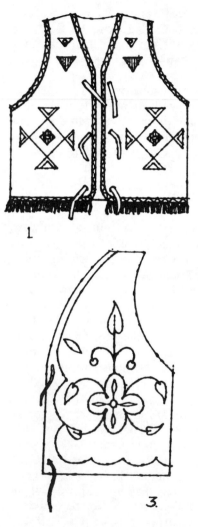

1

2

3.

## VESTS

The vest as worn by the Indians appeared early in Colonial times and was worn both as an ornamental piece of clothing and as a windbreaker. It was especially worn by the northern Blackfoot, the Chippewas, Sioux, and Crow Indians. This garment was borrowed from the Europeans; a completely beaded Indian vest was a work of art, and highly prized even in early times.

The vest can be made rounded, square, or even pointed in front. Vests of the Plain Indians were originally made of deer or elk skin; however, some vests of the Woodlands Indians were made of dark velvet, blue, black, or wine color, lined and embroidered with their typical floral designs.

You can use a commercial vest pattern, or make a paper pattern from one of your old vests. Make it at least an inch larger though, as the vest should fit loosely. They can be made of leather, wool, felt, denim, canvas, flannel, suede, or vinyl-leather. You could even take the lining from an old vest and decorate it and no one would ever guess its origin. Trace your pattern on some inexpensive material first, especially if you're going to make a suede vest. Sew the shoulders and sides together so your completed vest will look similar to the outline of Diagram 1. The vest can be bound in braid to look like beading, or rows of beads can be put around the armholes and bottom. Fringe can be cut or added to the bottom, or even to the armholes and front. For the pattern on your vest, bits of felt can be sewn or glued onto it, beads or braid can be added. If you make a canvas vest, you can make the decoration by using wax crayon. Be sure to press the canvas on the wrong side with a hot iron. Place a plain piece of material against the front design so the wax crayon will melt and set, staining the cloth rather than the ironing board. Diagrams 1 and 2 show the front and back of a Plains Indian vest with typical designs. Diagram 3 is a Woodland Indian vest of dark velvet embroidered in a floral design. Both are tied at the front with a thong.

75

# NORTHWEST INDIAN (CHILKAT) BLANKET
## WORN AS A ROBE

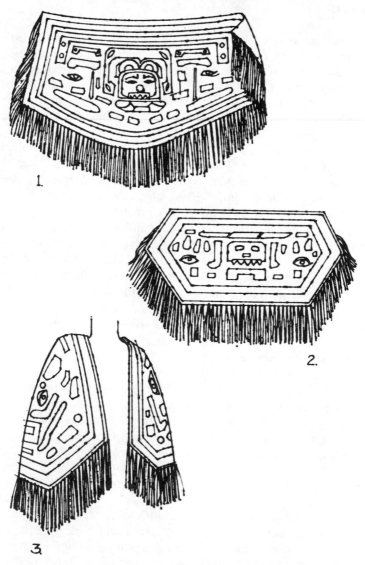

1.

2.

3.

# NORTHEAST INDIAN BLANKET

Diagrams 1 and 2 show two different shapes of the North-west Indian blanket which was worn as a robe or cape. The robes are woven of twisted cord or twine of cedar bark fiber for the warp, while the woof is of worsted spun from the wool of the mountain goat. The fringe is light, shimmery mountain goat hair.

This can be made of heavy cotton with the pattern painted on and finished with wide fringe. The designs of the North-west Indians are geometric; the motifs include mythological animals, usually in black, blue, white, and yellow; the total effect is highly formalized.

## ROACH HEADDRESS

A roach could be worn by an Omaha Indian warrior who had won three first honors of bravery. The roach type of headdress was used by many eastern tribes as well as those on the plains. The hair of the roach was woven and fastened to a bone spreader in such a way that when worn it stood straight up. A large feather was attached to its forward center and was originally held in place by drawing a lock of hair through a hole in the roach's forward end and then tying it in a knot.

Today a roach of this type can be made from a piece of long-haired black fur and red horsehair. Horsehair can be purchased from some hobby shops, or if you can't find it, use hemp binding twine, unraveled and dyed red.

Cut two to four pieces of felt, depending upon how thick and stiff it is. You can use a man's felt hat if you have an old one, otherwise felt or something equally stiff. These should be cut in the shape in Diagram 1, approximately 2 to 2½ inches at the widest, tapering down to the end. The length is 10 to 12 inches. Place one piece on top of the other as in Diagram 1A and sew the two pieces together. Trim the piece of fur so it is brush-like and bristly, and cut it exactly in the shape of the felt. Stitch the fur to the felt along the edges, as in Diagram 1B.

# WOMEN'S HAIR FASHIONS

## Hopi Women

A Maiden

A Matron

Plains
Indian Girl

# MEN'S HAIR FASHIONS

Navaho

Mohican

Hopi

Assiniboin

Dakota

Muskogean
Brave

# ROACH HEADDRESS

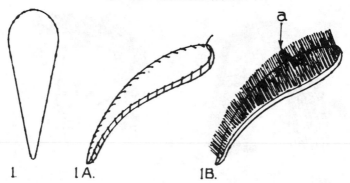

1.    1 A.    1B.

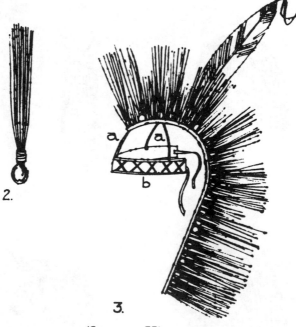

2.

3.

*(See page 77)*

The horsehair, or dyed binding twine, should now be cut in 12-inch lengths and put into bundles about ⅛ of an inch in diameter. Next bend the lengths of horsehair double and tie them above the fold-over, with thread, as in Diagram 2. These bundles are now sewn to the edges of the roach in a way to make them stand upright. Place them close together at the front and back and about an inch apart along the sides in between.

At the top of the roach a big feather is fastened so that it rotates in the wind. See Woodland Hats, Diagram 7 or 7A and explanation on how to attach socket and feather. Socket is attached at *a* in Diagram 1B. Prepare feather and attach into the socket as explained under Woodland Hats. The roach can be held on with tie strings, or sewn to a wig—or, as we show in Diagram 3, with a decorated headband. Attach a narrow black string to each side of the roach and from the front marked *a* in Diagram 3. Attach these to the headband (*b*) which is tied around at the back of the head and under the roach. Bead or paint the band, and at the tip of the rotating feather, sew a few strands of red horsehair. Your roach is now ready to wear.

## HEADBANDS AND HAIR FEATHERS

Headbands and hair feathers were used in some form by almost all tribes. They are interesting and easy to make.

Diagram 1 shows a type worn by the Plains Indians in the winter. It consists of a circle of fur and is decorated with a feather. Any old fur neckpiece could be used for this; simply sew it into a circle to fit your head and attach a feather at the back.

Diagram 2 is made of a tube-like circle covered with buckskin that has been beaded or painted with a design; a feather is fitted at the back. This can be placed upright or at an angle. You can either twist some strips of cloth until you have a circlet about an inch in diameter, or buy cotton rope belting, and cover it..

Diagram 3 is another type of fur circlet. This one is decorated at the back with tufts of feathers or fur tails. Three or four feathers are placed around the edge of the fur. These

# HEADBANDS AND HAIR FEATHERS

1.

2.

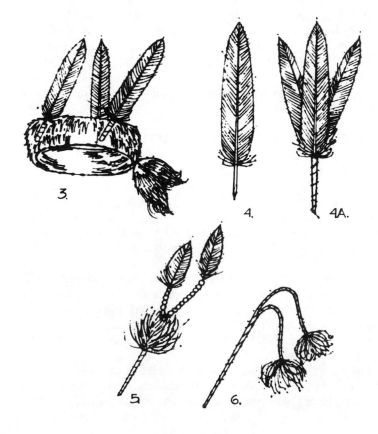

3.

4.

4A.

5.

6.

are placed in sockets and sockets are covered by the fur or wound with red flannel. The feathers can rotate in the sockets and give a rather distinctive air to the wearer as they move in the breeze. For instructions on how to make and place the sockets and put in the feathers, see Woodland Hats, Diagram 7 or 7A.

Hair feathers were tied or tucked into the hair and they were of many different types. The quill ends of the feathers were sharpened, or fitted with a splinter of bone or wood so it would slide into the hair. Sometimes one or two feathers were used, the two being wound together as in Diagrams 4 and 4A. Or quills were stripped, leaving only the feather end decorated with feather tuft, as shown in Diagram 5. Diagram 6 is made of rather stiff rawhide, wound with flannel, or beading. The ends are decorated with feather tufts (or yarn could be used). Hair clips could be sewn to the quill ends in order to hold them in the hair. Use your imagination as the Indians did, and individualize your hair feathers.

## WOODLAND INDIAN HATS

The ancient headgear of the Woodland Indians is simple to make and can be decorated in several ways. The Iroquois called this *gus-to-weh*, meaning "real hat." First make a foundation of leather straps to fit the head as in Diagram 1. Make the 1- to 1½-inch straps to fit the head comfortably, but not as tight as a skullcap.

For one type of hat, such as Diagram 4, cover the strap foundation with a circular cloth of velveteen of a dark blue, wine, or black color, or of soft leather or other similar weight material. Fit the cloth loosely over the top, as it must not be tight. Make a basting stitch of heavy thread around the hat 1 inch from the center of the top, and another 2 inches from the center. A third line can be basted around the hat below the 2-inch line, if you like. To this thread, feathers are attached in the manner shown in Diagram 3. The quill end of the feathers are cut at an angle after being softened with hot water. They are then fastened to the threads by passing the pointed end of the quill over the top and around the thread and then tucking it into its own quill as shown in Diagram 3A.

# WOODLAND INDIAN HATS

1

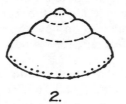

2.

2A.

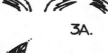

3.

3A.

4.

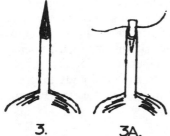

5.

5A.

6

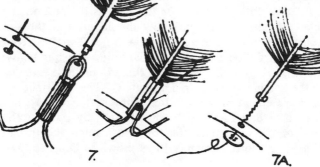

7.

7A.

The bottom part of the cloth covering is stitched lightly around the bottom edge and pulled in to fit the headband strap; this is then stitched to a tape or narrow piece the size of the headband.

In the center of the hat a small hole is made and a bone socket is put there. Today you can use a discarded holder for a ball-point pen or a section of colored plastic tube, anything that is hollow and open on both ends, and sturdy but not heavy. This will hold the top, or big, feather that rotates in the breeze, or as the wearer moves. Anchor this into the hat by running thread up through the hollow tube and down the side to be fastened to the cloth covering. Your hat will now look like the one in Diagram 2A. In ancient times this top feather was made so it could be removed while the Indians traveled through the woods.

Now make a circle of basting stitches very close to the socket. Catch this thread to the hat in only three or four places, so the feathers attached to it can fly rather freely. You now have two more circles of basting, and a third if you wish, although unless you have a rather large head you won't need another circle of feathers for this type of hat.

Small feathers, white chicken feathers with dyed tips, and small turkey feathers can be used, or you can buy commercial feathers at hobby stores. Place these feathers in overlapping rows, not too close together, and start at the circle farthest from the center socket. Place the pointed end of the quill over the basting thread and tuck it into its own quill, as already explained and as shown in Diagrams 3 and 3A. This leaves the feathers free to move in the wind.

Do the next smaller and higher circle of basting in the same manner. For the last or top circle near the socket, use small turkey feathers, marabou, or some other fluffy type feather. Now put the large top feather into the socket as shown in Diagram 7. Put a small nail through a small, narrow piece of leather. Next fit a wooden plug into the end of the feather and nail the leather thong to the wooden plug as shown.

Another way you can do this is to run a small wire through each side of the feather quill and then down through the leather thong and then through the eyes of a button where it will be held against the thong, but the feather will be free to rotate (see Diagram 7A). Now pull the thong with the feather down through the socket and catch the thong around the inside head straps so the feather is held at least halfway down into the socket (see Diagram 7). If this is done properly the feather will easily rotate at the slightest breeze. The hat is now finished by sewing a decorated band around its rim, as shown in Diagram 4.

A complete feather hat can be made using the same basic leather strap foundation as shown in Diagram 1. Over this foundation or frame place an old hat crown, or felt, something like a skullcap, but larger and not too tight. Make a small hole and place the big feather socket toward the front, along the strap which goes from the front of the head to the back. The socket and feather can be secured to this band. The outside is now covered with bits of fur or feathers. Use small turkey or chicken feathers, or buy commercial feathers. Start at the bottom of the hat and sew or glue a row of feathers around the bottom, then start another row above this, overlapping the feathers as you work to the top. Finally place the big feather in the socket as shown in Diagram 7 or 7A. If you like, glue (use household cement) or sew a tuft of feathers to the back of the hat.

Another version is made like the above, only fur is glued or sewn around the hat, then the feathers are added, one in the socket and a tuft of two or three at the back of the hat. A tuft can also be added at the front below the socket feather, or these could be straight squared-off feathers of different colors (see Diagram 5A).

A feather and fur hat can be made as in Diagram 6. Place a band of fur around the bottom of the basic hat, then put feathers above this, starting with a row of feathers nearest the fur and overlapping them as you place other rows of feathers to the top center of the hat, and the socket. Put a feather in the socket as previously explained and your hat is finished.

## CHIPPEWA AND DAKOTA INDIAN WINTER CAPS

These are made of skin or cloth, decorated according to tribe and individual taste, and are worn in cold weather. They

# CHIPPEWA AND DAKOTA INDIAN
# WINTER CAPS

Chippewa—Woodland Indian

Dakota—Plains Indian

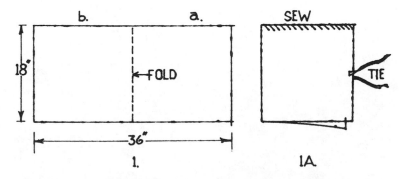

fit closely around the head, falling down over the neck and shoulders, and are tied under the chin to keep snow and rain from reaching the neck and throat. They are decorated with beading, embroidery, feathers, or a combination.

The simplest way to copy this Indian winter cap is use a commercial hood pattern. Make it of chamois, soft leather-

87

look fabric, wool, or flannel and then decorate it as shown; have it waterproofed for your own rain and snow cap.

You can make your own pattern by measuring from the top middle of your head down the side of your face and as far past your shoulder as you want the hood to fall. Whatever this measurement is, double it and this will be how long the material must be. Fold this long piece in half and sew along one side, put a tie on it, under your chin, and it is finished. For example if from the top of your head to past your shoulder is 18 inches, then use a length 36 inches, folded in the middle as in Diagram 1, sewed *a* to *b*. It will now look like Diagram 1A. Put a tie on each side, decorate it, and you are ready to wear your Indian winter cap.

# PART II

## INDIAN FOOD

*(Crafts begin on page 115)*

Sometimes we tend to think that much of the food we have came to this hemisphere with the early European colonists. We overlook the many food gifts given by the native Americans—misnamed Indians when Columbus thought he was in Asian waters rather than on the threshold of a new continent.

## SOME BASIC FOODS

Corn, which is a great natural resource of this country today, came from the Indian. How they developed it is a puzzle, as no wild corn has ever been discovered, and it grows only where man plants and tends it. The main types of corn were already growing here when Columbus landed, and the Indians were then eating popcorn which was often sweetened with maple sugar. This was probably the first version of what we know now as caramel corn. The Indians called corn "maize" (pronounced "mays"). It was cultivated not only for its grain but also as a forage for livestock. When the first white man arrived here, corn was being cultivated from Canada to Chile, and throughout the United States. From this hemisphere, the Spanish introduced corn into Europe, from whence it spread all over the world. Columbus spoke of the Indians as having an intoxicating drink made from maize.

The Indians have many legends about the origin of corn, and it is called "Mother Corn, the Giver of Life." The Pawnee believe that corn first came to earth as a beautiful yellow-

**SANTO DOMINGO POTTERY**
Bowl in tan with a black design is about 12 inches.

haired maiden whose locks are still preserved in the corn silk.

The food of the American Indian varied not only with the region inhabited but also with the season and with tribal preference. Some tribes had religious or superstitious beliefs that forbade them to eat certain foods. Almost every tribe had a totem or clan animal that could never be eaten or killed. The Navaho and Apache would not eat fish or the flesh of bear or beaver. Other Indians would not eat the turkey, believing it to be a cowardly bird, and that by eating its flesh, they too would become cowardly. Certain animals, considered brave, were eaten, as it was felt that to eat the animal or a part of it would give one the same brave characteristics.

While the men did the hunting and fishing, the women gathered the berries, nuts, and the "picked" type of food. Usually the women made this an outing and went in groups, ending with a picnic.

By slow experimentation, the Indians had learned just what native plants could be eaten and what could be cultivated and developed. They knew which mushrooms and puffballs to eat and which were poisonous. Mushrooms were usually cooked with meat or boiled down in grease. Oyster mushrooms were dried for winter use, or grated and used in soup.

The Indians knew which of the deadly nightshade family, such as the potato and tomato, were edible. And centuries before the arrival of Columbus, they cultivated the pineapple as a staple food. It received the name "pineapple" from the Spanish because the fruit looked like a pine cone. The Indian ate beans, peas, potato, squash, pumpkins, melons, and chili peppers. It was the Indians of Massachusetts Bay who gave the colonists many of the foods they later came to cultivate. It was here the first Thanksgiving day was observed, with the Indians bringing turkey, cranberries, pumpkin, and baked beans. Pumpkin pie soon became a favorite food, and these colonists liked the baked beans so well that Boston later became famous for baked beans—Indian style, or Boston baked beans.

Chewing gum also was used by the Indians as was tobacco, although tobacco was rarely just smoked for pleasure, but was kept for special occasions.

Blackberry, Juneberry, blueberry, cherry, and raspberry

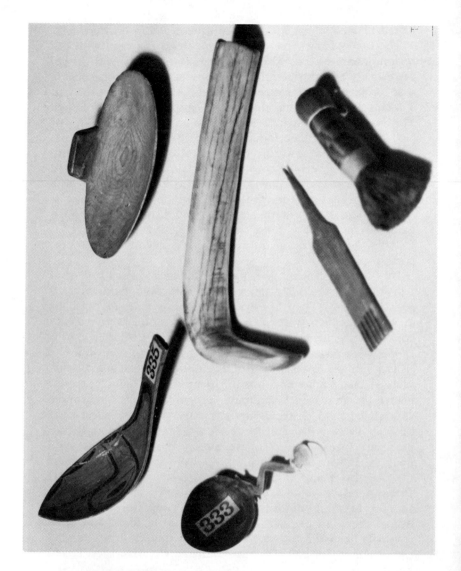

**VARIOUS INDIAN ITEMS**
Wooden spoon—tribe unknown
Wooden bowl—Woodland tribe
Wooden spoon—Plains tribe
Skin scraper—Plains tribe
Comb—tribe unknown
Hairbrush of fiber and bark wrapped—tribe unknown

were all important in the Indian diet. The strawberry, which was also important to the Indian was the ancestor of the wild strawberry found growing in so many parts of Great Britain today. It was introduced to England from Virginia in 1629. Berries were eaten either raw or cooked, and some were mixed with meat. All Indians, no matter what tribe, saved part of their food for winter use, and gathering food was of concern to all members of the tribe. Berries were left in the sun or were spread on sheets of bark or great basket trays to dry for winter use.

Nuts, which are a rich source of protein and the B vitamins, were a staple food with the Indians, and they even knew how to prepare the bitter, poisonous acorn so it could be eaten. These were never eaten raw, but were dried in the sun as soon as they had been gathered. Great care was taken to shake the drying baskets so the acorns would not become moldy. The shells were then cracked off and the inner kernels separated from the shucks. When the "meat" was to be used for food it was put in a stone mortar and ground into flour. This was frequently sifted and the coarse particles thrown back for repounding. Woven cloth or a fine basket was used as a filter and water was thrown over the meal. Sometimes the baskets were set upon gravel or sand so the water would drain through and trickle down into the stones beneath. This washed out the tannic acid in the flour and made it sweet and wholesome. When the water ran clear and the yellow stain disappeared, the meal or flour was ready. This was then saturated with water and was somewhat like dough when handled. When mixed in cold water to thin it, it was made into porridge which could be thick or thin. Acorn dough was also wrapped in cornhusks and placed in ashes to bake. The acorn lacked flavor, but it was a nourishing and satisfying food.

Chestnuts were boiled, roasted, or ground into meal. They were dried much like the acorn and, when shelled, were pounded into a coarse flour for making bread. Sometimes a little cornmeal was added, making a good combination. Chestnuts were gathered when ready, but some were always stored away for winter use.

The Woodland tribes ate hickory nuts, walnuts, butternuts, and hazel nuts. The western Indians used these nuts plus the

APACHE BASKET (Side view)
This basket that the Apaches delighted in using shows little figures of men and animals.

pecan and the buckeye. Not only were nuts cracked and the meat eaten, but they were also pounded in a deep wooden mortar until the shells were broken. This mass of nuts and shells was then thrown into water and the shells skimmed off. When all the floating particles had been removed, the liquid was boiled and, after frequent skimmings from the top of the boiling liquid, a milky fluid was left. This was preserved as an oily paste to eat with hominy or bread.

Hominy was made from Indian corn, after it was pounded, or cracked and boiled. Sometimes the kernels were merely hulled by steeping them in ashes or lye, then boiled. Hominy is another of the many Indian words we use today. It is from the Algonkin dialect of New England and Virginia.

For oil the Indians used the black walnut, butternut, and beechnut. These were crushed and then put into boiling water. The oily substance which floated on the top of the boiling water was skimmed off and used for frying meat.

In times of great hunger, the seeds of dropseed grass, picnic grass, or floating manna grass were used, as was the tiny seed of the cattail. The cattail fuzz was burned off, then the seed particles were ground and boiled. Seeds were freed from chaff by winnowing, then were parched and ground into flour. These were starvation rations, however.

Root food included the artichoke and the groundnut. The groundnut or wild bean vine has a root formed of long strings of small potatoes numbering from ten to forty. These were found in the bottom lands and were cooked like potatoes. They were small, but had an excellent taste. In the springtime the women gathered them from the overflowing springs, but in the autumn it was necessary to use a hoe to dig them out. Other roots used as food were the Canada lily, Turk's camp, broad-leaved arrowhead, water arm, or calla lily, as well as the showy orchid and the yellow pond lily.

To gather the yellow pond lily, long poles were used, or girls who were good swimmers would dive down and dig them out with their hands. Since muskrats were also fond of the lily roots, the Indians would sometimes rob the muskrat home for the roots. The pond lily was cooked by boiling or roasting.

The onion-shaped jack-in-the-pulpit was called "fire ball" by the Indians. It is as fiery as concentrated pepper and to

97

remove the acid taste the roots were baked, sliced, and dried, then, when thoroughly dried, were pounded into meal. The meal was again heated and set aside to dry out. Finally it was free of its hot fiery taste and ready to mix into meat for cooking. These roots were gathered in the fall and stored in damp sand to use for making winter bread.

The breadroot or prairie turnip was another source of food. It is about the size of a duck egg and when the skin is peeled off and the inside dried, it makes an excellent flour.

The leaves of the adder's-tongue, wild mustard, clover, brookline watercress, honeyworth, and wild onion were also eaten. It was believed that the eating of greens would keep fever away and prevent rheumatism.

The Woodland Indians living near the lakes found wild rice one of their chief foods. It grew in profusion in the shallow waterways and was gathered in canoes. The canoe was manned by a paddler and a gleaner. The gleaner bent the tall stalks over the side of the canoe and beat out the rice grains with a short stick, filling the canoe as it was paddled through the marshes. Gathering was the smallest part, for when the rice was prepared, it had to be freed of chaff by a roasting and winnowing process. The Chippewa and Menomini gathered the wild rice and used it as an article of trade. Today, wild rice sells at a high price and is considered a delicacy.

While some Indians ate salt and made trips to obtain it, salt was forbidden to the Onondaga. Some salt was obtained from the evaporated water of salt springs and of the ocean, and in the crystal from salt lake beds, or by trade. At times lye was used as a salt substitute by some southern Indians. Meat and fish were preserved by prolonged boiling in salted water.

Indians liked their food to taste good and knew that overcooking could ruin the taste. However the Indian seldom grumbled about a bad cook, although a good cook was always praised. The Indian woman who was a good cook was always in demand and was considered a prize. She might have only a few utensils to cook with, but she could turn a little meat, berries, and vegetables into a tasty dish.

Usually there were two meals a day, the main one being in the evening; however, Indians ate when they were hungry, as

**NAVAHO POTTERY BOWL**
Old pottery bowl with an inside star design has bands around the
rim in black and faded red.

there was generally food in the cooking pot. Since each person in the family, man, woman and child, was responsible for keeping his own eating utensils clean, there was no clutter of dirty dishes for the cook to do.

## METHODS OF COOKING AND PRESERVING

Food was always offered to anyone entering an Indian dwelling, no matter how little the family might have. It was believed that the Great Spirit gave the food for everyone, and like the water and the air, what was for one was for all.

The Indian woman fixed food in various ways. She might bake, broil, or fry the food, or dry it for later use. Fish, fowl, rabbit, and other small game were sometimes cooked by covering with clay that had been well worked and then spread two fingers thick. Great care was taken that the game being cooked was completely covered with clay. Fish were not scaled and birds were not plucked, except for the large feathers (the head and wings were removed), before being covered with clay. The game was placed in embers and covered with ashes and glowing coals. A fire was then built over the mound of clay and ashes and the cooking process began, continuing until the sun had moved a space in the sky. When the cooking was finished, the clay-covered game was taken from the fire and the clay broken off. The scales, feathers, or fur came off with the clay, leaving only the cooked game. Sometimes game might be dressed and stuffed with herbs.

A few of the tribes that had clay pots had a sort of pot roast dish. The pot was heaped around with embers, then covered with a flat stone. These pots were also used for deep-frying, the grease used being that of the deer, bear, buffalo, or the oil of nuts and sunflowers.

Boiling was done in skin or bark utensils or in beds of clay, by filling the utensil with cold water, adding the food to be cooked, and then dropping hot stones into the pot with long wooden tongs. Food was also boiled by suspending birchbark kettles over hot coals.

The earth oven used by many of the Indian tribes was

100

simply a hole in the ground into which hot stones and food were placed. The hole was covered with earth so that heat and steam would cook the food. The earth ovens of the Pueblos were largely community ovens consisting of a bottle-shaped cavity, dug into the ground and provided with a draft hole. Green corn was roasted in them. Similar ovens twelve to fifteen feet in diameter were used along the Salt River in Arizona. Small family ovens with draft holes were also used by the Hopi who set jars in the ground, then covered them with stones. These were treated by a fire of twigs. Cone-shaped ovens of stone plastered with clay were used among the Pueblo tribes, except for the Hopi. It is believed this form of cooking was introduced from Spain by way of Mexico.

The Indian fire did not blaze away in flames but was made of hot coals. It was simple to build these fires of hot coals in the tipi or dwelling. The fire was always directly under the cooking pot. Even when built outside, these fires not only saved fuel, but the minimal smoke did not attract enemies or set additional fires. Meat was stuck on spits and roasted over these open fires. There's an old saying, "A watched pot never boils," but the Indian woman did watch her pot because it was considered the sign of a poor cook if the woman wandered away from her cooking.

Indian cornmeal was white and flour-like, not like the yellow cornmeal we know. Corn was first pulled from the husk, then shelled and put into a solution of wood ash and weak lye water, which was just strong enough to bite the tongue. The corn was boiled until the covering of the corn looked loose and swelled. It was then dipped out and put into a washing sieve. It was then rinsed until the lye was washed out and the hulls became loose enough to float away. The half-cooked white interior was now ready for grinding or mashing in a mortar. The soft, wet meal, which was pulverized, was sifted in a fine mesh basket. The meal was then mixed with a bit of boiling water and molded into the desired shape, which was usually a circular pattie. The woman would dip her hands into the cold water and smooth it over the cake; this made the surface smooth and shiny and helped to keep the flavor in while the cake was cooking. The cakes could be wrapped in cornhusks and boiled, or wrapped in leaves and baked in a

101

fire. Sometimes, beans, berries, or nuts were added to the cakes to give them a different flavor. They were often sliced and eaten with sunflower oil, nut oil, or maple syrup, and they could also be fried.

Flavoring used in Indian food was made of wood ashes, sassafras, wintergreen, hemlock tips, bayberries, pepper pods, and wild ginger.

Along with nuts, berries, and root vegetables, there were all kinds of game and fish to eat. Many Indian foods were dried or smoked, preserving them for the cold winters or for times when food might be scarce. Fire and smoke hastened the drying process and also kept away flies and other insects. In hot areas the meat was allowed to dry in the sun. The term "jerky" comes from an Indian word which is from the Peruvian word *charqui* (pronounced char-key) meaning dried meat. For drying and smoking, the meat was hung on anything from a bush to a huge frame hung above the dwelling fire. Some tribes had simple square frames of poles with a fire beneath, used only for drying meat. Along the Northwest Coast regular smokehouses were built to hasten the drying process in the damp colder regions.

Fish was also dried in the sun, but smoked fish was less common than meat. Where the climate allowed, fish were frozen, and they were also preserved with salt. Some tribes pulverized the fish after it was dried and added berries to it, making it somewhat like the pemmican of the Plains Indians.

For the nomadic tribes of the Plains, buffalo was the main source of food. The hump ribs were the finest part, but all was used. Often the liver was consumed on the spot. The meat was cut into narrow strips and dried. Marrow bones or the bones of the hind legs were roasted, then cracked open and the marrow eaten. The buffalo had two stomachs and the contents of the first was believed to be a remedy for skin disease and especially frostbite. The one who killed the buffalo got the hide, as well as the fat hump and the tongue which was considered a delicacy. After a hunt, meat was always divided among the tribe; the aged, widows, and orphans were always provided for. Any fat left over was carefully put into skin bags for storage.

Wood was not plentiful on the prairie, so dried buffalo chips or dung was used for fuel. This made a hot low flame but little smoke. The Plains tribes used bent saplings, shaped like lacrosse sticks, as tongs to pick up hot stones and drop them into their cooking pots. Some of the tribes along the eastern Plains made pottery and a few to the west made baskets which they waterproofed with pitch. Some of the tribes in the Central Plains boiled their food in the buffalo stomach or in rawhide bags. Because of this method of cooking by putting hot stones in the cooking pot, the Assiniboin Indians received their name, "stone-boilers."

The wild turnip was a prize food of the prairie people, and large quantities were dug up in the early spring, to be peeled and dried for winter.

The Woodland tribes, while they might not always have a supply of fresh meat near the village, usually had smoked meat or fish, plus corn, beans, berries, nuts, pumpkins and maple sugar. Those who were near the lakes had wild rice also.

Maple sap gathering was always done by the women and children and was like a holiday with much chatter and fun. Flat spikes were driven into the bark of the tree and these conveyed the sap into birchbark buckets. The sap was then boiled in troughs made of bark or wood, and was then stored as syrup. Sometimes it was boiled longer and poured into molds to make crystallized sugar. The maple groves, like the hunting grounds, were owned by generations of clans, never by individuals.

The women of the Woodland tribes raised corn, beans, and squash, grown together in one big garden spot. Hominy was one of their main foods, often cooked with beans and any leftover bones, all in the same pot.

The Algonkins made clay pots for cooking, while the tribes to the north used birch, which could easily be folded into a container. Birchbark could be used as a cooking pot by dropping hot stones into it, or it could be hung over a fire for cooking, as long as there was liquid in the bottom. Birchbark could also be set directly over the fire; however, this ruined the pot for any other kind of cooking.

The cooking fire was generally made with the butts of three sticks. A cooking vessel was hung over the fire at the end of a slanting pole; this rested in a forked support, the outer end being held down by a big stone. Another method was a pole laid horizontally across two forked posts, the cooking pot hanging in the middle.

Bowls were made from maple burls which were round on the outside and did not split easily. The hollowing of the bowl was done by burning and scraping. Food trays, ladles, and spoons were also made of wood. Bark was also used as trays.

The southwestern desert tribes had learned how to make the desert yield crops. They had learned that water accumulates underground in low spots and that the roots of plants could reach it. They discovered where the underground streams were and planted their crops over them. Knowing that desert crops need a lot of growing room they placed their corn hills more than ten feet apart. The Pueblo men did the farming. The old men took care of weeding, and the women and children scared off the crows and other birds.

The whole process of cultivating and plowing was done with a single implement, a digging stick which was about four and a half feet long on which the stem of one branch had been left a few inches from the bottom to be used to place the foot when digging. The corn was planted twenty grains to a hill, and the growing corn looked different from any other in the land. A hill of corn gave the appearance of a low bush, its ears huddled near the ground under the leaves and out of the blaze of the sun.

Their corn was dried quickly in the hot desert air and then was ground into meal. In the grinding process, three women worked side by side, each one using a stone of different fineness. The stone was a flat slab, and when the Spanish saw them they named them "metate." The grinding was done by rubbing the grains across the stone with another stone, or a mono, in the hand.

It is believed the Pueblos knew over fifty ways of cooking corn. They made "piki" or paper bread which was made from a thin batter and cooked on a flat stone placed over the fire. The batter was sometimes colored yellow or red for special feasts, but it was usually gray from the wood ash which was deliberately mixed with the meal. To make good piki took great dexterity, as the stone was greased and became smoking hot. The cook would dip her hand in the batter, then with a

104

**HOPI POTTERY BOWL**
Hopi pottery bowl geometrically designed in black.

gesture that had to be sure and quick to save her from a blistered hand, she spread the batter thinly and evenly over the stone. The batter cooked almost at once. The piki was generally folded into neat rectangles as soon as it was taken from the stone.

Besides corn the desert people had squash, gourds, tobacco, and seven kinds of beans. They also had fields of cotton, the only ones in North America. There was a wild cotton native to this country, but it was not the same. The domestic American cotton, according to botanists, can only be duplicated by crossing this wild cotton with the domestic cotton of Asia.

The Southwest tribes were good hunters and added meat to their supply of food.

The Basin–Plateau people ate almost anything they could get nourishment from, which included wild seeds, roots, small animals, and bite-size insects. Piñon nuts were a staple food. They were ground into a coarse meal on stone slabs, which was made into a thin bread, sometimes mixed with berries or meat. Many plants found in this area have large fleshy roots in which water is stored, and these plants could carry the Indians though the rainless months as well as serving as food.

Rabbits were hunted and killed by throwing clubs at them, and there were rabbit drives in which many of the tribe took part. Long nets of yucca fiber were set up in sections to form a semicircle. A pit was dug between each section and each pit was watched over by an elder man of the tribe, armed with a club. Children would fan out for a great distance and then drive the rabbits, first into the nets, then into the pits where they would be clubbed.

Antelope was a luxury in this area. They were stalked by men wearing antelope hide and shot at a very close range with bow and arrow. Where the antelope was more plentiful, a shaman would take advantage of the animals natural curiosity and lead them into a trap.

Grasshoppers and Mormon crickets were driven into a trench, then gathered into baskets. They were roasted until completely dry, then ground up and stored. Snakes also went into the cooking pot.

In the California area, acorns formed the main diet, being stored in the shell to be used when needed. The acorn was

106

bitter and the tannic acid had to be removed to make them edible. Small game and fish supplemented the diet in this area.

Along the Northwest Coast, salmon, whale, and porpoise were eaten as were strawberries and raspberries. The porpoise and seals were harpooned from canoes in tribal hunts. Salmon was preserved by splitting and drying them, but in the south the dried salmon was pounded up fine and packed in basketry bags for future use. Berries, roots, seaweed, and crabapples were all cooked in fish oil, and these were the only vegetable foods. Cooking was done mainly by the hot stone method.


# CACHES


The Indian moral code forbid stealing from a friend or a friendly tribe, but it was considered a virtue to steal from an enemy. This, plus the need for food during a lean time, led the Indian to hide part of his food and equipment which was put in a place that came to be known as a cache, from the French word *cacher* meaning "to hide."

When the Indians of the Northwest hid their dried fish they stored it in a cache built of split cedar and planks supported on the branches of the trees far above the ground. They also put clams on strings of cedar bark to dry for future use. Acorns were kept in a brush storehouse on top of the homes. For holding liquids and small seeds, vessels of rushes, plastered inside and out with piñon gum and pitch, were used. People living along the Columbia River pounded fish between two stones, then stored them in baskets made of grass and rushes lined with salmon skin. The fish were pressed down and covered with fish skin, each basket weighing from ninety to one hundred pounds.

Plains Indians kept food and valuables in buffalo hide cases. The Indians along the Missouri River made caches by first removing the soil from a circle about twenty inches across, then excavating a pit having the form of a kettle, which was gradually enlarged to a diameter of six or seven feet. The hole was then lined on the bottom and sides with sticks. Food, skins, and other items were stored in these kettle-like pits. The

**APACHE WATER JUG**
Jug shows convenient carrying strap and is pitch-lined.

pits were then filled with dirt or sod to make them appear as natural as possible. This was also done in the Southwest and by some of the western Plains people. A jug-shaped pit was made, eight to nine feet deep, the only entrance a ladder through an opening two to three feet wide. The southern Indians made a kind of crib, erected on posts and then covered inside and out with loam or clay. These would keep out the smallest vermin. Mesquite beans, piñon nuts, acorns, filberts, and hickory nuts were stored in brush enclosures. These structures were possibly the originals of the slatted corncribs still in use today.

The Winnebago women stored part of their wild rice harvest by burying it. Some tribes, instead of burying the grain, put it in cedar bark-lined bags, which held about three fourths to one bushel. The Ottawa and Potawatomi used this method, but they also buried the bags when it was necessary to hide them.

Even water was cached. The Zuñi made trips to the high mountains where they made huge snowballs, then melted them to obtain water when it was needed.

When the Hopi were going on a long trip or on the warpath, they had several women follow them part of the way. Each woman carried gourds of water and at certain intervals would bury the water-filled gourds, then turn back to camp. When the men made their return trip, they would have sufficient water in case it was needed.

## HUNTING AND FISHING

To the Indian, hunting was not a sport, but part of his fight for survival. Much of the hunting was for food, clothing, and lodging. It was the first duty of every man to provide food which the woman cooked. The pursuit of game was divided into two sets of activities, trapping and hunting, which many times corresponded to military strategy and tactics, including a series of traps and hunting weapons.

Game was sometimes captured by hand, without the aid of weapons or apparatus. It consisted mostly of picking up marine

**BUCKSKIN BOW AND QUIVER CASE**
Hunter's principle trappings. Approximately four feet long, this one is very plain and decorated with fringe, the skin is dyed yellow.

animals stranded on the beach, robbing birds' nests, or seizing birds from their roosting place at night. This called for utmost cunning, agility, and strength. Often the hunt was a tribal one in which many took part, as, for example, when all the tribe would surround a herd of animals and drive or coax them into a gorge or corral.

Hunting weapons were used for striking, bruising, or breaking of bones; these included stones held in the hands, clubs and other hard objects, some attached to a line or in the form of a sort of slingshot. Some tribes took great care in carving the clubs for hunting and decorated them with special symbols.

Slashing or stabbing with edged weapons was another method. Stones, reeds, and wood were all used to make weapons of this type, as little metal was known in early Indian history. Chipped and ground weapons were used, with or without handles, but were not as common as the piercing weapons, which included pointed sticks, stones, spears, harpoons, and bows and arrows. These were all held in the hand, hurled from the hand, or shot from a bow or blowgun, and some were slung with throwing sticks. Weapons of this kind went through many changes and transformations, depending upon the game hunted, the material at hand to make the weapon, and the skill of the maker, as well as the skill of the hunter and tribe.

Pits, snares, and traps were another method of hunting. The Plains tribes and the ancient Pueblos often used this method of pitfalls in capturing deer, antelope, and wolves.

Some Indian tribes used dogs, but with few exceptions dogs were not trained specially for the pursuit of game. Fire and smoke were sometimes used; as in other parts of the world, the use of fire almost assured the conquest of animals. Smoke drove the animal out of hiding, or torches were used to dazzle the eyes of the deer and to attract fish or birds.

At times drugs were used to capture animals, such as the bark of the walnut root which was used as an anesthetic for fish in freshwater pools in the southern states. This allowed the fish to be caught easily. In other parts of the country soap root and buckeyes were used in the same way.

There were a great many rules and taboos connected with hunting, perhaps because the survival of the tribe depended on the hunters. From early childhood every boy was taught to become a hunter. Along with the weapons, he had to learn the taboos of things he must and must not do, as well as the things which must not be killed. Along with the taboos were the laws which forbade the eating of certain foods. Some tribes could not eat food that smelled, such as leeks, or wild onions, before a hunt. Tobacco was saved to be used in ceremonies, including those of the hunt. Hunters had to be familiar with the calls of birds and animals and be able to imitate them. They made decoys, whistles, and masks like the animal to be hunted. There was a proper hunting season as well as ceremonies and fetishes, laws and taboos for the hunting of each animal. Every hunter had to know something about the anatomy of each animal so that he would know where to aim his arrow or spear for the kill. He also had to know how to cut up game.

Among some tribes, the hunter had to take purges and cleansing baths in a sweat lodge, and rub his body with certain leaves before going on a hunt. An Iroquoian hunter had to live alone for at least a week before a great hunt. He could have nothing to do with his wife, including being near her, touching her, or even eating food she had prepared.

In the winter, game was hunted on snowshoes in the areas where this was possible. Snow would slow up the animal and sometimes the larger animals would become stuck in the snow. Only small groups of Indians would make up these winter hunting parties.

With the arrival of the horse on this continent hunting methods changed for those Indians who adapted to the horse. The bows became shorter so they could easily be handled from the back of a horse. The arrows of the Plains horsemen had some iron heads, but most were of stone, bone, copper, and even hard sinew. The head of the arrow was small and was eared at the rear end to aid in lashing it to the shaft. The neck end of the Plain arrow where it met the bowstring was wider than the shaft and was kind of Y-shaped. Much of the arrow was feathered, and under the feathers the arrow was marked with stripes to represent kills. These arrows also had grooves, often three of them running from the arrowhead to the feather.

They could be straight but were usually wavy. These were believed to represent lightning and make the arrow fly faster, better, and to hit its mark. Also it was thought they made the game bleed freely. Many of the Plains Indians could shoot an arrow right through a buffalo, and the force of the arrow was said to be almost unbelievable.

Among the Woodland Indians, the hunting grounds were usually marked off and recognized as belonging to certain tribes. In some tribes the hunting grounds were subdivided so that each clan had its own area, marked with its totem cut on trees along the boundary line. Hunting grounds were usually far from the main village and expeditions went to the hunting grounds and camps for a whole season. Much of the trip was by canoe since it was easier to get the meat and hide back to the camp by this method. If there were no streams, or they were filled with ice, the game was dragged back to camp by men on snowshoes. Much hunting was done in the winter, as the fur pelts were much thicker and better and game was easier to find and track in the snow.

While most Indians did not have dogs for hunting, the Woodland Indians did have a short-legged, rather short-nosed little dog they took with them in the canoe. These were a kind of burrowing dog that would go into the beaver lodge or fox den and chase out the animal. Winter hunting was tedious, as the animal had to be stalked downwind so the hunter could get within a few feet of it. This was necessary as the Indian's bow and arrow didn't have a long range, its maximum being about 125 feet. To make the arrows perfectly straight, a drilled wood or bone tool was used. The quivers were usually made of skin or fur with a wooden stiffener or two placed in them to hold the shape. They hung upright from the left shoulder held by a band which passed over the right shoulder and under the left arm. A good hunter could easily accomplish what is called a mortar shot, in which an arrow is shot upward to fall back to earth and strike its mark on the ground; also they could get ten arrows in the air before one had fallen to the ground.

On the hunt, fire was made by means of a bow drill or a pump drill spun about by unwinding a wrapped thong very

113

rapidly. However, they were large to carry and often the Indian carried a little fire with him. This was done by lining a large shell with clay and filling it with powdery rotten wood, the best being yellow birch. A pea-sized ember started this spunk smoldering and its nearly airtight container kept it burning slowly. The shell was carried in a bag and would keep fire all day.

Sometimes birds and rabbits were chased into nets where their heads were caught in the meshes, carefully calculated for size. The nets were made of Indian hemp spun on the thigh and were eight feet tall and often thirty feet long.

Nets were also used for catching fish in some areas, as fish, in fact almost everything edible that came from the water, was consumed by the Indians of this continent, except for the Apache, Navaho, and Zuñi who held fish to be a food taboo.

The coastal tribes ate a great deal of shellfish in their daily diet. Shellfish were dug up or taken by hand when wading or diving. Some were always dried and stored away for future use. For the tribes of the Northwest Coast salmon and herring eggs were a staple. In the larger streams fish were speared from canoes, and in some places a regular platform was built in the water. The fisherman would stand on this with a spear and catch the fish as they swam by.

Large fish and marine mammals were killed by means of harpoons, while smaller ones were usually killed with a bow and arrow, gigs, nets, or traps. Fire or torches were used along the shore or from boats. The gleam would attract the fish to the surface where they were then caught by hand or in a net.

The Indians of the Great Lakes region fished in the winter by chopping openings in the ice with stone hatchets. Huddled in their furs, they would erect shelters over the holes; then the men would wait patiently, a lure in one hand and a spear in the other. The fish would be speared and put aside on the ice where later the women would come around and collect them.

The swallow-and-gorge hook was often used, as well as bone hooks tied to long lines of sinew. Almost every young Indian boy could catch a few fish for a meal.

For bait, crickets were used for bass and trout, grubs and May beetles for sunfish and perch, and katydids were used for almost all types of fish.

114

# BASIC FOODS AND RECIPES

As with all people, some tribes were famous for one type of food while others cooked something different. But one food, or a form of it, was basic among most Indians, and the Plains people depended upon it to take them through a hard winter. This food was called pemmican. In the old days this was made with dried buffalo meat and berries mixed with melted marrow fat, but today it can be made with dried beef.

## RECIPE FOR INDIAN PEMMICAN

*1. Run dried beef through a food blender.*
*2. For each pound of dried beef add ½ cup of raisins.*
*3. Put the beef and raisins in a shallow pan and pour melted suet over it. Be careful in pouring; use only enough suet to hold the beef and raisins together and no more, as it will be too fat for modern taste.*
*4. Mix thoroughly, then allow it to cool.*
*5. After cooling it can be cut into squares, strips, or however you want it stored. This will keep for some time.*

You can vary this by adding other dried fruits with the raisins or in place of raisins. You might want to add more fruit per pound of dried beef. You can experiment, as every Indian woman seemed to have her own personal recipe for pemmican, which made it just a little different from her neighbors. If the recipe was a tribal one, then each tribe secretly guarded their special recipe.

## BROTH AND POTATOES

*2 pounds new (or small) potatoes, well washed*
*6 cups water*
*Beef broth (follow directions on package for amount to use; usually one cube or teaspoon per cup of water)*

Place potatoes in broth and simmer for about 45 minutes, or until potatoes are tender. Serve as soup, with a potato. Makes about 6 servings.

## SWEET POTATO PANCAKES

*4 large sweet potatoes*
*3 eggs*
*1 cup flour*
*1½ teaspoons salt*
*⅛ teaspoon pepper*
*2 tablespoons cooking oil*

Parboil potatoes until tender; peel and mash. Mix eggs, flour, salt, and pepper. Heat oil on griddle until a drop of water sizzles. Drop potato batter from a large spoon, and brown on both sides. Flatten pancakes as you turn them. If needed, add more oil to griddle. They can be served with honey. Makes about 15 pancakes.

## FRIED MEAT PIES

*1½ pounds ground beef*
*Dash of salt*
*Dash of pepper*
*2 tablespoons green pepper*
*2 tablespoons onion*
Make meat balls about the size of a walnut.

Batter for meat balls:

*2 cups flour*
*3 teaspoons baking powder*
*1 teaspoon salt*
Enough warm water to make a very thick batter.

Roll meat balls in batter and drop in very hot oil or fat. Brown on all sides.

## BAKED MEAT PIES

*1½ pounds ground meat*
*Salt and pepper to taste*
*2 tablespoons water*

Make dough of:

*2 cups flour*
*1 teaspoon salt*
*2 teaspoons baking powder*
*1 level tablespoon shortening*
*1 cup milk*

Roll mixture in small rounds and place a bit of meat in one half of round, then fold over and crimp edges together. Place in well-greased pan and bake in moderate oven until brown.

## MAPLE CRANBERRY SAUCE

*1 cup maple sugar*
*1 pound fresh washed cranberries*
*1 cup white sugar*
*1¼ cups water*

Put maple sugar, white sugar, water, and cranberries in a large saucepan. Bring to a boil, then reduce heat and simmer for 25 minutes, or until skin of cranberries pops.
Cool and serve at room temperature or chilled.

## SUNFLOWER CAKE

*3 cups sunflower seeds, shelled*
*3 cups water*
*⅛ teaspoon salt*
*6 tablespoons cornmeal*
*½ cup oil or shortening*

Put sunflower seed, salt, and water in a large saucepan, cover, and simmer for about an hour, stirring occasionally. Put this in a blender and puree.

Mix in the cornmeal, a tablespoon at a time, until the dough is stiff enough to be shaped by hand. Cool.

After dough is cool, shape into firm, flat cakes about 3 inches in diameter.

Heat oil in large skillet. When a drop of water sizzles, the skillet is hot enough. Brown cakes well on both sides and drain. You may need to add more oil as the cakes are cooking.

Makes about 15 cakes.


## TOMATO SOUP

4 pounds tomatoes, washed and halved
2 yellow onions, peeled and sliced
2 sprigs mint
1 cooking apple, peeled and sliced
6 sprigs dill
2 bay leaves
1 teaspoon salt
2 quarts water
2 packages chicken broth or 2 cubes chicken broth (beef cubes or packages may be used if wished)

Place all ingredients in large keetle, simmer for about 3 hours, stirring occasionally. Remove bay leaves and serve hot or cold.


## FRIED HOMINY GRITS

1 cup hominy
5 cups water
1¼ teaspoons salt
Pepper
Butter
⅓ cup oil or bacon drippings

Bring water to boil and gradually add hominy, stirring continually. Add salt and pepper, and butter and boil about 20 minutes. Wrap in foil paper and chill overnight. Then remove paper and slice the hominy grits about ½ inch thick. Put into frying pan and brown on both sides in the oil or bacon drippings.

## WILLOW AND ROPE FISH TRAPS

Fish traps were made of long willow poles and rope, formed into the shape of long baskets. A rope was tied at one end of a willow pole, about 3 to 4 inches from one end. The rope was twisted with left-handed turns for about 3 or 4 inches and then another pole was tied with rope, and again at 3 to 4 inches another pole until the willow poles were arranged in a circle of the size wanted, with the loops and twists of rope connecting them, as in Diagram 3. Six inches or so below the first circle of rope another rope was twisted around the poles, and so on to the end of the poles. As each circle or rope was twisted into place the willow poles were pulled closer together, like a funnel. Where the ends tapered to a point the poles were tied together at that end, as in Diagram 1.

Next a shorter funnel was made in the same manner as above; however the tapered end was not closed but was pulled together so that an opening was left, as in Diagram 2. This small basket was placed inside the larger one, as shown in Diagram 1, where the large openings are tied together.

The fish trap was then placed in water and fastened down so that the opening faced upstream. When fish entered the trap they swam through the bottom opening of the smaller inside basket and were trapped in the bottom portion of the larger basket. After the fish were caught, the fisherman untied the lower end of the larger basket and emptied the fish into storage containers.

## WOODEN FISH HOOKS

Probably the simplest hook to make of wood is the swallow-and-gorge hook. Any 2 to 3-inch hardwood twig can be used

# WILLOW AND ROPE FISH TRAPS

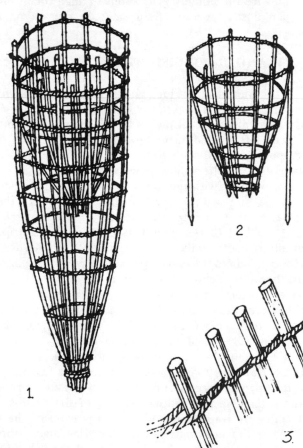

1

2

3

*(See page 119)*

to make this. Whittle a sharp point at both ends, and smooth down the twig. In the center cut a small notch, so that the line can be tied here (see Diagram 1). Be sure you do not cut this notch so deep that it will break here when the fish is caught. Tie your line at the middle notch as in Diagram 2. Cover the wooden hook and the tied notch completely with

# WOODEN FISH HOOKS

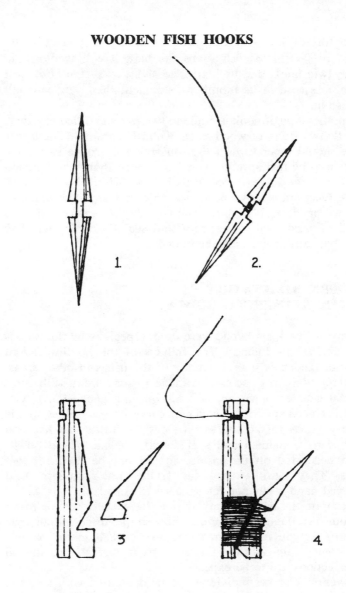

some sort of bait—worms, suet, or whatever your favorite might be. When the fish snaps the bait, it will swallow the entire twig hook, and as it tries to swim away the hook will catch crosswise in its mouth or stomach; then you can pull the fish in.

Another type of hook is made in two parts and tied together. Whittle two stems of wood as shown in Diagram 3. The larger piece should taper toward the top where a groove is cut for the line to be tied around. The other piece should be notched to fit into the larger piece and the end whittled to a sharp point. Diagram 4 shows how the two pieces are fitted together and wrapped. A little pine pitch (today a waterproof glue could be used) will waterproof and seal the wrapping. The hook part of this must also be baited.

## MODERN ADAPTATION OF INDIAN HOUSEHOLD BOWLS

Bowls of bark and wood were used, especially by the Woodland and Plains Indians. The Indians of the Southwest had clay pots and bowls, as did many of the tribes in other areas.

Adaptations of these can be made for use today with commercial wooden bowls and a wood-burning pencil set. If you are extremely ambitious, you can carve or trace lines in the wooden bowls for an Indian-type design. Bowls that have no finish can be painted and sealed with shellac. These bowls, when decorated on the inside, should not be used for wet foods. They can be used for fruits, nuts, popcorn, and wrapped candy, but not for salads with salad oil.

Decorate the bowls in any Indian design you like, or make up your own. Diagrams 1 and 2 show simple-to-do Indian-style patterns. If you make a mistake, just leave it in the pattern and keep going; only the Great Spirit is perfect, and mortal imperfections are to be expected.

Diagram 2 shows individual bowls decorated with a turtle, a horse, and a bird. You could use a butterfly, a moon, stars, the sun, in fact, whatever you want. Following Indian custom, this becomes your own personal bowl.

# MODERN ADAPTATION OF
# INDIAN HOUSEHOLD BOWLS

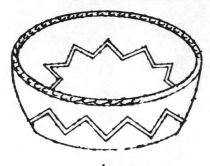

1.

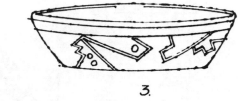

3.

2.

1.

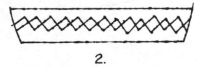

2.

3.

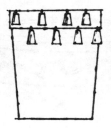

4.

5.

## MODERN ADAPTATION OF
## INDIAN HOUSEHOLD BASKETS

The Indians used baskets for storage, for carrying items, for gathering seeds and berries, and for trays. Their baskets were not only useful but added a colorful bit of beauty. Baskets are lightweight, easy to store, cannot be broken when dropped, and have countless uses. Why not adapt this very useful Indian item to your own kitchen? Plain baskets can be found at most markets; you can decorate them as the Indians did and use them. Wind yarn or strips of colored ribbon (reds, yellow, blue, green, white, and black) around the edge and hang small yarn puffs at intervals as in Diagram 1.

A tray basket can be decorated by using a darning needle threaded with yarn; make a pattern around the side as in Diagram 2, using the above colors or your favorites.

Diagram 3 shows a deep basket which could be decorated with tin cone jinglers (see Part V for directions on making tin cone jinglers); attach them in twos or threes around the edge. The Indian baskets you see in museums are decorated in this manner.

Diagram 4 is a small berry basket. Actually it could be made from the small woven plastic baskets that grapes and small tomatoes are sold in at the market. Weave yarn or ribbon in and out of the large open spaces, in different color combinations.

Diagram 5 shows a large storage basket made from a bushel basket, covered with cutouts of felt, with felt glued around the edges and around the handles. Cardboard baskets could be painted a base color and then decorated with lines and paint in geometric designs. These make wonderful storage baskets for everything—wastepaper, toys, vegetables, newspapers, magazines, overshoes, or as a clipping basket for all the loose odds and ends.

Start using colorful baskets as the Indians did and you'll never be without them.

# PART III

## CEREMONIES, MYSTERIES, AND MEDICINE MEN

*(Crafts begin on page 145)*

Ceremonies, mysteries, and medicine men were all part of American Indian life. Ceremonies were divided into groups; those that the entire tribe took part in; those of a secret nature; those that only men were allowed to take part in; those for men of special rank, such as the medicine man or a warrior; ceremonies for women; ceremonies involving only one individual.

## CEREMONIES

Ceremonies of a public nature were often in the form of a play or drama, while the secret ones were usually perfomed in some specially constructed lodge, room, or chamber, with none but those taking part, and the priest or medicine man, as witnesses. Some tribes, such as the Pueblo, had special symbolic altars representing the earth, the heaven, or a god.

A semipublic ceremony might be a footrace, the winner being the one favored by the gods; he might receive some tangible object which possessed magic potency. The public ceremony was usually ushered in by a stately procession of priests or medicine men, who sang the traditional songs. There were the rites of smoking, sacrifice offerings of food, and offerings of prayer. The dance was a prominent feature, as were the costumes worn. Dancers wore masks or regalia which told the story of why the ceremony was being held. The time for each ceremony varied; they lasted a few hours, a few days, or a week, being held after a battle or the gathering of crops, or annually.

Among the Plains tribes the Sun Dance was a ceremony that was held annually by the Ponca and some of the other Siouan tribes. However, among the Cheyenne, Arapaho, and others, it was performed as the direct result of a vow. Nonetheless, the Sun Dance ceremony had the following features in common, among all tribes: it was held in a secret tipi; there was a procession of priests or medicine men; and there was a ceremonial construction of the great lodge, of which the raising of the center pole was the prominent feature. The dance could last from one to four days, and the dancers painted their bodies with symbolic designs. Each ceremony had its songs, musical instruments, and magic equipment.

The Pueblo tribes of the Southwest are noted for the length of their ceremonies. The Hopi have thirteen big ceremonies, each lasting nine days. Their secret rites are always held underground in chambers called kivas. An elaborate altar is erected, with special items placed upon it; each masked dancer is a symbolic figure. There is the winter solstice ceremony and the new fire ceremony, among others; and in all of these, the Hopi have a large number of Kachina, or masked dancers.

The Navaho and Apache have long ceremonies which are the property of the medicine men and must be regarded as medicine dances. Many of these are very complicated. Elaborate and intricate symbolic masks are worn. There is dancing, chanting, and the making of dry pictures, or sand paintings, which are destroyed when the ceremony is over. It is believed the sand paintings absorb whatever bad influences may be around a person, and for this reason the sand from the painting is sometimes carried a great distance from the one involved in the ceremony. In this way, the bad influence is removed far enough so that it will not have any effect.

The California ceremonies usually last only a single day and contain little symbolism. The tribes of the Northwest Coast have ceremonies lasting from one to four days. The object of the winter ceremony is to bring back youthfulness, or rejuvenation.

# MYSTERIES

Mystery and magic were as fascinating to the Indians as they have always been to all people. Many Indians were well versed in sorcery, good at prophecy and telepathy, and generally good magicians, especially at sleight-of-hand tricks. Illusion, hypnotism, suggestion, and sleight of hand were used in the healing of disease as well as on other occasions. A common method of sleight of hand in relation to cures was to pretend to suck foreign objects from the body.

The fire ceremony was an astonishing performance; many people of different tribes seemed able to handle hot items with little effect. A Chippewa sorcerer could handle, with impunity, red-hot stones and burning bands, or could bathe his hands in boiling water or syrup and never seem to be burned. Such magicians were called fire dealers or fire handlers.

Navaho performers, naked except for a breechcloth and moccasins, their bodies daubed with white clay, would run at high speed around a fire, holding great fagots of flaming cedar bark. As they ran, they applied the burning fagots to the back of the runner in front. They would run until the fagots were nearly consumed, but they never seemed to be burned or injured by the flames. That cedar bark does not make a very hot fire and that the clay coating could have partially protected the body has been pointed out by skeptics.

Some tribes handled venomous serpents without harm. It is believed that Hopi children are given a small scratch of snake venom, so that by the time they are ready for the dance, they are immune to its poison.

Navaho dancers, in the ceremony of the Mountain chant, pretend to thrust an arrow far down their throats. In this feat an arrow with a telescopic shaft is used; the point is held between the teeth, and the hollow part of the handle, covered with feathers, is forced down toward the lips; thus the arrow appears to be swallowed. The Navaho also pretend to swallow sticks.

Magicians are usually men, but among the Iroquois, women often are the magic makers. Many tribes have people who are bound hand and foot and then, without any visible assistance or effort on their part, release themselves from the bonds. There are rainmakers, and those who claim to make corn or beans grow in a matter of moments—feats of illusion.

While magic had both its serious and fun aspects, among the Indians visions were considered the most imporant moments of a young boy's life. Having a vision was part of a young Indian's maturing, and the vision search was something of an ordeal. A vision was a sort of message from the gods to an individual. Solitude, fasting, and praying were the path to a vision, a contact with a supernatural visitor. The Iroquois called it "Orenda," or special strength; the Algonkins called it "Manitou" and the Siouan called it "Wakonda." A strong vision could lead a young man to become a shaman, or medicine man, in which case he could read the future, give news of people at a distance, and diagnose illness and even cure it. Hunger, loneliness, pain, and expectation led most of the young men to have a dream experience. After the vision, objects from it would be put together and this was called the medicine bundle, which offered lifetime protection. From the vision, a young man would learn songs, chants, and dances which were then his individual medicine or charm. If a man could not obtain a vision he might buy an old vision and the medicine of someone else who had been especially blessed. A successful dreamer would permit others to copy his charms and he would teach them his songs and dances. If a young man had a bad vision, he might commit suicide. The worst vision was one in which he would never be a man. If, in his vision, the moon came to him holding in one hand a warrior's bow and arrow and in the other a woman's pack strap, and if as the young man reached out to take the weapon, the moon crossed hands and the young man touched the woman's emblems, there would be nothing he could ever do but turn pseudo-woman.

## MEDICINE MEN

Every tribe had medicine men and, in some cases, medicine women. These individuals were regarded as having supernatural power, and in many tribes they ranked next to the chiefs. Some were healers, some were seers, and others were a bit of both. The medicine man was a person of mystery who had obtained his power through a vision which had come to him when he was either asleep or awake. His vision could have been in any form, such as a bird, animal, object, symbol— something that is done in the vision and understood as a message. Special chants and prayers were given through the vision. Because of all this power the medicine man was both feared and respected.

There were four requisites for the medicine man. He must recognize the sanctity of human life. He must meditate between the Great Spirit and the people. He must never depart from the truth. And in addition, he must be slow to anger, prudent in speech, and deliberate.

Illness was believed to be caused by the fact that one's soul was lost or had been stolen by a ghost, an enemy sorcerer, or an unfriendly medicine man. Illness would remain while the soul was gone, and if it wasn't returned death would result. Death was also believed to be caused by the intrusion of evil ghosts or demons into the body, so a strong well-developed body was better able to resist ordinary ailments.

Drums, gourd rattles, and a horn cupping apparatus were sometimes used in healing work. Some tribes believed in the cure of roots and herbs, while the Omaha of the Plains felt that bleeding was important, the gashes being made between the eyes.

With a fair knowledge of anatomy, the medicine man could set bones; after setting the bone, he placed a piece of rawhide that had been soaked in water until it was soft, around the broken bone to hold it in place. As the rawhide dried, it shrank, molding itself to the broken limb and making a cast very similar to the plaster cast used by the white men. Deep wounds were sewn up with fine strands of sinew, the needle being a very fine sliver of bone.

Each medicine man had his own medicine bag, usually made from an animal skin, containing roots, paints, white clay, deer tails, leg bones, claws of eagles, and on the Plains, the maw bone of the buffalo, as this was supposed to contain the life or soul of the buffalo, considered big medicine. These medicine bags were handed down from father to son. The Sioux believed that the medicine man lived among the thunder before his mortal birth and there he gained the knowledge of his work on earth. Many of the Indian medicine men were very accomplished, even by our standards. They not only could set broken bones and cure illness with their knowledge of herbs, they also knew a great deal about psychology, and much of the contents of the medicine bag was devoted to this end. They knew the benefit of distracting the patient's mind from himself, and even their dress was something formidable, often a bearskin reaching from heels to head, covering the head. At other times they might wear a costume of finest beadwork or quill work, decorated with much fringe, and a horned bonnet or turban headdress of wolfskin.

The medicine man usually carried something of nature with him because it was believed that everything in nature lives and has being, and that there are both good and evil spirits. A medicine man possessing magical powers supposedly could control these spirits, knowing what chants to sing and the medicine to use to discourage an evil spirit from taking hold of one.

The Southwest tribes often set up an altar in the home of a sick person and the medicine man stayed with the person until he recovered or died. Medicine men did not assist with childbirth in these tribes, but after the birth the father would ask the medicine man to take the child out into the sun and name it. The child would be carried to the east edge of the mesa and just as the sun rose, the infant was held to the east and given a name.

Unlike the Pueblo, the Navaho did not have curing societies. If a young man wanted to become a medicine man he found one he wanted to imitate and asked him to become his teacher. If he was accepted, he must pay a fee to his teacher, then later he must gain public approval.

Illness could be caused by so many things, such as bad dreams or fright, if taboos were violated, that the idea of a Navaho cure was not so much to cure an illness as it was to avert it. In fact they practiced preventive medicine. If a man had a bad dream, he would go to the medicine man. The curing ceremony often lasted nine days and relatives would come

134

for miles around to attend. Altars were set up, and sand painting were made along with the chants and stories which accompanied them. There were games, feasting, dancing, magic displays, and much gossip. It was felt that the curing ceremony and chanting not only helped the patient, but would also benefit all who were there, and eventually the whole tribe would be blessed.

Today's curing ceremony is based on tradition and is unchanged since antiquity. Throughout the ceremony, each day is linked to the next by means of a song sequence containing several hundred songs. These, and the prayers, are intoned like a litany, or chanted, and have great power. By means of prayer sticks, carefully made of wood, the supernatural ones are invited to come.

The ceremony might be as follows: on the first day of the ceremony the medicine man sets up sacred objects after praying at dawn; these distinguish this special chant or ceremony. Next a large fire is built and a sweat bath is taken by all who want to participate. Later prayer sticks are made, and when they are ready, the patient, who should never see them being made, symbolically lights the sticks which are then wrapped. Holding the sticks, the patient repeats after the medicine man a prayer, phrase by phrase. The prayer sticks are then placed in spots where the gods will see them. On the first night, the house is blessed and objects from the medicine bundle are applied to the patient's body as prayers are chanted. The same ritual is followed for the next three days, while prayer sticks to different deities are made each day. On the fifth day, the sacred items of the medicine bundle are put outside the ceremonial house, with a prayer to attract the gods. These things are left there until a sand painting has been completed inside. The sand painting is quickly made by the medicine man and his assistants upon clean sand spread in the center of the ceremonial house. On occasion the painting can be done on buckskin or cloth. This is not painting, as we think of watercolors or oils, but a dry picture made by letting colored sand flow through the fingers onto the ground. Great control and skill are needed to make lines, dots, and circles from sand flowing from the hand.

The sacred bundle items are then brought in. The patient is

positioned in the middle of the sand painting and these items are applied to his body. The sand painting is a symbol of the special gods being prayed to, and now the patient becomes one with these gods represented in the sand. Miraculously he shares in their power. The years that it has taken the medicine man to learn the chants, the sequence of prayers, all of the ritual for establishing the harmony of the ceremony now works to restore, heal, renew, and bless the patient and those who take part in this sacred and beautiful performance. The painting is wiped away; the sand is carried out.

This sand painting ceremony is repeated each day for the remaining eight. At the end, some of the sand can be given to those who have come to take part in the ceremony, and this is put in small pouches which are sometimes worn around the neck for special protection and medicine.

## FETISHES

This small medicine bundle of sacred sand from a sand painting is much like a fetish. Actually a fetish could be of stone, wood, bone, feathers, almost anything that was believed to have a special power for that particular individual. It could be large, small, natural, or artificial. Sometimes a small rock which looked like a bird, a fish, or some animal would be tied with feathers and bits of coral or turquoise for a fetish. These were usually worn about the person, often carried in small bags, for protection and good luck. Whatever the fetish might be, it was regarded as being animate and possessing immortal life. In fact almost everything was considered to be animated: water, rocks, plants, trees, earth, sky, stars, wind, clouds, sun, and moon. Lakes and seas might writhe in billows, but they could not traverse the earth; the rivers might traverse the earth, but even these could be held in bond by the mighty power of the god of winter; mountains and hills might quake, but they were held in check by a powerful and mysterious spell, proving that all things, while related, are equally under the guidance of the Great Spirit.

The fetish was usually acquired by a person, family, or

136

tribe for the purpose of promoting its good luck and welfare. In return the fetish required that its owner give it prayer and protection and consider it in a sacred light. Some fetishes were more powerful than others, and should a fetish lose its repute as a promoter of welfare, it would become useless and be only a charm, amulet, or talisman and finally fall into the category of mere ornament. A fetish was different from the tutelar or guardian spirits, as the fetish could be bought, sold. loaned, or inherited, except among the Iroquois.

Most of the articles found in the medicine bag of the shaman or medicine man bore the title of fetish. These were commonly otter, snake, owl, and other bird skins, bark, roots, berries, many kinds of potent powders, and other items. Among the Hopi, a splinter from a tree that had been struck by lightning had the reputation for great power in the treatment of fractures.

There are numerous hunting fetishes, some of stone naturally in the shape of animals or birds, others are small carvings made to resemble various predatory animals, with eyes inlaid with turquoise, and one or more arrowheads bound at the back or side, the whole smeared with the blood from the slain game.

The fetish could be inspired by a dream, a gift from the medicine man, a trophy taken from a slain enemy, a bird, animal, reptile, a small bag of pebbles, or a strangely twisted bit of wood. It could be anything that the owner had imagined or dreamed about, but it always had some symbolic connection with occult power. A fetish could be fastened to the scalp lock as a pendant, attached to some part of the costume, hung around the neck in a small pouch, hung from the bridle bit of the owner's horse. It could be concealed between the covers of the shield, or hidden in a special place in the dwelling. A mother might tie a fetish to her child's cradle, to protect it.

The Hidatsa used the teeth of the beaver to tie around the neck of a little girl, believing this would make her more industrious. When a Hidatsa brave went to war he would, at times, slit the hide of ,a wolf in such a manner that when it was pulled over his head, the head of the wolf hung over his chest and the tail and back over his shoulder and down the back. This was considered a powerful fetish, as was the hide of a white buffalo. If the hide of a young buffalo not over two years old could be taken off completely and tanned with the horns, nose, hoofs, and tail, it was a magical fetish to be worn on special occasions.

Among many Indians, there was a belief in witchcraft. As the shaman was the mediator between the world of man and of the spirits he was considered to possess supernatural powers and was often a wizard or a witch. However anyone could practice witchcraft if he knew the correct formula. Witchery was usually learned from an older relative, and there was a special "witch bundle" or bag which held the special medicines.

There were several ways of casting a spell. One way was purely mental, which consisted of strong wishing thoughts. The witch, or sorcerer, would work himself into a frenzy, then seek to make his mind cast a spell upon the object of his wrath. Sometimes bark or wooden images were made and used. A woman envious of the weaving skills of another might concentrate on the other's hands, in the hope they would lose their skill. Young women used witchcraft to attract certain warriors or for revenge against a rival.

## MASKS

Masks were used by some tribes as a means of intensifying the idea of the actual presence of some mythic animal or supernatural person. Once the mask was believed to have been used as a face shield or a protective covering, and from this it evolved into the high fancy headdress or a symbolic mask.

The most simple form of mask was made from the head of an animal such as the buffalo, deer, or elk. These realistic masks did not represent the actual animal but the general type and, when worn, endowed the wearer with certain distinctive qualities which identified him with the supernatural spirit represented. Many of the masks of the Northwest Coast were made with double faces to illustrate this belief. This was done by having the muzzle of the animal fitted over and concealing the face below. There were also compound masks, or faces within a face. A string would pull open the first face and another of a different expression would be revealed.

There were sacred masks that required prescribed methods of handling and use. The Hopi put their masks on and off with the left hand. Before painting the masks, which were made with leather, cloth, or basketry, and decorated with wood bark, hair, woven fabrics, feathers, herbs, and bits of gourds, they had certain rites of bodily purification. The decorations were taken off at the close of the ceremony and deposited in some sacred place. Other masks were simple face coverings, concealing only the forehead. Some of these had a helmet attachment which was symbolically painted. The Hopi did not always wear their masks in the ceremonies, but at times would put them on a pole, and these were carried by another.

As with many things of tribal life, certain masks belonged to the clan and were held in their keeping. Some masks could never be touched by pregnant women, nor looked upon by a child who was not yet initiated into the clan to which the mask belonged. There were masks which were constructed in such a way that the tongue could be stuck out and pulled back; the eyes could blink, the mouth open and close. Parts of the masks were hinged to enable the wearer to change its aspects throughout the different phases of the ceremony.

The Iroquois had two kinds of masks, those carved of wood and the ones woven of cornhusks. Those called the false-face masks were believed to be evil spirits or demons, without bodies, arms, or limbs, having only faces of a most hideous character. These were grotesquely carved and showed a combination of skill mingled with a sense of horror as well as humor. The Iroquois even carved in outline the face of a mask on a living, growing tree, the idea being that as the tree grew, so would the face and thus it would take form. When the tree was cut down so the mask could be completed, it was believed that it had absorbed the life of the tree and was a living thing. After the mask was hollowed out and the features formed, the mask was usually painted red, or red and black depending upon the type of face carved. Long wisps of hair were put into place, holes were drilled for the thongs which fastened the mask to the wearer's head, and medicine tobacco was tied to the part in the hair.

139

Boys of the Siouan tribes made weird masks to disguise themselves. They made a mask of rawhide to represent the head of the thunderbird. When the first thunder was heard in the spring, the boys covered their head and face and went to the tipi of an uncle, where they imitated the sound of thunder and struck the doorflap with sticks. After a while the uncle would invite the boys in and give them gifts. The Sioux warriors made masks of buffalo skulls to use in their sacred dances.

The Pueblo Indians called their masks Kachinas, and they were supposed to represent the spirits of mythical beings or long-departed ancestors. These masks covered the head completely with ornaments projecting above the face section. They were of many colors and it was believed that the wearer of the mask would absorb the nature of the mask, with his personality becoming merged into the character represented, and the spirit of the mask entering into the wearer. The word "Kachina" is used by the Hopi in three ways—for the small wooden doll carved in the likeness of the masked dancer, for the masked dancer impersonating the spirits, and also as a name for the large clan of supernatural spirits.

There are two types of Kachina masks: the one that covers the whole face or part of it, and the other a helmet-shaped mask that covers the entire head. These basic forms are then decorated with paint, fur, horns, eyes, noses, and other trimmings.

The costume worn is basically the same for any Kachina, and is designed individually by the wearer. The male dancers have their moccasins stained red, brown, or green, and wear an embroidered cotton kilt held in place with two wide belts which have a fox skin hanging down the back from the waist. The bodies of the dancers are bare and painted in various designs.

It was believed that the masks for the Kachinas were introduced by the early Spanish from Mexico, but two sets of prehistoric wall paintings in underground ceremonial rooms disprove this, as these show figures wearing masks, in some cases identical with those in modern use.

The Kachina dolls are little figures, carved and painted to indicate in miniature the elaborate headdresses, decorated face

**KACHINA DOLL**—Southwest tribe
Old-type doll has some bayeta at the top of its head. A feather is
attached to it.

and body, and clothing of those who represent the Kachina spirits.

## PIPES

Pipe and tobacco have been used by the Indians as sacred objects rather than items for pleasure. Smoking was indulged in only on special occasions to bring good and to arrest evil. The pipe was smoked to prevent storms, to gain protection from enemies, to insure a good hunt, and to invoke the blessings of supernatural powers, and for peace and friendship.

Certain pipes or pipe stems, which were seldom made for actual smoking, were known as calumets. These pipes got their name from the French word *chalumeau* meaning "tube" or "reeds," and were at first simply a bundle of reeds or a shaft. This was one of the most sacred objects among most Indian tribes, and was important in all religious, war and peace ceremonies. When the long stem of the pipe was decorated with red feathers instead of white it indicated war.

Originally the pipe was a ceremonial trademark of the Woodland Algonkin tribes in the upper Mississippi area, but it quickly spread to the Great Plains. Southwest tribes often used pottery tobacco tubes, or long cornhusk cigarettes in place of the calumet.

The pipe was a passport among the tribes, allowing safe travel. It was used in ceremonies designed to conciliate foreign and hostile nations, and to conclude lasting peace treaties. It was used to attest to contracts and treaties which could not be violated without incurring the wrath of the gods.

The Pawnee believed the sun gave the calumet to them. A man was prohibited from smoking the calumet when his wife was with child, since it was believed that the child would die, or the wife would die in childbirth.

The Sioux made journeys to the pipestone quarry in southwest Minnesota to obtain a red clay stone for the pipe section. The Comanche, Ute, Bannock and Shoshoni used a soft stone of greenish color for their pipes. The Iroquois pipes were mostly of varied hues of light and dark yellowish, reddish, and brownish gray, the latter almost black.

142

**KACHINA DOLL** (Side view)
More modern doll is painted yellow and black with a bit of red.
Note the fur around the neck and the feather on head.

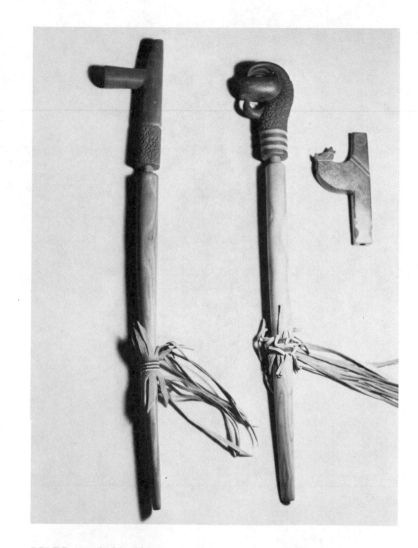

**PIPES—probably Sioux**
Left, red catlinite bowl with red rawhide tied around wooden stem.
Center, pipe with carved catlinite bowl on wooden stem.
Right, horse bowl is carved from catlinite, or red clay stone.

Pipes varied according to locality. Some were a single piece, while others had a detachable stem. The type of pipe most widely used was a straight tube, usually plain on the outside and only occasionally elaborately ornamented. The crudest pipes of this type were made from the leg bone of a deer or similar animal. They were often reinforced with a piece of rawhide, which was wrapped on wet; it contracted in drying, and this helped to prevent the bone from splitting.

The Pueblos had a pipe called the cloud-blower. This was a straight, tubular pipe, varying from a few inches to a foot in length. This small-sized pipe was usually made of clay in the same manner as their pottery. Large cloud-blowers were usually made of stone and did not differ in form or decoration. This pipe was used only for ceremonial purposes, the smoke being blown by the medicine man toward the four directions of the earth.

Some pipes held only a thimbleful of tobacco, while others would hold an ounce or more. The pipe stem could be straight, curved, twisted, round, flat, long, or short. The women of the tribes often made elaborate ornaments for the stems from beads, quills, feathers, or hair. The men, however, always put the actual decorations in place. The design of the pipe was characteristic of the tribe using it, and it was recognized by friends or enemies.

The medicine man had a special pipe usually regarded as powerful medicine, which was used for curing the sick as well as for bringing success in war.

Men of the Plains tribes had elaborately beaded and fringed bags to keep their pipes in. At night they hung in the tipi over the owner's head, and in the daytime over the door or on a tripod at the rear.

## KACHINA DOLLS

Kachina is a Hopi word with three meanings. First, it means a large group of supernatural spirits. It is also used for masked dancers impersonating these spirits, and for the small painted dolls.

It is believed that the more than two hundred Kachina

# KACHINA DOLLS

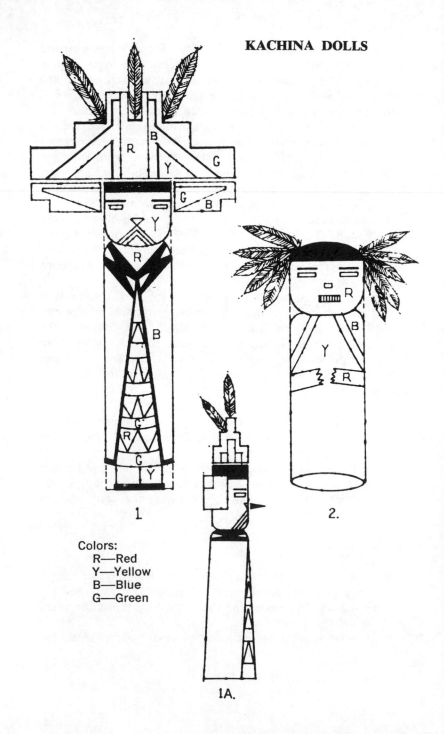

1

1A.

2.

Colors:
R—Red
Y—Yellow
B—Blue
G—Green

spirits live the latter half of the year on the mountain tops, and the first half of the year with the people. They serve as messengers between people and the great, important gods. Most of them are believed to be friendly, although some are ogres. They are both male and female. Among the Hopi there are five main religious ceremonies, each lasting nine days, and a larger number of smaller ones lasting one day. It is at these ceremonies that the dancers appear wearing the masks representing male and female Kachina spirits. It is believed that when a man puts on a mask representing a spirit he becomes that spirit.

Kachina dolls are sometimes called by the Hopi word *tihu* (tee-hoo), and it is believed that although the idea of Kachina spirits and masks is ancient, the making of the Kachina dolls is a relatively new development, probably less than one hundred years old. Any man can make the dolls, but usually the work is done by older men who become expert. In general the dolls are made of cottonwood root, a soft white wood common in the Southwest. They are carved with pocket knives, or small chisels and are then painted. Ears, noses, headdresses, and horns are usually separate pieces attached with glue or tiny dowel pins. Feathers that are not glued or stuck on are tied on with cotton string. The intricate design of the face, actually the mask, is painted on. Native mineral colors used to be used, after a coat of white clay had been applied. More recently commercial poster paint or opaque watercolor is used. The dolls made before, or about 1900, were more simple in form, with cylindrical or oval bodies and heads. The heads of these early dolls were very oversized. Later dolls are more in proportion, with natural-looking arms and legs, if they have them at all. Heads are more natural in size, and the painting is brighter than on the older dolls. The average size of a doll is about 8 to 10 inches high, but they can be up to 2 feet— although this is rare—and they can be as small as 3 inches. Much of the height is due to the elaborate headdresses that many of the dolls wear.

During the celebrations of the masked dancing, the dolls are given to the children, along with other gifts. The dolls are carried around by the little girls, as is the custom of little girls all over the world. However the Kachina is more than a toy, it is to help teach the children something of the beliefs and practices of the religion. Aside from being children's playthings, they are also found displayed in the homes.

An adaptation of a Kachina doll can be made from a round piece of wood, perhaps a used handle from a broom. This would make up into a smaller size about 3 or 4 inches. It would need only a notch whittled at the neckline, then painted, and some side feathers glued on at the side top of the head as in Diagram 2. This would be similar to the old-style dolls. Paint the body white, then when it is dry, trace the design in black and paint according to the diagram, or use your own combination of colors and designs. Bits of fur can be added to the doll's headdress, and the face can be painted in any other design to represent a mask. If you have a cylindrical piece of wood that tapers at one end, as some handles do, use the larger end for the head part, and then proceed as explained above. The larger head will make the doll look even more like the old-style Kachinas.

Diagram 1 shows how a doll can be carved from a rounded bit of wood, or from a flat 2 by 4 piece of soft wood which can be bought at any lumberyard; or a tree branch can be used, although green wood is hard to carve. There isn't too much carving other than the headdress. The legs and feet can be cut out as shown or left straight, as in Diagram 2. Carve a small notch around the neck and draw the face. A triangle or round nose can be made to stick out from the face by attaching with glue, as shown in Diagram 1A. Otherwise merely paint the nose with the rest of the face. Cut the three pieces of the headdress and glue the two pieces to the side and the one to the top, or they can be put on with tiny dowels. Feathers can be added to the top of the headdress as shown, or they can hang from the side of the headdress. Color the doll completely white, then when dry, trace the pattern with black lines and paint according to the color chart given, or use your own colors. Poster paint or watercolors work very well.

Adaptations of Kachina dolls can be made from cardboard, or you can carve a Kachina doll from a bar of white soap—it may intrigue a young bather.

148

# FETISHES

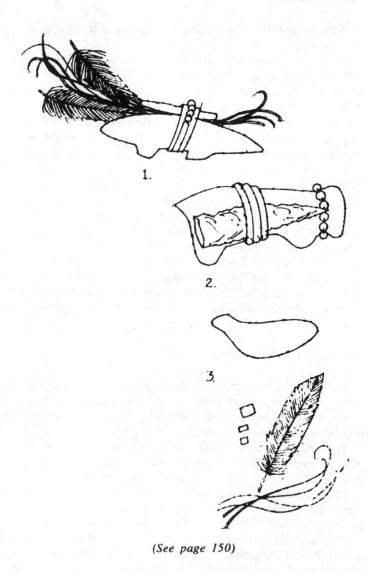

1.

2.

3.

*(See page 150)*

## FETISHES

A fetish can be of anything that appears to give power to the owner.

Diagram 1 shows a natural stone about 1¼ inches in length and ½ inch wide. A mother-of-pearl shell is tied to the back or top of the stone, together with two feathers and a bit of hair. On top of the tie are beads of coral and white.

Diagram 2 shows a carved stone, tied with an arrow on one side and a necklace of small shells. This is about 2½ inches long and because of the arrow, represents a hunting fetish.

Diagram 3 shows a natural stone or rock, some small beads, feather, and strands of hair. Tie these together with cotton cord and you have a fetish similar to the one in Diagram 1.

A rock with strange markings can be a fetish, as can a coin or a shell. Whatever is put together to make a fetish must have a special meaning, or represent something to the owner, such as that in Diagram 1 which represents the sky, the earth, and the water—the feathers, the stone, and the shells and coral, plus a few strands of the owner's hair, making it thus a general protective fetish, bringing the owner into harmony with the universe and its unknown forces.

## CALUMET OR INDIAN PIPE

The term "calumet," strictly applied, refers only to the long, elaborately ornamented stem. Later the name came to mean the stem with a pipe attached. This is a very sacred object, used in most rituals.

The stem, usually made of light wood, is painted and adorned with beautiful feathers, fur, wrappings of bead, and quill work. Sometimes the stem is also carved.

The bowl was carved from catlinite, or pipestone, which when first quarried, can be carved with a knife. Later, with exposure to air, it hardens. The stone was usually red.

The calumet was used in the ratification of treaties, which is why it was frequently referred to as a "peace pipe." It was used to greet strangers, as a symbol in the declaration of war or peace, and to insure its bearer's safety among alien tribes.

150

# CALUMET OR INDIAN PIPE

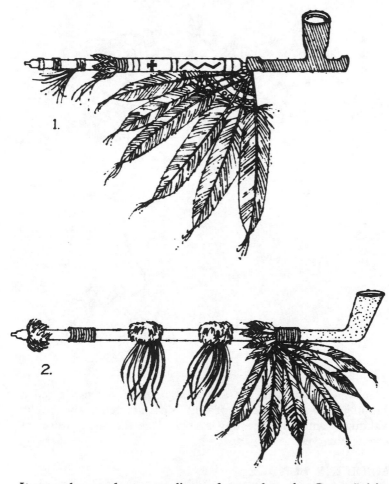

It was also used as a medium of appeal to the Great Spirit, to bring blessings or lessen bad events.

The calumet in Diagram 1 is decorated with wrappings of beads and small feathers, with a great eagle feather fan. The stem is carved with the symbol of the four corners (north, east, south, and west) and with lightning. The one in Diagram

# MEDICINE BUNDLE

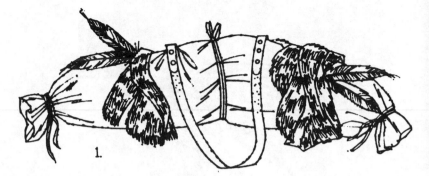

1.

2.

2 is ornamented with fur and wrappings of red cloth and a fan of feathers. The bowls of both pipes are relatively simple, although sometimes the bowls as well as the stem, were intricately carved.

## MEDICINE BUNDLE

The medicine bundles contained fetishes and cures, such as bones, feathers, claws, hair, images of mythical animals, representations of the sun, lightning, stars, vegetal medicines, plants, roots, herbs, leaves, bark, and dried small animals, such as crickets and lizards. They could be made of buckskin shaped into a bag, or a piece of buckskin could be wrapped around the items and tied with fur and feathers, with a carrying strap. They could be made in a round shape like a quiver case, or box-like, depending upon individual taste (see Diagram 1).

Small medicine pouches were made to be worn on the person, around the neck, or attached to the clothing. These contained the personal medicine of the individual (Diagram 2). A medicine pouch or bundle could also be attached to the shield, the horse, hung in the tipi, worn on the person all of the time, or only for special occasions.

## NAVAHO SAND PAINTINGS

Sand painting is a very ancient Southwest Indian art. It is a dry painting on the ground, and on some occasions on buckskin or cloth, made by letting the sand flow with control and skill through the fingers. Most of the dry sand paintings are destroyed within a twelve-hour period. The ritual of sand painting is usually done in a sequence which is termed a chant and lasts from five to nine days, but never less than three. A new sand painting is made each day, as long prayers and invocations are chanted.

There are two types of sand paintings: those that belong to the night rhythm and those belonging to the day rhythm. A day painting begins at sunrise and is finished and destroyed by sunset of the same day, with the sand taken away from the ceremonial lodge. A night painting is from sunset to sunrise. The patient is chanted or sung over and symbolically the sand painting is transferred from the ground onto the body of the patient who is sitting in the middle of the painting. This chanting seems to have a miraculous effect on the patient, for the healing power of the painting and what it represents is good for a sick mind and sad heart. Even if the ceremony does not cure the patient, he resolves his inner conflicts, has a more peaceful mind, and feels more in harmony with the world about him.

On some occasions the people present may take a little of the sand to put in pouches about their neck, but usually the medicine man gathers most of it and, going from the dwelling,

153

# NAVAHO SAND PAINTINGS

(Gods)

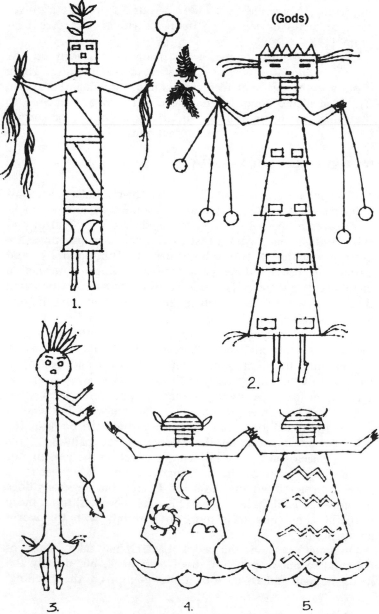

1.

2.

3.

4.

5.

# MASKS
## Zuñi Masks:

### The Clowns

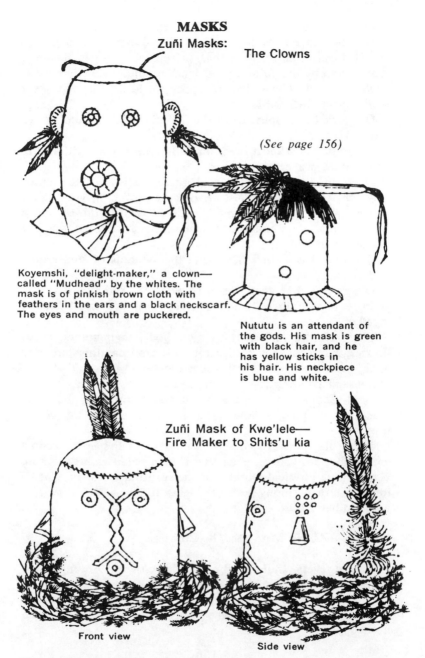

*(See page 156)*

Koyemshi, "delight-maker," a clown—called "Mudhead" by the whites. The mask is of pinkish brown cloth with feathers in the ears and a black neckscarf. The eyes and mouth are puckered.

Nututu is an attendant of the gods. His mask is green with black hair, and he has yellow sticks in his hair. His neckpiece is blue and white.

### Zuñi Mask of Kwe'lele— Fire Maker to Shits'u kia

Front view

Side view

The mask is worn during the winter solstice ceremonies. It is black with large plume decorations. Bells of white paper hang on each side of the mask. Spruce twigs are around the neck.

scatters the sand first to the east, then the south, north, and west. Then to Father Sky and Mother Earth. The paintings can be from three to more than fifteen feet. East is generally represented by the color white; south by blue; west by yellow; north by black. Generally the upper world is blue, the lower world black with white spots.

Diagram 1 is a Spirit from the Shooting Chant, holding rattles and reeds.

Diagram 2 is a Spirit from the Mountain Chant, with rattles and feather prayer offerings.

Diagram 3 is a Curer of Disease, called Qastceelci or Yaybichy. This god can also invoke the power for good crops and abundant rain. It is shown with a corn headdress and a small animal, the animal representing the sickness coming out of someone.

Diagram 4 is Father Sky, with the symbols of sun, moon, and stars.

Diagram 5 is Mother Earth, showing the radiations of life-giving energy. Father Sky and Mother Earth are usually shown together.

There can be variations in these gods, their colors, headdresses, and what they hold, as no two sand paintings are ever alike, even though they represent the same gods and stories. On a sand painting the background is always beige or sand-colored. Should you want to paint one or more of the gods, black, white, blue, yellow, and red are generally the colors used.

These diagrams are all representatives of the Spirit People who help man. It is believed that if man balances his thinking between the physical world and the spiritual world he will be in rhythm or harmony with the higher forces, with Father Sky and Mother Earth.

## MASKS—ZUÑI MASKS: The Clowns

Almost every Indian tribe had its clowns. Among some tribes these were grotesque figures who feared neither blasphemy nor obscenity, so great was their supernatural powers. The Hopi would use clowns to ridicule the citizens who needed it.

# Wooden Masks

Northwest Mask
Tsimshian Mask of the Moon

Southeastern Mask
Old type, worn in Deer Ceremony

Wood Haida Mask

Many times the clowns would dance between the ceremonial dances. They belonged to honored organizations and would create the gaiety in the tribe. The clowns, no matter what tribe, were always the ones who were amusing. They would sometimes wear masks and paint their bodies, or they would dress in old ragged clothing.

They would pretend to be hot in winter and freezing in summer. They would sometimes ride a pony, falling off and tumbling about. Some clowns would pretend to be chased by a black bear; when they captured it they would open it up and take bits of corn, berries, and other things the bear might have taken.

Some of the masks had noses 6 inches long and mouths from ear to ear, great eyes, and huge tongues.

Mudhead, or Koyemshi, was such a clown; he would dance about and miss a step. Or there might be several clowns, each dancing about, falling down, going the wrong way, all whooping and running about. They would get in the way of the other dancers, sit on the ground, and rock their bodies to and fro. They would pretend to lose things, then search for them anxiously. Their job was to amuse the audience.

# PART IV

# HOME IS WHERE THE INDIAN'S HEART IS

*(Crafts begin on page 178)*

Indians had many kinds of dwellings, some permanent, others movable. The Ojibwa of the Woodland Indians built four different types of homes. In winter they lived in either a domed wigwam, or one with a peaked roof. Their summer homes were rectangular bark huts or conical-shaped frames covered with bark slabs or animal skins. As the wigwam was their permanent dwelling it was carefully made with long slender poles as a frame, then covered with bark slabs and reed mats, reinforced with animal skins.

## DWELLINGS

Some Woodland tribes such as the Mahicans and a few Algonkins had a bark-covered communal dwelling, somewhat like an apartment building. The Iroquois called these "long-houses" because they were of various sizes, but could shelter from fifteen to twenty families. During their construction, young boys, who were light in weight, would climb around the dome placing the poles and lashing them together. The sleeping shelves, on the inside of the house, were eighteen inches from the floor and each family had a space eight to twelve feet long and from five to six feet wide, as their own apartment. Above each sleeping shelf was another shelf supported by poles that rested on partitions. Personal belongings were stored here and the poles also served as a hanger for curtains of tanned deer hide which covered the front of the sleeping platforms. The space below the platform was used for holding the family cooking pots and utensils. Two families usually shared the same fire. The roof, along the ridge, was cut with a series of square openings. These were designed to admit light and allow the escape of smoke from the cooking fires. The smoke holes could be partially or completely closed against the wind and rain by pieces of bark on top of the roof which were controlled from within by pushing with long poles. Each end of the longhouse had a vestibule ten to fifteen feet long, running across the width of the building. These rooms were used for storage and as meeting places for the people living in the house, a sort of apartment lobby. In summer the bark was removed from this part of the framework, converting this meeting space into porches.

Some of the tribes of the Southwest lived in permanent dwellings, laid out around a plaza. Some had private gardens, but the land was owned only during occupancy and could never be purchased or sold. The hogan of the Navaho was constructed with a forked piñon support log ten to twelve feet long, then earth to a depth of six inches was placed over the structure, with a smoke hole left in the center. The entrance was always to the east.

The Creeks lived in fortified towns, surrounded by a stone wall with garden space on each side of the inside wall, and a council house in the center. They constructed both gabled roofed and domed roofed houses around the council lodge. Just inside the gate was a sentry house, as well as a sentry box just outside. The homes of most of the southwestern tribes were solidly built of wood, bark, thatch, and reeds. Some of the early settlers in the southern area copied the solidly built homes of the Indians.

The Plains tribes lived in three types of dwellings, the tipi (the best known of the three), the earth lodge, and the grass lodge. Tipi is a Dakota word meaning "place to dwell." Some tipis were made taller than others, and the decorations varied from tribe to tribe, but their basic design was the same. A conical frame of poles covered with animal skin, and later canvas. The earth lodge was a circular dome-shaped structure roofed with earth and entered by a covered passage. One lodge could hold as many as forty people, and was said to last from seven to ten years. The grass lodge was the permanent communal dwelling of the Wichita. It was a conical skeleton of stout poles bent inward and overlaid with grass thatch until it looked something like a haystack. The Osage lived in oval or oblong houses; covered with mats or skin, they were often thirty to one hundred feet in length and fifteen to twenty feet wide. However, on hunting trips, the Osage lived in tipis.

The California tribes lived in dome-shaped houses approximately sixteen feet in diameter. They also had communal dwellings about sixty feet in diameter.

The tribes of the Northwest Coast lived in permanent wooden houses, which in ancient times were put together without nails or pegs, all parts being fitted and grooved to support one another.

Indians were artists at utilizing what was at hand, so while they had little regular furniture as the white man had, what they did have was especially functional and suited to their environment.

All tribes had some kind of seats. In many dwellings these were placed around the walls of the structure. Mats of various types were used as seats, pillows, and even beds. Among the Woodland tribes these were made of plaited bark and woven rushes. In the Plains, animal skin, dressed only on one side, was used. Seats were stuffed with hair, feathers, or grass, and many tribes felt the skin of the bear made a seat of honor.

The Pueblos of the Southwest had stone seats, or rectangular stools made from a single block of wood. Some of their benches went completely around the dwelling. The tribes of northern California used circular stools, and the Northwest Indians had long settees which faced the fire.

Where the tribes lived in stationary dwellings or lodges the seats were often used as beds at night. Beds were also made of willows stretched upon a low platform which had tapering ends raised and fastened to tripods, forming head and foot boards. Skins of the buffalo, killed in winter when the fur was thick, were cut to fit this willow bed and used as a mattress, with other skins thrown over it as a cover.

Pillows were made from skin or woven reeds. The Indians

BABY CRADLE—Hupa tribe of California
Example of sit-down cradle.

of California made pillows of wood, which were only used in quarters occupied by men. The Woodland Indians embroidered their pillows with elaborate designs.

Baby beds were sometimes constructed on the plan of a portable box and adapted to the age of the child. Another cradle or bed was simply a hammock made by folding animal skin around two ropes and hanging it between two posts; it was used to rock the baby to sleep.

Household items differed according to the area lived in. Wood, pottery, baskets, and bone were all used for spoons and bowls. In most tribes the cooking and eating utensils were kept by the woman in a space provided for them. If a spoon or other dish was highly decorated, it was usually used for ceremonial purposes and was a treasured heirloom, passed on through the family and tribe.

Most Indian tribes had central cooking and a large dish for the main meal, with smaller dishes to hold salt and condiments. All could come and eat from the tribal cooking pot. The meal was usually served on a tray large enough for the entire tribe and piled with corn, other vegetables, and fish or game. Some tribes had soapstone dishes and efficient and beautiful dishes of seashells, many carved in the shape of animals. The Iroquois made dishes of wood, attaching handles to them.

Brooms made of coarse grass or twigs were used to sweep the home, and a brush from a bird wing was used to keep the central firepit clean. Many Plains tribes and those of the Rocky Mountains used a wooden spade-like implement to remove snow from the ground near the entrance of the lodge.

## ETIQUETTE AND FAMILY RELATIONSHIPS

The entrance to one's home was a sacred place to the Indians, and all who came were made welcome; among some tribes, even an enemy was safe within the tribal circle. The Indians had a highly advanced concept of hospitality, and it was this trait of welcome and sharing on the Indians' part which enabled those early settlers to survive the cold, hard winters. In Massachusetts, Pennsylvania, Virginia, and other parts of the land, those first intruders were made welcome and even helped to stay alive by the Indians.

It was the custom among most Indians to offer food to anyone who entered their dwelling, and to refuse was an insult. The food must at least be tasted and thanks given to the woman of the home. This was repeated at any hour of the day, and a person who visited much could be offered many meals in one day. Orphans were unknown among the Indians, and even captive children where adopted and raised within the tribe. The aged were cared for, not only by their own family but by the whole tribe, and they were deeply respected for the wisdom age had brought to them.

Rules of etiquette varied. A Comanche host would be offended if his guest did not enter the lodge first and take the place pointed out to him. A guest in an Indian camp usually had the place of honor in the lodge, and he was always offered the choice bits of food and drink. Some tribes passed the calumet around among visitors as a sign of friendship, hospitality, and peace.

Hunger and want could not exist at one end of an Indian village or in any section of an encampment, while elsewhere there was plenty. A successful warrior could not claim more than his due, but must share his hunt and gains with the less fortunate of the tribe. A great warrior considered this an honor.

Long before 1600 the Algonkins were sending out "dinner invitations" in the form of specially cut blocks of wood about the size of the little finger. All those who received the bits of wood with their curious picture-message knew that they were invited to attend the feast and celebration being given by the Algonkin.

Correct use of language indicated the rank and standing of a man's family. Being too frequent a visitor was considered bad manners and a sign of ill-breeding.

A man was expected to precede a woman when walking or entering a lodge, in order to see if the way was safe. Respect to elders was shown at all times in speech and action. No child could interrupt another when speaking, nor be forced to

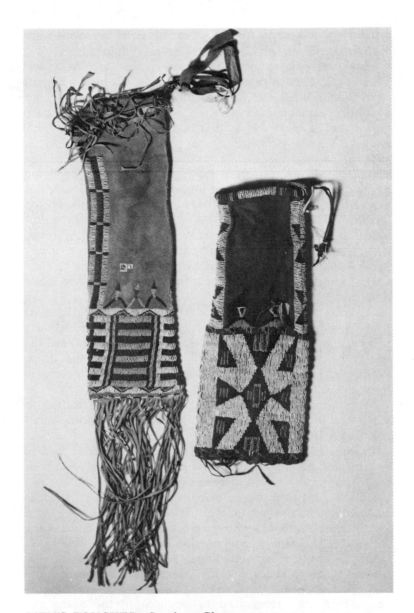

**MEN'S POUCHES**—Southern Cheyenne
Larger fringed buckskin pouch is beaded in white, red, and blue
in the Lazy Stitch.
Smaller buckskin pouch is beaded in white, dark blue, and yellow.

speak if he wished to remain silent. Personal questions were seldom asked, and private matters never mentioned.

Family care was a social duty and extended to all relatives. The regard for each member of the family was most apparent in the home. While the interior of most dwellings was without partitions, each member of the family had a distinct space and it was as inviolable as if it had been separated by thick walls. Here the personal articles were stored in packs or baskets, and in this private section was the bed. Children played in their own space, or ran in and out of that belonging to the mother, but they did not intrude elsewhere and were not allowed to meddle with another's possessions. Besides each member of the family having his own space, guests were provided for, with a space generally set aside for them. A visitor, when entering a lodge, must not pass between the host, or any person, and the fire, without asking permission. If one brushed against another, or stepped on a foot, an apology was made immediately.

Standing and sitting also had rules of etiquette. In most tribes, a woman stood with her feet straight and close together; if her hands were free, the arms hung down a little toward the front, the fingers extended and pressed against the dress. Women sat with both feet under them to the side, or sat on their knees. Men sat cross-legged.

Many tribes had a mother-in-law taboo, which forbade a son-in-law to speak directly to his mother-in-law. Some tribes also had a father-in-law taboo.

In some tribes, if a cooking vessel was borrowed, it had to be returned with a portion of food in it, usually what had been cooked, to show how it had been used.

Honesty and truth were valued traits. There were no locks on the doors and very little theft. If one was to be gone for a length of time, a pole was put across the door to indicate the absence of the family, and no one entered the dwelling. A family, when leaving something, would put a possession marker nearby and leave it for several days, before coming back to pick it up. Truth, honesty, and the safeguarding of human life were recognized as essential to the peace and prosperity of the tribe.

Crime was not a big problem among the Indians. Murder was sometimes punished by exile, or by leaving the punishment up to the relatives of the slain. Punishment for adultery depended on tribal custom. Among the Apache, a woman who committed adultery had her nose or ears cut off. Some tribes banished the woman or killed her, and at times the man was also killed or banished. A council of respected elders and warriors usually carried out the making of laws and dispensing of justice in the tribe.

## COURTSHIP AND MARRIAGE

Courtship and marriage were usually conducted according to tribal customs. Indians of the Northwest Coast had a clan system, and marriages between clan members was strictly forbidden. In some tribes the women made the arrangements, marrying the girls to older men who were good hunters, and the boys, when possible, to older widowed women who had cornfields and also were known to be good cooks or craftswomen. Other tribes had a gift system. Gifts were sent to the parents of an eligible girl, and the parents of the girl would send gifts of equal value back to the parents of the boy. This indicated they were willing for the marriage to take place.

The young people of the Plains tribes seemed to have more free choice. The boys and girls would see each other around camp and would meet while picking berries or doing chores. If a boy was attracted to some girl, he would sit wrapped in his blanket in front of the girl's tipi and play his flute. If the girl came out and sat with him, pulling his blanket around both of them, it indicated she had selected him, and it was an engagement of sorts.

The Hopi, Navaho, Zuñi, and others of the Pueblo tribes of the Southwest had a clan system, and marriage was arranged by the parents; however, at times the young people themselves made the arrangements. A Zuñi suitor took gifts to the father of his betrothed and became his adopted son. Married life then began in the home of the bride. She was mistress of the

169

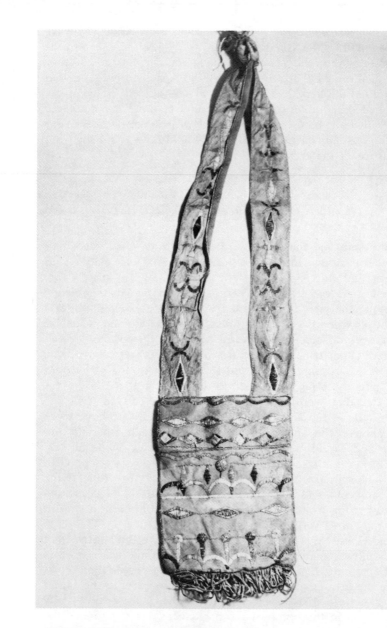

SHOULDER BAG—Basin-Plateau tribes
Quill work on buckskin in red, white, and yellow and fringed at
the bottom.

home, and the children belonged to her clan. A wife could order her husband from the home at will.

Some Plains tribes weren't as free as others, and a young girl was guarded until the Maiden Ceremony, which was something like a coming-out party. Often a young couple would elope, or a young man would simply kidnap a girl and ride off with her; when they returned they would be considered married. Polygamy was the custom and often the second wife would be the sister of the first wife; or, should a man's brother be killed, he would take the brother's widow into his tipi as his wife. The Hopi were monogamistic and faithful in marriage.

There were tribes in which the men had absolute power over the women, but separation and divorce were nonetheless common. Among the Cheyenne and Arapaho a young man might go to live with his wife's parents as a sort of hired man for a period of time, but this was not a set rule. A Blackfoot or Crow couple would live near or with the man's parents. Omaha, Kiowa, and Hidatsa girls were almost always consulted about the choice of a husband. A wife could leave a cruel husband, and each could remarry. The children went with the mother.

Descent of name and property was in the female line among the Iroquois tribes. When an Iroquois girl saw a young man she liked, she told her mother. Her mother, if she approved, became friendly with the young man's mother. If all went well, the young girl would bake twenty-four double loaves of ball biscuit which she put in a basket and hung on the young man's door. If he ate even one of the biscuits, he was compelled to marry the girl.

Most women had clear rights, and few were treated badly or worked any harder than pioneer woman. In fact an Indian woman probably didn't work as hard as some of the pioneers, as Indians worked in groups, which made the work more pleasant. Most women had a voice in tribal affairs, and there were many women sachems, or medicine women. Most women owned the home and whatever was in the home. The man owned the horses and what he produced or secured with his own hands.

171

# CHILDREN

Children had certain rights too, and they were treated with kindness and affection. Among the Indians there were no neglected nor abused children. Children were seldom spanked or whipped, as the Indians believed that to strike a child was not only insulting, but could break his spirit. To punish a child, cold water was thrown on his face, and no Indian child could ever get his own way by crying or having a tantrum. Self-restraint, obedience, respect for elders, neatness, cleanliness and orderliness were taught to the children from the time they were infants. Training started early, relentlessly, and firmly, but with love and understanding.

It was an unwritten law of the Lakota that at least six years should elapse between the birth of children. It was felt that the entire care of the parent was required for that period in order to rear a child properly. Both the father and mother took part in the child's training. Children were taught to acquire wisdom by listening and observing, and to give respect not only to people but to animals. It was believed that animals as well as men were watched over by Sanka Tanka, the Great Grandfather, and that all creatures had souls or spirits worthy of consideration.

Among most tribes, the newborn infant was immediately given a bath, whether in summer or winter, and turned over to another matron or nurse until the mother's health was restored. The Hopi rubbed ashes or sacred meal over the infant. Little clothing was worn by the baby until he was about four or five years old.

Names given at birth were often discarded and a new one given the child later. The initial name was usually given because of some happening at the time of the child's birth, like an eagle flying near camp, or a storm. Some tribes gave a child a name based on something the child did, or a characteristic it had. A Hopi baby was given a name twenty days after its birth, and then this was done at sunrise.

Twins were regarded as uncanny and were feared to possess occult powers. Some of the Oregon and coast tribes considered

**DOLL CRADLEBOARD**—Shoshoni tribe
Toy measures 18 inches overall and has nailheads on the two narrow boards converging at the base, each board projects above the bag. The beadwork is white background with red, blue, and yellow beads.
Basket on the left is from the Modoc tribe.

the births abnormal, and one or both twins were put to death at birth. If a child was born deformed, it would be put to death immediately. This was not cruel, because in a society such as theirs a sick or deformed person could not contribute his bit toward the survival of the tribe. However, if a child was crippled by accident, it would be taken care of and treated tenderly by the family and the whole tribe.

Among the Plains tribes, a boy started wearing his breech-cloth at about nine or ten and this was observed with rejoicing. Some tribes had the first marks of tattooing at this time. The Powhatan of Virginia would render a boy of ten years unconscious in order to take away his memory of childish things so that he would awaken a man. Boys of the eastern and central tribes would go on solitary feasts at the age of fifteen; this was in order to gain communication with the medicine spirit, which would be a special protector throughout their lives.

In most tribes girls reached womanhood at about thirteen or fourteen years of age. They were given a special celebration and puberty dance, which marked the end of their childhood days.

Because of their training, children were fond of pets, and little girls would dress up puppies and carry them around on their backs in little cradle boards.

Toys were given to children according to their age and sex. Little girls had tiny clay dishes, or lumps of clay to make dishes, tiny bits of hide to tan, doll's clothes to make, and beadwork and quill work to put on the doll's clothes.

Boys were given bows and arrows, along with other weapons of war and hunting. They were taught to ride, hunt, fish, and find their way through strange territory. Boys were taught by their fathers, or a special uncle. After reaching manhood, they did not remain much around their mothers. If a boy aimed his arrow, or other weapon, at any member of his tribe, or at another boy, as children will, he was no longer allowed to play with his toys, until he learned the proper use of them.

Each child had a special place for his toys and playthings. Untidy boys or girls had their toys swept into the trash hole, and it was a long time before a similar toy was made for them.

Children were taught the traditions and religious ideas of

their tribe. They learned to be polite, as an ill-mannered person was considered unfit to associate with others and was shunned by all. An unpleasant child was ignored by children and elders alike, and this was usually a most effective treatment. Children soon changed their manners.

Indians did not laugh at or ridicule their children but treated them with respect, listening to them, and reasoning with them. An Indian parent felt the child's own experience was the best teacher. Children, as well as parents, had to abide by certain tribal rules.

Boys were taught the art of public speaking, and would go with their uncle and father to the council meetings to hear the great orators; there were at least one or two in every tribe. Then the boys would try to imitate them.

As almost everything was shared within the camp circle, there was little quarreling among the children about ownership. If a child was punished, he knew why. Since a crying baby could scare away game or alert an enemy, babies were taught very early not to cry. In the first few days of his life, a baby would have his nose held gently at the first sound or cry, and he soon knew not to weep or cry at certain times.

An illegitimate child did not forfeit social standing or legal tribal rights, because his parents were unmarried. It was not considered the fault of the child and was not held against him.

## EDUCATION

The education of the Indian was religious, vocational, and physical. The religious education began with the mother. The lullabies she sang, the stories she told of the Great Spirit, and the expressions of thanks she offered as she prepared the food were not lost on the child.

The games the child played were a part of his vocational education. The games were competitive: footraces, contests in jumping, swimming, and climbing. Both boys and girls enjoyed these. The boys played games of tracking animals and games of war. The boy who excelled in these soon became the leader. Girls did not play war games, but played they were tanning

175

BAGS
Smaller bag is decorated with cowrie shells and beads. Tribe
unknown.
Larger bag of the Northeastern Woodland tribe. The floral design
includes beads of blue, red, and green.

hides or going berry picking. In play, they also learned to find and classify plants. A boy would be sent out alone to observe wildlife, and upon his return would be asked to imitate the sounds he'd heard and to describe what he'd seen.

There were tribes that had organizations for teaching. Women who were good at beadwork would teach the young girls, other women taught cooking, tanning, and the making of moccasins.

## NAMES

Most Indians believed that their name was sacred, and sometimes it was never told; to ask someone's name was impolite. A warrior would ignore the question, although if a friend appeared he might tell his name, with the friend present.

There were true names corresponding to the personal name, and names that were similar to titles and honorary names. The first name defined or indicated the social group into which a man was born, plus his family background such as any honored accomplishments of ancestors; the second name marked what the person had done himself.

Names were given or changed at important points in one's life: birth, puberty, the first expedition, some notable feat, the elevation to chieftain, and retirement from active life. There were also vision names, or those obtained or told to one in a dream or vision. There were also give-away names, where an old warrior gave his name to some young person. Warriors of the Plains Indians used to assume battle names, some having as many as four or five.

A Pueblo might have several names, but one secret name he kept always. A name could be loaned, pawned, or given away. Usually the possession of a name was jealously guarded, and at times it was considered insulting to address anyone directly by name. It was felt that each one should have a name so perfectly expressing his innermost self as to be practically identical with him. It was for this reason that many Indians refused to give their real names, and many Indians who went away to school would not give their real names.

177

Indian names are often mistranslated in essence. For example, "Takaihodal" in Kiowa means "stinking saddle blanket." This sounded repugnant to the white man, but to the Kiowa it was an honored name. It meant a great warrior had fought so many battles that he did not have time to take off his saddle blanket.

## LAWS AND CUSTOMS

Suicide was not uncommon among the Indians. A man might commit suicide rather than suffer a slow death as a prisoner, and a woman might take her own life because her husband left her in her middle age. Taking a poison plant was the most common way for women. A man might shoot, stab, or strangle himself.

Insanity was treated with respect. Indians would never bother a person they believed insane, fearing an evil spirit had entered him. Traders sometimes used the trick of insanity to escape being taken prisoner by the Indians.

Indians had their own laws. One was not to bother another about his beliefs, but let all believe as they wished. Other laws included:

Never leave camp with trash about.

Never destroy the land and its beauty.

Never stare at strangers.

Respect all, but never grovel.

No one is responsible for another's bad deeds.

Thank the Great Spirit for each day.

A person is bound by his promise, so never give your word unless you can keep it.

Be kind and hospitable.

Don't ask personal questions of guests.

In another's lodge, follow his ways.

### TIPI

The home of most of the Plains Indians was a conical tent called a tipi. This is a Sioux word, *ti* meaning "dwelling"

# TIPI

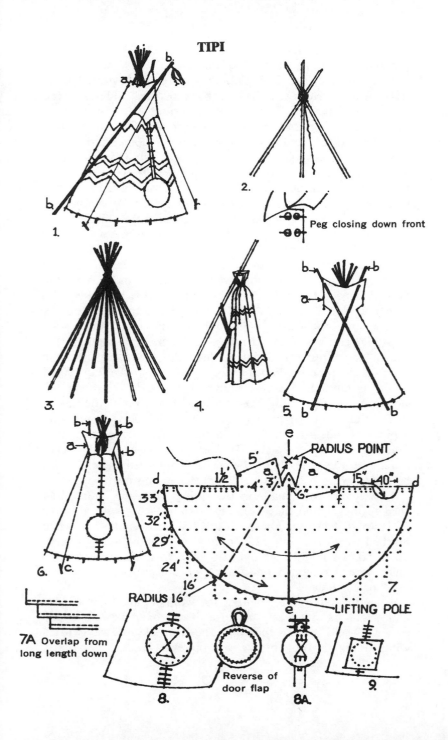

Peg closing down front

1.

2.

3.

4.

5. b b

6. c.

RADIUS POINT

5'

d  1½'  a  a  15"  40"  d
33'  4' 3'  G  f
32'
29'
24'
16'

RADIUS 16'

e

LIFTING POLE

7.

7A Overlap from long length down

8.

Reverse of door flap

8A.

9.

and *pi* meaning "used for." It is also spelled tepee, as it is pronounced. These beautiful serviceable lodges were especially suitable for the area in which they were used. Actually the tipi is not a true cone, as the back or west side is much steeper than the front. In the Plains country the wind is almost always from the west, therefore the door and smoke hole face the east, and many of the lodge poles slope from east to west, bracing against the pressure of the wind on the steep west side. Because of this prairie wind which even today can blow smoke back down a chimney, the smoke hole of the tipi is a piece of engineering genius, albeit extremely simple. An opening is left at the top of the tipi to allow the smoke to escape, and the wind is kept from blowing down this opening by two flaps or extensions of the tipi which rise on either side of the smoke hole. These can be adjusted to the direction of the wind by means of two poles reaching up to them from the ground outside the tipi—see Diagram 5 and 6 *b–b*, the poles which adjust the smoke hole flaps (*a*). Diagram 5 is the back of the tipi showing the poles holding the smoke flaps wide open; Diagram 6 is the front of the same tipi, showing the smoke flaps from the front as they are held open. Note *c* which is the rope holding the bottom of the smoke flap staked to the ground. Diagram 1 shows the pole *b–b* holding the smoke flap (*a*) partially closed toward the front of the tipi.

The tipi is entered through an opening which is closed with a piece of hide stretched over a light round frame of wood, much in the shape of a shield. This opening was usually decorated with the symbols of the owner. The opening could also be closed with just a hide or blanket hanging over it.

New lodges were made in the spring when the buffalo had shed their hair and their skins were thin. A tipi with a radius of 18 to 20 feet took about 10 to 12 skins to make and when finished weighed about 125 pounds. A large council lodge of up to 40 feet might take over 50 skins to make. Later, when there were not enough buffalo left on the prairie, canvas was used, or cowhide.

After the skins were tanned, the woman called her friends and neighbors to a feast, and after it was over they all helped in sewing and cutting the tipi. The most skilled was trusted with cutting the tipi, or the old tipi was used as a pattern.

180

Usually, though, the woman who cut the skins could do so entirely without a pattern. Care was taken not to waste skins in cutting or sewing, and the work was usually done in a day. The cover is a rough half circle (see Diagram 7) with two flaps projecting from the straight side (see 7a); between these is a tongue. This is where the lifting pole is placed (7 e-e).

Old poles are used, or if new ones are needed they are made of pine, cedar, spruce, or any straight slim tree. Flexible wood is not used for poles. The trees are cut down, peeled, and dressed down. The women did most of the work, although the men sometimes helped. The poles were from 10 to 40 feet long, but usually the average length was 25 feet. They tapered from a diameter of about 2 inches at the top to 6 inches at the ground end, which was sharpened. Poles were kept as long as possible and became dark and polished from handling and smoke. New tipis were nearly white, but became darkened with smoke and were almost black around the smoke hole.

Pins (for holding the cover together above and below the opening) and stakes were cut from slender, strong pieces of wood. These were usually a foot or two long and half an inch thick. In winter, stones and earth were piled against the bottom of the tipi to help anchor the stakes tightly, and to keep out drafts and moisture. If the tipi was to be left in one place for very long, the dirt floor inside was then excavated to a depth of two feet or so.

It is said that a tipi can be put up in a matter of minutes by Indian women, but it takes practice. Every little Indian girl had a tipi for her dolls, in the manner of a doll house, so she started early learning how to put them up and take them down. There were even small dog-house tipis for the family pet which were moved when the family did.

In putting up the tipi, the cover is spread flat on the ground, and the foundation poles are laid on it in order to measure at what height they are to be tied together (see Diagram 2). The poles are marked so that the next time they will not have to be measured. They are tied together with a rawhide band or rope. The long end of the rope is left hanging so that in windy weather it is fastened to stakes driven near the center of the lodge. The three tied foundation poles are placed on end (some tribes use four foundation poles, which is said to make

181

a more beautiful tipi but not as sturdy). One pole faces east and forms the south door post. The other two are placed behind the door pole and are closer to each other than to the door. When the foundation is firmly fixed, the other poles are put in place. The first pole makes the other door post and the next four to six are set up to the north of it. The next group are placed south of the foundation door pole. The remaining poles go between the two back foundation poles. All but the last group rest in the front, or east crotch of the original poles. There is usually about one pole every 30 inches around the circle.

The last pole, or lifting pole, is next laid across the tipi cover on the ground, along the center, from the bottom to the small tongue between the smoke flaps (Diagram 7 *e–e*). Tie this pole at the tongue and place this pole, with the cover attached, to the west or back of the poles, in the west crotch (Diagram 4). The two sides of the cover are pulled around the poles until they meet in front. The left or south side is placed over the other and the two are pinned together with wooden pegs put in from right to left. These are placed about 6 inches apart and extend from the bottom of the smoke hole, which goes partway down the east or front of the tipi, to the top of the door opening. If the opening is placed a bit above ground level, pins are placed below the opening as well.

When the pins are in place, the women enter the tipi and push the poles out against the cover until there is no sagging. When the cover is tight against the poles, the bottom edge is staked to the ground.

The smoke flap poles are now put in place, the ties staked down either on separate stakes, or the two flap ropes tied to one taller stake or half pole set a bit to one side and in front of the door. To keep the smoke poles from going too far through the hole, tie a small crossbar about 18 inches or two feet from the top end. By moving the smoke flap poles, the smoke flaps can be moved according to the direction of the wind, and in bad weather they can be completely overlapped.

If you want to make a tipi, make a small-scale model first and then you'll be completely familiar with the method. Today tipis are made of canvas or waterproofed muslin which is lightweight. A 16-foot tipi takes at least 50 yards of 36-inch wide material. Cut the material into five lengths as shown in Diagram 7 (the dotted line). The longest length, along the straight edge, is cut at 33 feet, the next is 32 feet, then 29 feet, 24 feet, and 16 feet. Place the lengths as shown, overlapping from the long one down (see Diagram 7A). If you sew the lengths in a flat seam overlapping in this manner, water will run off the tipi rather than into it. From the radius point marked $X$ on Diagram 7, just above the center tongue of the cover, measure 16 feet. With a long 16-foot tape measure or a string and marker, hold the end at $X$, the pivot point, and mark an arc or half circle. The radius point is usually about 30 inches above the center of the top or long length. This half circle is shown as $d$–$e$–$d$ on Diagram 7. (If you have a tarp large enough to mark off a radius of 16 feet you won't have to sew the strips together, or perhaps only two of them.)

Cut two smoke flaps 1½ by 3 feet and 4 by 5 feet. The 5-foot length on the slant as in Diagram 7. From the center point on the long straight length measure 6 inches to each side. This is where the tongue will be sewn. This is a 12-by-12-inch square, rounded off on the one side. After this is in place, sew the smoke flaps to each side as shown. At the narrow end of the smoke flap make a 6-inch slit at $f$ (Diagram 7), to allow for overlap down the front, above and below the door opening. On all cloth, reinforce the slits with extra stitching or binding. If you have enough material it is advisable to double the smoke flaps, and tongue, and sew them down along the seam, joining it to the main cover, or at least reinforce the material around the holes on the smoke flaps for the poles, and on the tongue where the lifting pole is placed.

Cut door openings on each side, an oval approximately 15 by 40 inches. This leaves a total door width of about 18 inches when the front is lapped over above and below the opening. You can cut the door wider if you wish, but remember to allow for the 6-inch overlap.

When sewing the strips together it is easier and turns out more even to start at the center of each piece and work out to one side, then back to the center and sew out to the other side. Double-stitched flat seams are best.

Sixteen to eighteen poles about 18 to 20 feet tall will be needed. Pick out the best three poles for the tripod, two slender poles for the smoke flaps, and a good solid one for the lifting pole.

The tipi can be decorated with symbols, animals, geometric designs, lines, stars, or just dots. The best time to decorate the tipi is after it has been sewn and is laid flat. Draw your design on a small scale so you have an idea how the total design will look. Fold your small-scale model into a cone shape to be sure your design looks right when the tipi is standing. With chalk or marking pencil draw the design, then paint it. Textile paints can be used, or if the material is waterproofed, ordinary paint can be used. Spray the waterproofing material on the tipi while it is flat, and let it dry before painting.

The door opening is closed by a skin or material pulled over a hoop which hangs over the closing peg just above the door and swings easily to one side or the other (Diagram 8 and 8A). Another type is a square of skin or material stretched from a pole hung to a closing peg above the door (Diagram 9). This is more of a flap-type closing. Either kind are usually decorated with some symbol of the owner, sometimes a figure from the owner's dream vision. The smoke-flap poles and lifting pole are decorated with streamers attached to the top of the pole, where they can fly in the breeze.

## TIPI LINING OR DEW CLOTH

The tipi cover and poles do not make a tipi, or at least not a cozy one. The cover cannot be staked exactly to the ground all the way around, leaving an inch or two here and there for drafts. If it rains, water runs down the poles and leaves everything damp around the edges. A tipi lining is the answer. It keeps out drafts and dampness, keeps rain from running down to the floor from the poles, creates insulation, helps to keep the inside air in the tipi clear of smoke, and adds color to the interior. The lining keeps dew from condensing inside, so it is often called a dew cloth. After long use, hide tipis became almost transparent and the lining was a sort of curtain. The journals of early travelers often described the beauty of the glowing tipis at night. With a fire burning brightly in the center firepit at night, the tipis were lighted up like giant lanterns, and those inside cast shadows on the walls for all on the out-

184

# TIPI LINING OR DEW CLOTH

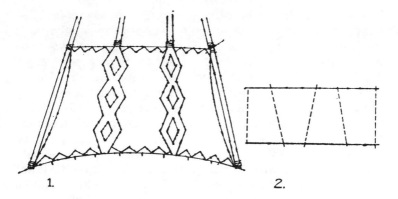

1.

2.

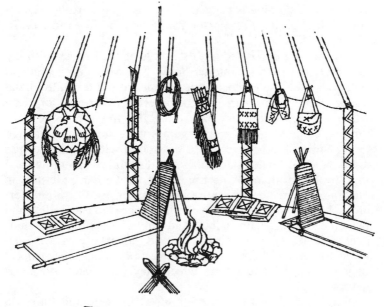

3.

side to see. But if the lining was in place, no lurking enemy could shoot an arrow at a shadow inside the lodge.

The lining should be of a lightweight waterproofed material, about 5 to 6 feet wide and long enough to go all around the inside of the tipi. This can be made in sections of several pole lengths, as in Diagram 1, or cut to fit each pole length and sewed together. In the latter case, cut the material as in Diagram 2, then turn every other piece right-side up, so the top of the lining is smaller than the bottom. This is more work but there will be less sag in the lining. A rope can be run all around the tipi poles, and the lining hung to this, or the lining can be attached directly to the poles. Turn the bottom under, and with the floor robes down, cold air will be kept away from the lower part of the tipi, where the beds are, and where the children play. In fact, the lining turns the cold air, which enters under the lower edge of the tipi cover, up along the sides to the top of the smoke hole. In extremely cold weather, dried grass can be stuffed between the outer cover and the lining for extra warmth. If the lining is pegged down tightly all around the inside of the tipi, it will keep the inside of the tipi almost draft-free.

Linings were decorated with symbols of the owner, with figures that told of his exploits. Some had a striped pattern at each pole, others, a geometric design all around the bottom and the top. Decorations were painted on every other pole, or every two poles, depending upon how big the tipi was. Scenes of hunting, of horse races, and of games were sometimes painted on the lining. Linings were also decorated with beaded stripes and dangles of feathers and claws. These tipi decorations were hung by the woman of the tipi, much as we hang pictures in our houses to make them more appealing to us. Certain decorations having to do with the buffalo were considered "good medicine" by the Plains tribes, and only women of good character and ability as craftworkers and housekeepers were allowed to display them on or in their tipis. These women belonged to a special society to which they were elected because of these qualities.

Diagram 3 shows the interior of a tipi with the lining in place. It shows how the equipment of the family was hung around from the poles, adding their color to the interior. War

# DIAGRAM OF INSIDE AND OUTSIDE ARRANGEMENT OF A PLAINS INDIAN TIPI

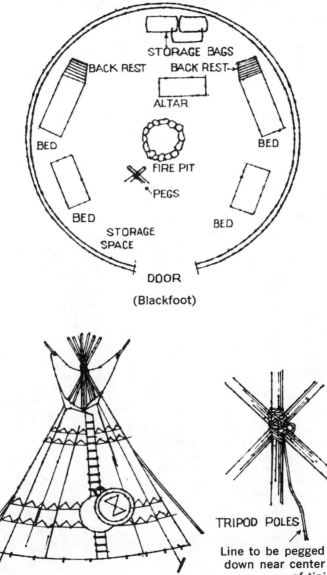

STORAGE BAGS

BACK REST    BACK REST→

ALTAR

BACK REST

BED    BED

FIRE PIT

PEGS

BED    BED

STORAGE SPACE

DOOR

(Blackfoot)

TRIPOD POLES

Line to be pegged down near center of tipi

# TIPI DECORATIONS

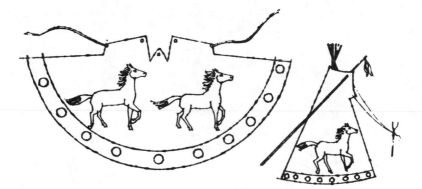

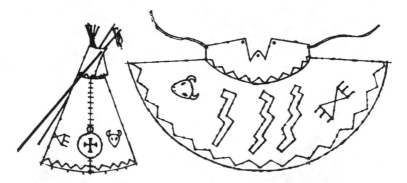

When you are tracing your decorations on the tipi as it is laid flat, take into consideration that it will be in a conical upright position when finished. If you do not remember this you could have an animal sideways when the tipi is put up.

For example: the left horse on the first pattern would be climbing up the tipi when the tipi is upright in a conical position.

# FORTIFIED CREEK VILLAGE

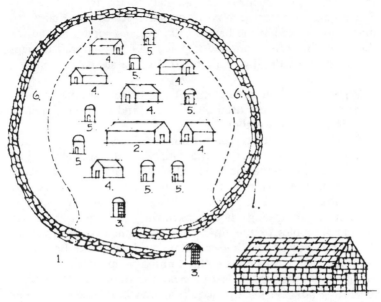

1. General Plan of the Village    4. Gabled Roof House
2. Council House                 5. Domed Roof House
3. Sentry Box                    6. Gardens

shields, war clubs, horsehair lariat, quiver, pipe bag, extra moccasins, and pouches were all tied to the tipi poles. Parfleche bags, the storage boxes and suitcases of the Plains Indians, are stacked at the back of the tipi and sometimes beside the beds. The rope from the tripod poles is anchored to pegs just in front of the fire. This holds the tipi steady in a strong prairie wind.

When the buffalo were plentiful and there were many robes in each tipi, they were used on the floor and kept the tipi snug even in the worst weather.

Beds with backrests for sitting or sleeping were usually placed around the sides of the tipi, with storage spaces just inside the door and to the back, where the parfleche bags could be stored. The firepit was to the back, past the center and under the smoke hole. In front of this were the anchor pegs. Equipment and things not packed in the bags were hung around the poles of the tipi. The altar space is just back of the firepit. Not all tipis had an altar, but if they did, here were kept the sacred objects of the family. Sometimes a sacred medicine bundle would be tied near the door, or attached to the lifting pole, so the tipi would always be blessed as it was put into place.

## CRADLE BOARDS

Most Indian tribes used a baby-board or carrier of some kind which was for the restraint and transportation of babies. They differed, from tribe to tribe, in the way they were made and used. A Pueblo woman carried the child's cradle board in her arms, a Plains Indian mother strapped the cradle board to her back, or, as these were good horsewomen, the cradle board was slung from the saddle when traveling.

Actually the cradle board was much like our baby carriage and the baby was only in the cradle board while being transported, or perhaps when the mother was berry picking. Sometimes the cradle board was hung on a tree within sight of the working mother, eliminating the worry of where the infant might crawl. Moreover, if the tribe was on the move, or escaping a war party, the baby was little trouble when it was transported in this simple way. The cradle board was the

# CRADLE BOARDS

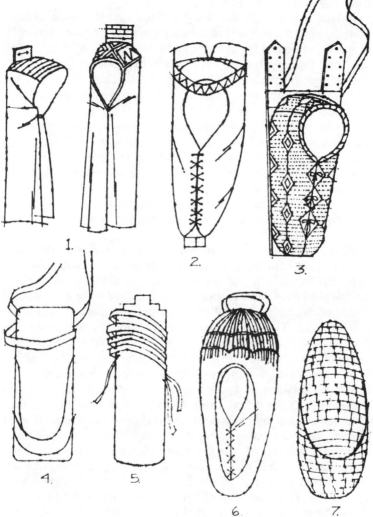

1.

2.

3.

4.

5.

6.

7.

baby's first lesson in restraint, discipline, and endurance, all traits essential to Indian life.

Babies weren't left for long periods in the cradle boards, though, unless absolutely necessary because of forced moving or wars, just as babies today aren't left in the baby carriage all the time. Indian children were much loved, their grandparents played with them at every opportunity, teaching them to walk and to talk during those times when they were out of the cradle boards.

Cradle boards differed even among neighboring tribes, but basically they consisted of a flat surface or bed, covering, padding or pillow and other devices for the protection for the head, a foot rest, the lashing, devices for suspension plus trinkets and rattles to amuse the baby.

The material used depended upon what nature provided in a given area; the decorations were individualistic, but within the tribal designs.

Skin cradles were used among the Plains Indians where the buffalo was plentiful. One type simply consisted of a rolled-up hide, the hair left on for warmth, making a sort of pocket for the baby to fit in. Sometimes this was lashed onto a triangular wedge of flat boards, or stiffened rawhide reinforced with small willow sticks. The baby was wrapped and tied into this sack or pocket. The head was protected by a bow-like arc which circled out from above the head, protruding out in front of the baby's head. This not only protected the child should the cradle board fall forward, but was a good place to hang trinkets and rattles to keep the infant amused. Some of the boards had very little decoration, others were more elaborate with almost solid beading (see Diagrams 2 and 3).

Often a woman of one tribe would marry out of her tribe into another, and it was natural she would make things as she remembered them but adapted to the style of her new home. The one in Diagram 2 might have been such a cradle board. It has the flat board typical of the western Rockies, with a skin pocket arrangement like the Plains, and the head-protecting half hoop on the outside, similar to Woodland cradle boards. The baby is laced into a soft deerskin as is done among tribes of the western Plains. Only the head loop is decorated, otherwise the cradle board is quite unadorned.

Diagram 3 shows a beaded Sioux type cradle board, made of a deep, straight-sided bag of skin, heavily beaded, and attached to a pair of narrow boards, whose pointed upper ends extend far beyond the top of the bag. These upper ends are trimmed with brass-headed tacks. Straps supported the frame so it could be carried on the mother's back, or hung from a horse's saddle, or put in a travois basket when camp was moving.

Diagram 1 shows another form of Plains cradle board. To the flat baseboard is attached a sort of triangular hood which is stiff and heavily beaded or quilled. From this hangs a large rectangle of skin or cloth. When the lower corners of the hood are tied together, it forms a head covering like a sun bonnet. The baby is laid on this, its head fitting into the bonnet, and the cloth bottom is folded around his body and legs.

Diagram 4 shows a basic Woodland type cradle: a flat board with an angled wood bow projecting forward from near the top, a small foot board, and low sides of wood or bark around the middle and lower section of the board. Sometimes this curved piece is not so long but is merely a foot rest. Cloth or skin is attached to the sides of the board and laced over the baby.

Diagram 5 shows a cradle board of the southwest Pueblo, a flat board with an eye shade, sort of like a folding awning frame. The top of the board is carved into terraces which symbolize the clouds and life-giving rain.

Diagram 6 shows a type from the Basin–Plateau tribes: a flat board cut into a long oval, wider at the top than the bottom. The board is covered with skin or cloth, usually beaded. The covering is tight over the large top section and the edges, but made into a shallow bag, to hold the baby, on the narrow lower portion. Sometimes a shade of coarse basketry is added over this.

Diagram 7 shows the basket or wicker cradle board used among the California Indians. The baby is wrapped and laid in the basket which is very much like a cradle. Sometimes a small cone-shaped basket-hat shade was perched over the top of the cradle basket.

Among the Northwest Coast Indians, babies were placed in

little boxes of cedar, carved out with the adz in the same way that their canoes were made.

Another type of cradle board was made from a number of rods or small canes and sticks arranged in a plane on an oblong hoop and held in place by lashing with splints or cords. The bed is of shredded cottonwood bast, the baby held in place by an artistic wrapping of colorfully woven bands.

Padding under the baby is adjusted around the head and shoulders, in some cases to flatten the head, in others to allow its normal development, and for more comfort. Some tribes put moss between the heels of the little girls so they would toe inward, and moss was adjusted around the feet of tiny boy babies so they would walk and toe straight. Scented herbs were also placed in the cradle boards and wrappings.

Babies used the cradle board for a year or more, but when the mother worked around the home the infant was laid on a robe or mat and allowed to kick and play. Some tribes made a new cradle to exactly fit each new baby, but among the Pueblos the cradle was a sacred object, handed down in the family, and the number of children who had used it was shown by the notches on its frame. It was never sold, as this might bring about the death of a child. Should a baby die while in the helpless infant stage, the cradle board was thrown away, broken up, burned, or placed on the grave. Some tribes buried the corpse laced up inside, as in life. The grief of a mother at the death of her baby was intensely pathetic, as this was the one time an Indian woman could show her emotions; the father too could show his feelings at this time.

Dolls and doll cradle boards that were replicas of the regular boards were made for the little girls to play with.

## INDIAN BAGS AND POUCHES

Every Indian tribe used bags and pouches, in fact they were necessary in almost every phase of their life. They held many items of daily life as well as ceremonial things. They were made of soft skin and decorated according to tribe, individual taste, and use. The Plains tribes used geometric designs while the Woodland Indians favored floral motifs.

Diagrams 1, 2, and 3 are designs of the Plains Indians. The

# INDIAN BAGS AND POUCHES

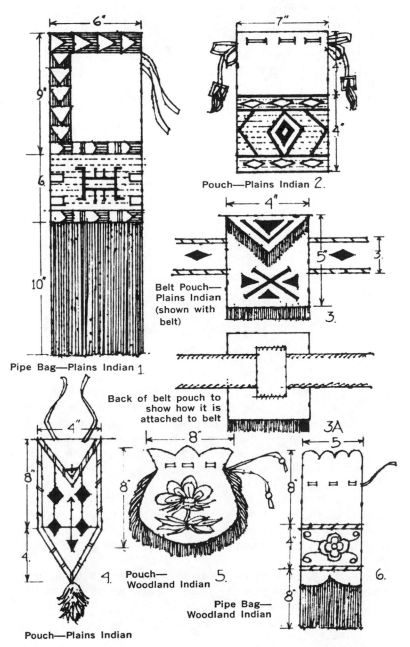

Pipe Bag—Plains Indian 1.

Pouch—Plains Indian 2.

Belt Pouch—
Plains Indian
(shown with
belt) 3.

Back of belt pouch to
show how it is
attached to belt 3A.

Pouch—Plains Indian 4.

Pouch—
Woodland Indian 5.

Pipe Bag—
Woodland Indian 6.

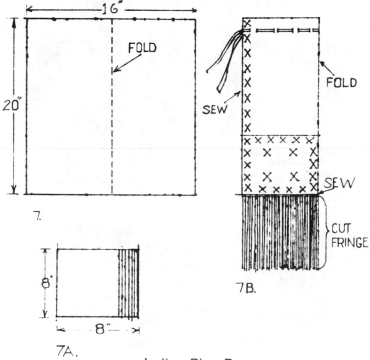

Indian Pipe Bag

first is a pipe bag, one of the most prized of Indian items as it held the special ceremonial pipe and tobacco. These were usually beautifully decorated and fringed. The overall length of the bag in Diagram 1 is 25 inches by 6 inches. These can be made in one length, with the fringe cut at the bottom, or the fringe can be sewn on; or they can be made in three parts, the upper portion lightly decorated so the bag can be closed with a drawstring. The middle portion is heavily beaded or decorated in some way, and the lower part is fringed. Diagram 6 shows a pipe bag decorated in the floral designs of the Woodland Indians; the overall dimensions of this one are 20 inches by 5 inches.

Diagram 7A and 7B show how to make a pipe bag with one piece of material 16 by 20 inches folded lengthwise in the

196

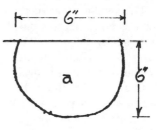

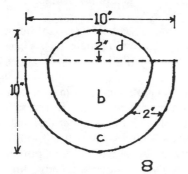

8

8A.

8B.

8C.

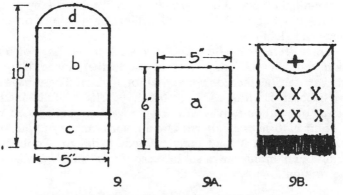

9.

9A.

9B.

Strike-a-Light Pouches and Personal Pouches

middle and sewn along the one side. A smaller piece, 8 by 8 inches, is slipped between the fold at the bottom of the larger piece and sewn down, then this piece is cut as fringe. It is then decorated where marked with X's.

The smaller bags or pouches are used to hold personal items such as body paint, small trinkets, and sewing materials. These are usually decorated with favorite symbols and only short-fringed, if fringed at all.

The belt pouch is designed to wear on a belt as in Diagram 3; Diagram 3A shows how it is attached to a belt. Diagram 4 shows a small pouch with the pendant bottom decorated with a tuft of feathers. Diagram 5 shows a Woodland type pouch.

Diagram 8 shows how to make the rounded type pouch; *a* (see Diagram 8A) is to be sewn over *b* along the heavy line, *d* is the flap, and *c* will be cut as the fringe. Diagram 8B shows the decoration and Diagram 8C illustrates the slits in the back side of the pouch where it can be slipped onto a belt.

Diagram 9 shows a rectangular pouch: *a* is to be sewn over *b* along the heavy line. The back side with flap *d* is 10 by 5 inches. The front part to be sewn on is 5 by 6 inches. Diagram 9B shows the completed pouch with the lower or *c* portion cut as fringe.

Another type of pouch, made like any of these, is called the strike-a-light pouch. It is smaller, usually 3 or 4 by 5 or 6 inches and was used for carrying flint for making fire; every household had one.

These were generally made of buckskin and later of buckskin and canvas. Today you can use leather, suede, chamois, canvas, felt, leather-look material, or flannel. These bags can be decorated with beads, embroidery, bits of felt glued or sewed on, and on canvas you can use wax crayon, pressed with a hot iron to set the pattern. Use a favorite motif of your own, or look in Part V and copy an Indian design. Commercial fringe and braid can also be used for a simple and quick decoration.

## PARFLECHE: INDIAN CARRYING CASE

Among the Plains Indians this rawhide case was used to carry and store meat, and larger ones were used to store and

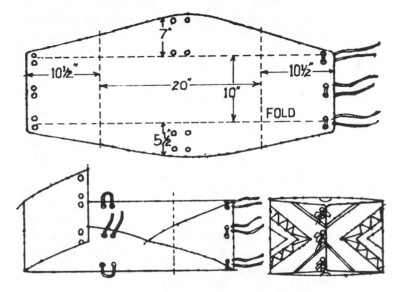

carry clothes. They were made in different sizes, but usually in pairs so, when traveling, they could be slung one on each side of the pack saddle. The pair was decorated exactly alike, in a geometric pattern. The rawhide was a light cream in color when new, but it darkened with age; the colors used on these cases were usually red, blue, green, yellow, black, and brown. Before obtaining commercial colors from traders, paints were made from colored earths, charcoal, and various plants, and were often mixed with grease. The parfleche was decorated or painted on the tops of the end flaps, and less commonly on the inner flaps and backs.

The name "parfleche," pronounced "parflesh," comes from the early French explorers who called rawhide by this name. The Plains Indian shields, made of heavy rawhide, could turn an arrow, so the name from the French, *parer*, "to parry," and *flêche*, "arrow," came to be applied to the rawhide containers as well.

When folded, these cases are usually twice as long as they are wide. Today they could be made of heavy canvas, imitation leather, heavy felt, or any heavy material that can be painted. Follow the diagram for cutting. On the long sides, measure the correct width at the center and at the ends, then when cutting, taper the sides from the center to the edges; this will give you the somewhat irregular shape. The end sides are straight. Fold on the dotted line as shown in the diagram. The long sides are folded first, then one side over the other, and tied with narrow cord or thong where the holes are marked.

Other things made from rawhide are buckets, dippers, cups, and even mortars for pounding meat and fruits.

## RAWHIDE ARTICLES

Plains Indians made all sorts of articles, using rawhide; among these was a mirror case. In the beginning the mirror was a reflecting bit of tin, fitted into a frame of rawhide, attached by a thong to a case. The mirror slipped into the side of the case which was decorated by painting in the manner of the parfleche cases (see Diagram 1). Indian men carried the mirrors not only to be used as looking glasses, but also for signaling. Women also carried these small mirror cases; they were very prized and some of them were highly decorated, with personal and good luck, or medicine symbols.

These can easily be made today using imitation leather or felt. The size will depend on the mirror. If you use a small mirror from a purse, add about 2 inches to the size of the mirror, then cut this double the size so it can be folded over in the middle. Cut tabs at the end, or sew these on later from scrap material. For example, if the mirror you use is 2 by 2 inches, one side would measure 4 by 4, so in order to double

# RAWHIDE ARTICLES

Mirror and Case

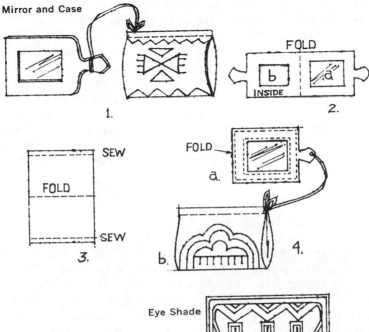

FOLD

b INSIDE

a

1.

2.

SEW

FOLD

SEW

3.

FOLD

a.

b.

4.

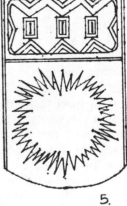

Eye Shade

5.

the material, cut a piece 8 by 4 and when this is doubled you have a piece 4 by 4 for a 2 by 2 mirror, or 2 inches of frame around the mirror. Paste the mirror on one side of the material (see Diagram 2, *a*). On the other side cut out a space ¼ smaller than the mirror (see 2, *b*). When the material is folded over, stitch around the outside of the material and ½ inch from the edge of the mirror, as in Diagram 4, *a*.

For the case, measure the material so the mirror is ¼ smaller than the case when it is folded, plus an extra inch where the case is sewn at the top (see Diagrams 3 and 4, *b*).

Diagram 5 shows a rawhide eye shade. This is a sort of cap with a wide visor and no crown. Instead of a crown, a hole is cut from the rawhide and a series of notches made, which grip the head.

## POSSESSION MARKERS

Possession markers were used by most Indian families to identify firewood just gathered and ready to be moved. A possession marker was put in the ground beside the wood, so that anyone coming by knew who had gathered it. A possession marker put beside a travois just unloaded was the same as a locked door; no one would bother the things stacked on the ground and all knew who owned them. The only time possession markers weren't needed was on a hunt, when a man's personally marked arrows identified the animals he had killed. When his wife came out to skin the animal, her husband's arrows pointed out to her which animal she was to work on.

Possession markers are easy to make. Start with a peg or stake from 2 to 3 feet tall. Feathers, fringe, yarn, bits of fur, streamers, paint, can all be used to make possession markers.

The one in Diagram 1 is made with three crossbars, tied to the upright stake. Lightning designs have been painted on the upright stake, with feathers tied to the ends of the crossbars.

The marker in Diagram 2 has one crossbar decorated at the ends with long buckskin fringe. A band of fringe is tied around the stake just under the crossbar, and three feathers are tied upright at the end of the stake.

The one in Diagram 3 is decorated with a tuft of fur at the

202

# POSSESSION MARKERS

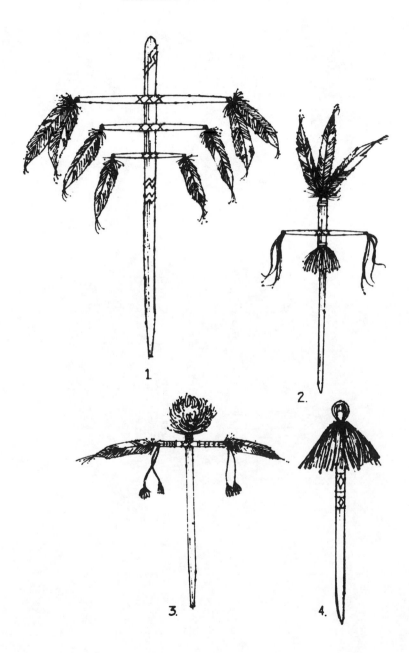

# TOYS: CORNCOB DOLLS

top of the stake and horizontal feathers at the ends of the crossbar, tied on with colored yarn.

In Diagram 4, one upright stake is decorated with beaded bands and fringe at the top and a piece of bone.

## TOYS: CORNCOB DOLLS

Corncob dolls were simple and quick to make, amusing for the children, and if they were lost in play or while moving, it was no great loss. Some dolls, probably made by loving mothers and grandmothers, were beautifully done, with hair and beaded faces for eyes, nose, and mouth. The dresses and costumes were identical with adult clothes, heavily beaded and fringed, even the tiny moccasins.

The diagrams show how the corncob can be utilized. Yarn hair is glued on. Eyes, nose, and mouth can be painted or inked in. Dresses can be made of pieces of fringed chamois, as can the little boy's costume. Felt hands and feet can be glued onto the chamois. A Seminole Indian doll can be made out of two circular pieces of material decorated with small bands of colored yarn or tape. Glue a small band of feathers to the top of the corncob, paint eyes, nose, and mouth, wrap a bit of fur around the cob for a robe, and you have a chief or a medicine man.

# PART V

# ARTS, DECORATIONS, AND SYMBOLISM

*(Crafts begin on page 224)*

To call Indian art primitive is misleading, for that would imply a lack of refinement, and this is not true, as most of their art is the result of long and continuous development. Over extended period of time, Indian artists and craftsmen perfected special skills and styles uniquely their own. Most traditional Indian art can best be considered folk art, as it was always an inextricable part of all economic, social, and ceremonial activities of the society. The tools of the Indian artist were limited, and in utilizing them he employed simple materials; because of this, what he made was simple in form, although the design might be intricate.

Much Indian art is symbolic, but a lot of it is purely decorative. While some tribes had specific designs and names that were descriptive and could be identified, other tribes simply made things they felt were pretty and useful.

Many Indians possessed an almost microscopic eye for delicate work and had a wonderful sense of form and color. The soft shades of the sky, lakes, forests, birds, and flowers all suggested design and color to the Indians.


## NATURAL DYES


The dyes for coloring varied with the tribe and with what was available in each area. Natural dyes were used in coloring yarn for weaving, in baskets, quills, blankets, painting, and for personal adornment.

The Navaho dyed all the wool for their blankets. Of the ancient natural dyes, yellow was the easiest of all to obtain and ranged in color from clear yellow to a greenish yellow.

Golden yellow can be made with 3 pounds of sagebrush and ½ cup of raw alum. The sagebrush, leaves, and twigs are put in 5 gallons of water and boiled for 2 hours. This mixture is strained and the raw alum is added to the dye water. Let this stand for 10 minutes. The yarn is then washed and, when still wet, added to the dye, stirred and boiled gently for about 6 hours. After boiling it is soaked in the dye for about 8 hours more, then removed and rinsed.

Black can be made from 2 pounds of sumac including leaves, 3 cups of piñon pitch, and 3 cups of yellow ocher. The sumac is rolled in large rolls, in winter, and allowed to dry. The dried sumac is boiled with 6 gallons of water for about 3 hours; the longer it boils the faster the color sets. The ocher browned to a cocoa brown, the pitch is put in a little at a time and stirred as long as it smokes. It becomes shiny like gunpowder and has a bluish color. The ocher is cooled until just warm; it must be kept away from the fire now, as it is inflammable. Strain the sumac and add to the ocher and pitch. This mixture is stirred and boiled for 15 minutes. Then the wet yarn is added and boiled for 2 to 3 hours. Later the yarn is shaken to remove the loose powder.

To get a pinkish color, 4 gallons of very thick brick-colored rain water from the red mesa are used. The water is dipped from the puddles immediately after a heavy rain. The wet yarn is added to this, and, after stirring, it is boiled for 4 hours, with clear water being added to the dyebath as needed to keep sufficient water in the pot. Then the yarn is rinsed. The redder the clay, the deeper the color.

The shade of the color depended upon the plant used, and the longer the dye was boiled, the deeper the shade. If the yarn was allowed to remain in the dyebath overnight, the color would be brighter, and also produce a faster set. Some dyes were not boiled with the yarn, such as that made from cactus fruit. Also there were certain berries and flowers which would lose their color if boiled. These were allowed to ferment into the yarn. Yarn was always rinsed several times after the dye, so any absorbed dye would be removed.

Dyes were also made from stone, bark, leaves and stems, roots of plants, and minerals. Before the arrival of the white man, the Tlinkit of the Northwest Coast obtained black color from sulphur spring mud, hemlock bark, and iron scraping in salt water. Two shades of purple were obtained from huckleberries. Red came from alder bark and wood, sea urchin juice, and hemlock bark. Yellow was from wolf moss; greenish blue from hemlock bark with oxide of copper; blackish purple from maidenhair fern; straw color was from grass, and brown was spruce root.

The black color of the basket designs of the ancient Pima, Papago, and western Apache was made from the devil's claw seed pod. The Apache used a variety of colors—yellow, green, brown— all from various parts of the yucca plant.

Painting on carved wood, Kachina dolls and masks, and Northwest totem poles was done with earth colors. Earth and rock with iron or copper compounds supplied most of the color as iron tinged the earth with red, brown, yellow, and orange, and a fine white clay, kaolin, produced white. Actually the range of earth colors is almost unlimited.

As quill work began to be used less after beads were available, the dye used for quills was almost forgotten. All shades of red were made from the root of the buffalo berry, squaw currant, tamarack bark, spruce cones, sumac berries, bloodroot, and hemlock bark. Black was made from alder bark, wild grapes, hickory or walnut and butternut bark. Blue was made from the larkspur.

Black for pottery was made by combining vegetables and minerals. To obtain a shiny black, sooty smoke was brought in contact with red-hot pottery.

The Chilkat mountain goat wool blankets of the Northwest Coast have three colors: black from the hemlock bark; yellow from the lichen wolf moss; and green from copper oxide.

Bird feathers were often used as color in decorations; the woodpecker, for red; the mallard, for green; oriole feathers, for orange; the meadow lark, yellow; the quail, black; the feathers of the thrush, for brown; the heron, for white; the turkey, for iridescent shades; and the parrot, for green.

# MEANINGS AND USES OF COLOR

The four cardinal points are symbolized by color among many of the Indian tribes. In addition to the four horizontal points, or regions, of the universe, three others were sometimes recognized which may be called vertical points and were termed the upper, middle, and lower worlds.

Among the Navaho there were two color schemes. One applied to the songs, ceremonies, prayers, and legends which pertain to the surface of the earth, the celestial regions, and the places of life and happiness. These first colors are: east—white; south—blue; west—yellow; north—black. The second color scheme applied to the songs and things which refer to the underground, to the region of death, witchcraft, danger, and where the gods or wizards dwell. These colors are: east—black; south—blue; west—yellow; north—white.

Other tribes and their four-direction colors are as follows:

| Tribe | East | South | West | North |
|-------|------|-------|------|-------|
| Apache | Black | White | Yellow | Blue |
| Cherokee | Red | White | Black | Blue |
| Creek | White | Blue | Black | Red or Yellow |
| Hopi | White | Red | Yellow | Black |
| Isleta | White | Red | Blue | Black |
| Omaha | Red | Black | Yellow | Blue |
| Sioux | Red | Black | Yellow | Blue |

Color was used by all tribes and was usually divided into four categories. First, color for decorative use; second, color used in ceremonies; third, color in connection with death and mourning; and fourth, color connected with war and peace.

Even the naming of a person was connected with color. It could denote social status by being descriptive; for example, a person was like a Red Hawk, or strong as a Black Buffalo. Sometimes the Indian would give a color name to the place he lived.

Color was used as a sort of cosmetic body paint. The Mandans painted their bodies reddish brown, then painted deeper red or black figures on their arms. They would paint their faces, putting yellow around their eyes, and vermilion on their chins. They usually painted their faces for war; and when a person died, many of his relatives painted their faces as a sign of deep mourning.

Among the Sioux and Cheyenne, the bodies were painted. When a Santee Sioux warrior wanted to be left alone he might paint his face black, then make a zigzag line from hair to chin by scraping off the paint with his fingernails. This could also indicate the warrior was going trapping, or it could signify he was melancholy, or he was in love. The size of the line often indicated which one.

When a warrior was courting he might paint yellow or blue around his eyes. If a Santee woman wanted to be attractive she would paint a half-inch red streak from ear to ear across the bridge of her nose, and also a red streak in the part of her hair. Some Indian women painted their hair red or yellow to attract the attention of men, or some special man. However, among the Seneca this was forbidden. When a girl of the Arikara was in love she painted her cheeks with several dots, or one large dot of ocher. Iroquois women used an absorbent, soft, fluffy red powder with a pleasant scent. This was made from the red dry rot of the heart of the wood of the pine. Warriors painted their faces with red streaks on their cheeks, and when a prayer had been invoked by the god of thunder, the man would paint four lightning-like streaks from his eyes down to his chin.

The Zuñi used shades of red which varied from pale pink, to red, to deep maroon, and they used several shades of blue, yellow, and even purple. They associated color with butterflies and music, believing the god of music created the mythical plant, "tenatsli," which had blossoms of the four cardinal points. For special ceremonies, they also selected corn which had the colors of the cardinal points—white, red, yellow, and bluish black.

The Navaho believed in the symbolism of sex based on colors and the cardinal points. Things male were larger and more robust, noisy and violent, and for this reason things black in color belonged to the male. The San Juan River was male water because of its turbulence. Things feminine were finer, gentler, smaller, and more peaceful. Their color was blue. The Rio Grande was considered female because it was a more peaceful river.

The posts in the Grand Medicine Society of the Ojibwa were painted various colors; a band of green about the width of a hand was painted on a red post. The reason for the red is uncertain, but the green seems to have had some connection with the south, the source of heat and abundance of crops. The thunderbird comes from this direction in the springtime and brings rain which causes grass and fruit to grow. Some of the red posts had white spots and some black spots. On one post something like a cross was painted white on the east side, green on the south side, red on the west, and black on the north. White was considered the source of light, facing the direction of the rising sun; green the source of warmth, rain, and abundance; black to the north pertained to the regions from which comes the cold, disease, and desolation; red on the western side related to the road of the dead, perhaps because it is the direction of the setting sun.

Many tribes painted their dwellings, and the most spectacular and original was probably the tipi of the Plains tribes. Each owner exercised his own preference in color, though the usual colors used were green, red, blue, black, yellow, and white. White signified snow or winter. Blue was a favorite of the Sioux, and in later days the women would boil old blue blankets to obtain the color.

Blue, used so often in the yokes of the dresses, represented a lake or body of water in which the sky was reflected. Sky blue was also used for the background of baby cradles. In ceremonies blue would represent the sky, wind, clouds, the west, lightning, thunder, the moon, water, or day. Black represented night and also victory over enemies.

The Sioux used red to paint their faces, and red on a garment represented many wounds inflicted, as well as wounds received. Anyone who had been wounded had the right to wear a red feather. A red border on a tipi indicated that those who came there would be fed, or a tipi where a feast would be held. Red was also used on saddlebags, saddlecloths, girls' puberty robes, on moccasins and cradles.

The Chippewa men painted their faces black as a sign of mourning and death. The Salish tribe painted the faces of their dead red and black. The Sioux often wrapped their dead in a green blanket, while they were sometimes dressed in red, sig-

214

nifying they were going to the Happy Hunting Ground. Blue was the color used by the Cherokees to signify grief or depression of the spirit. The Winnebago painted the faces of their dead according to their clan. The Thunderbird clan painted a red line on the forehead, with a black one under this, and red dots under the lines and across the forehead. Red was painted on the mouth, the chin, and across the throat. The Warrior clan painted three lines across the forehead, the top and bottom, red, the middle black. A circle of red was painted from the corner of the mouth around the chin. The Eagle clan painted a black line across the forehead and down the bridge of the nose and from the corner of the mouth around the chin. The Bear clan had the top line on the forehead red and the bottom one black, with the chin painted red. Another branch of the Bear clan had two heavy black lines across the forehead with two red lines on the chin. The Wolf clan painted a thick blue line in the middle of the forehead. The Buffalo clan had two lines over the left eye, with the top blue and the lower one, red. The Elk and Deer clans painted circles of blue and black on the cheeks while the Water Spirits clan painted a circle of blue in the middle of the forehead.

The Algonkin Indians used a red feather on their pipes to signify war; other colors indicated peace. When going on the warpath, the Cherokee painted their faces with red or vermilion, then made a circle of black above one eye and white around the other. The Modoc warrior painted his face black before going into battle to symbolize victory over death. Many Sioux painted their faces red from the eye down to the chin before going into battle, and blue was often used to decorate the standards they carried into battle.

Black usually symbolized night, and red the day. Many tribes did not distinguish between black or dark blue, green and light blue, and white or natural color.


## TRADITIONAL DESIGNS

Designs varied greatly among some tribes. The Northwest Coast Indians had many designs based on animal and human

**HOW TO BEAD INDIAN ITEMS** *(See page 226)*
Plain moccasins beaded by the author.
Design was drawn on chamois bag then beaded.

figures. They were skilled in carving both in relief and in the round, and carving was the most important art in this area. The special characteristics are the curving line, not moving in regular geometric forms, but enclosing the various parts of the animal designs in subtle and irregular curves. Straight or angular lines are rarely seen, and the colors here are soft and rich.

The Southwest had a variety of art techniques and design styles. The latter included birds, butterflies, human forms, animal forms, curves, and straight lines. The Indians of this area were multi-talented in painting, carving, the making of pottery, the weaving of cloth plus bead and quill work. Many of the designs of the Southwest have been preserved on their pottery.

The Woodland people made designs of plants, animals, and beautiful floral patterns. Theirs was a semirealistic style, because while each flower or leaf may be quite true to nature, they often put many types of leaves or flowers on one plant. The tribes of this area also used birchbark as a basis for their decorations.

## BEAD AND QUILL WORK

Bead and quill work seems to have been done by many tribes, and is still sought after and copied. Before trade beads were available, the beads used consisted of bits of shell, bones, chips of rock, seed, nuts, beans, teeth, claws, fish and lizard scales, pearls, bits of crystal, agate, quartz, topaz, turquoise, jade, and various other stones. Beads were also made from clay or porcelain, some of them painted and engraved.

Beads or quills were sometimes worked in elaborate patterns, at other times in very simple designs. Tribes living close by one another might have totally different types of beadwork, while a tribe living a great distance might have similar patterns.

The tribes of the Southwest used a great deal of turquoise beads in their decorations, while the Indians living along the Pacific Coast used abalone shells. The people of the Atlantic Coast used the round clam, quahog, or pearls.

Pony beads were another decoration. These beads were

WEAVING—Southwest tribes
Woven cloth in a red, green, and black design.

about ⅛ of an inch in diameter and made of opaque china. They were quite irregular in shape and size and seem to have been used around the mid-nineteenth century. White and medium sky-blue were the most common colors, with black being next. Beads of deep buff, light and dark red, and a darker blue were also used.

In the 1840's to 1850's smaller beads, referred to as seed beads, appeared in beadwork. They were of a soft rich color with the edges thicker than the center. Translucent beads did not appear until later. In 1885 glass beads colored silver or gilt were introduced in the trade goods to the Indians.


## WEAVING

Both the Pueblo and the Navaho wove their own cloth. Among the Navaho, women were the weavers, but among the Pueblos it was the men. Pueblo handspun was a bit coarser than the Navaho, but was more even.

The Navaho used "bayeta" cloth later in their weaving. This was usually red, but could be blue, green, yellow, or white. The old story that the Indians obtained bayeta cloth by unraveling Spanish uniforms may be so, but the cloth was also available in large bolts from traders.

Saxony yarn was imported from Saxony in Germany in 1850, or before; this can usually be recognized by its silken sheen and the very even twisting of three fine plies. This yarn was red, and blankets made of Saxony are perhaps rarer than those made of bayeta. Germantown yarn reached the Southwest about 1875–1880 and was used by the Navaho for the next twenty-five or thirty years. It was dyed with aniline dyes, the colors are bright, somewhat harsh, and fade.

Cotton was used by the Hopi who carried on weaving in prehistoric times. They wove cotton, yucca fiber, fur stripes, and feathers. It is believed the earliest weaving of the Pueblo began around A.D. 758. Sheep were brought by the Spanish around 1540, and by 1600 the Pueblo began to weave with this wool.

# BASKETS AND POTTERY

Baskets were made by many tribes. The Northwest Coast Indians had finely twined cylindrical baskets as well as flat types. The background was straw-colored, the decorations being made of colored thread. The Hupa and other tribes of California made beautiful baskets, and also a brimless cap with red or black geometric designs on a light background. Some tribes made baskets with feathers woven into them; in fact most tribes could be identified by their basketwork. The baskets of the Basin–Plateau tribes were not so well made, and there was little basket-making among the Plains Indians.

Pottery was made by many tribes, and each area had its own symbols. In the Southwest, rain was always of great importance, so much of the pottery was decorated with the rain symbol. The pottery of the Acoma is very thin and can be distinguished by this characteristic. Their pottery is decorated with birds and flowers, the birds having curved parrot beaks, single or double wings, usually upraised, and a few thick tail feathers. The roadrunner is found on Acoma pottery. These birds have small heads on short necks, and round bodies with elaborate tails and short legs. Realistic flowers and leaf forms are frequently drawn with these birds.

Among the Hopi, the potter is usually a woman, and the design is painted freehand, the idea for the design being created in the mind of the painter. An outstanding feature of Hopi pottery is the color, which ranges from a light cream, through yellow to orange, to red. Many of these shades blend into each other, with designs of conventionalized birds or parts of birds. Masked Kachina figures, or their masks alone, are common on small flat tiles.

The pottery of the Isleta was red up until the 1880's, the design heavy and daring. The work of these California Indians shows a great variety of design. The base is usually red and the designs are red and black, or black. The Tsia bird, used on this pottery, has a small head with a thick, wedge-shaped bill, long neck, round body, single upraised wings, a few big

220

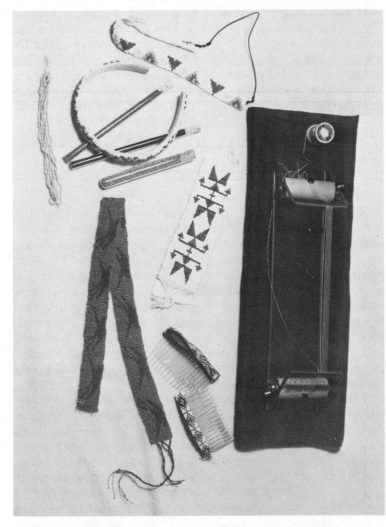

**MODERN BEADWORK AND COMMERCIAL LOOM**
Headband is attached to a hat rubber and beaded in various colors.
Large piece is for the starting of a belt.
Beaded band is attached to plastic hair band.
Combs sewn with decorative beadwork.

tail feathers, and long slim legs. It is red or yellow. Realistic deer are also drawn. Broad, double red bands, drawn in big curves, are found on water jars. Plants with black leaves and red flowers and berries are found arranged in graceful sprays.

Zuñi pottery can be recognized by its color and design, the designs often being dark brown-black or medium red. The lip is clear white which darkens with age. Often the Zuñi design is marked off into sections within which the design is placed. Their pottery shows deer, crudely drawn, little squatty birds with long elaborate tails, and large flowers like disks or rosettes that stretch from the neck to the base of the jar.

## JEWELRY

The Navaho learned the art of silversmithing from the Mexicans, and the first dated silversmithing of the Navaho was about 1853. The concha belt so popular in the Southwest was derived from the concha of the Plains Indians. The Ute, Kiowa, and Comanche, all traditional enemies of the Navaho, wore round and oval plaques of German silver as ornaments strung on leather belts. The Navaho obtained some after battles with the southern Plains tribes. It is believed the Plains tribes learned to make the silver ornament from the Delawares and the Shawnee. These tribes were skilled in the art of silversmithing, and when they moved from the East to the Plains they brought the skill with them.

Turquoise used to be mounted in a very different way on the silver; the bezel, or rim into which the stone was set, was deep and level with the top of the stone. This rim was often bent over the top of the turquoise, forming a small cup which held the stone securely in place. Sometimes there was notching on the edges of these crude bezels, giving a pleasant saw-tooth pattern which formed a decorative relief against the turquoise. The shallow bezel, extending halfway up the stone, was developed later.

The squash blossom necklace did not come into being until about 1880. The squash blossom is similar to one of the little units that go to make up the center part of the sunflower. Some

# TIN CONE JINGLERS

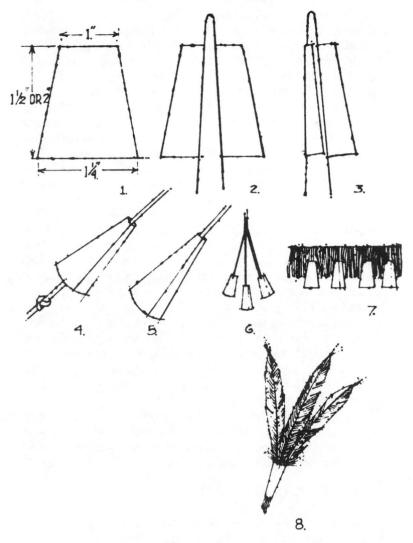

1.

2.

3.

4.

5.

6.

7.

8.

*(See page 224)*

Navaho believe the naja (a pendant) found on the necklace is really the bow of Nayenezgani. The Navaho used the Mexican beads as their example when making the squash blossom necklace, and their word for beads of this shape is really "beads that spread out." It is not a symbolic meaning but merely that the beads look like a flower.

Both the Navaho and Zuñi prefer, above all other turquoise, the stones that are a clear, deep, robin's-egg blue. This turquoise the Navaho call male turquoise; the more common greenish hue is called female turquoise. They also prefer the plain-colored stone and not those marked with matrix. Turquoise has been colored or dyed a deeper blue in some cases, and an inferior grade has been given a deeper color by soaking in grease. However, if these stones are left in the sun they will become greasy as the grease sweats out. Turquoise of deep blue, such as the Indians prefer, will retain its color, while the softer stone, of lighter blue, or of a greenish cast, will become a dull and unattractive green. The stone, which has a high polish and evenness, is not characteristic of those that are polished by the Navaho and Zuñi, who use crude tools and not those of the lapidaries.

Copper was used by the Indians for weapons, adornment, and even dishes; however, the use of copper soon passed out of existence after the arrival of the white man. The Northwest Coast tribes made copper neck rings of heavy twisted rods, and also used this metal in making masks. Designs on copper were usually birds and animals.

Most Indian art, decoration, and even symbolism is alive and vibrant, a useful part of their daily life. Everything was made as beautiful as possible to show appreciation to the Great Spirit, the giver of all things.

## TIN CONE JINGLERS

Many later items of Indian use were decorated with these small tin cone jinglers, cut from tin. These were used to decorate baskets, drums, clothing, cradle boards, in fact were used as metal fringe on some things, or tied in with fringe for the small sound they made. Several were attached to a stick to make a rattle. They were sometimes slipped over the quill

# METHODS OF BEADWORK

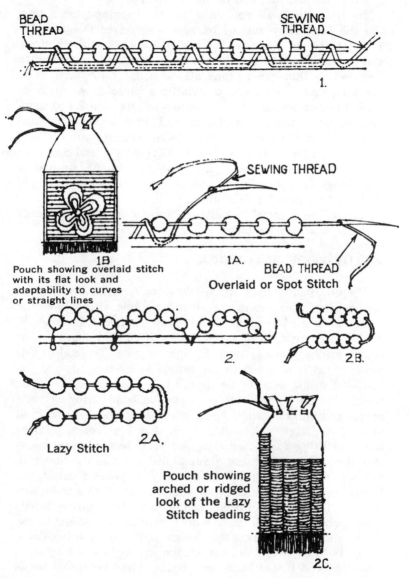

BEAD THREAD

SEWING THREAD

1.

SEWING THREAD

BEAD THREAD

1A. Overlaid or Spot Stitch

1B
Pouch showing overlaid stitch with its flat look and adaptability to curves or straight lines

2.

2B.

2A.

Lazy Stitch

Pouch showing arched or ridged look of the Lazy Stitch beading

2C.

*(See page 226)*

of a feather, as added decoration, or to hold several feathers, as fringe on pouches, and on moccasin ties.

To make these, all you need are tin cans and tin shears. Cut the pieces in a sort of triangle shape (see Diagram 1). They can be cut 1 inch at the top, 1¼ inches at the bottom, and on the sides 1½ to 2 inches long. Cut them according to their use, as they can be long and slim, large or small. Next use a tapered metal form, or whittle a piece of wood to be used. Lay the tapered piece as shown in Diagram 2 and hammer the tin around it as in Diagram 3. Pull the tapered wood or metal from the cone, tie a knot in one end of cord, and pull this through the cone as shown in Diagrams 4 and 5.

Use the metal jinglers in groups (Diagram 6), or tied in with fringe (Diagram 7), or pulled over feather quills to hold groups of feathers for decoration.

Uses of these metal jinglers are numerous; you'll probably discover new uses for them.

## METHODS OF BEADWORK

The Overlaid or Spot Stitch takes two separate threads and two needles. The beads are strung on one string, and the other one is used to stitch the beads to the buckskin or cloth. A thread is strung with a few beads; it can be one, two (as shown in Diagram 1), or up to eight or nine. The end of this bead thread is attached to the article to be beaded, and the thread is strung with the beads and laid along the article. The sewing thread is then stitched over the bead string at right angles and into the article being decorated, where it is carried along (see Diagram 1, dotted line), then emerges to go over the bead string again (see Diagram 1A). In sewing on buckskin the under thread was never pulled through the material, but within it, as shown by the dotted line. When finished, the beads are closely pushed together and conceal both strings or threads. The number of beads strung on the bead thread before it is stitched down will make a difference in the fineness of the work, and depends upon the design and what is being decorated. With fine work and curves, the sewing thread may cross over the bead thread every two beads. The number of beads between stitches depends upon the pattern. In straight rows of

# SIOUX BEADWORK DESIGNS

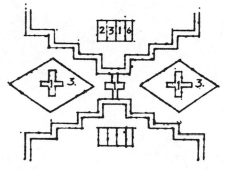

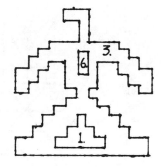

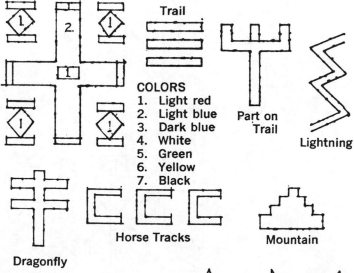

Trail

COLORS
1. Light red
2. Light blue
3. Dark blue
4. White
5. Green
6. Yellow
7. Black

Part on Trail

Lightning

Dragonfly

Horse Tracks

Mountain

Tipi

Clouds

# SIOUX BEADWORK DESIGNS

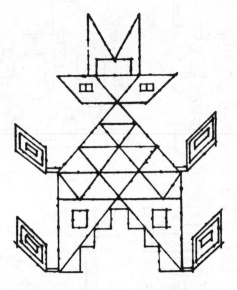

For dresses and shirts

For dresses, bags, and shirts

the same color seven or eight beads can be used between overlaid stitches. Where a color changes, there should be a stitch (see Diagram 1A). Elaborate flower designs can be made like this, and also solid work where a curving design is made and then the background filled with closely laid lines of beads, straight or curving (Diagram 1B). This is adaptable for floral designs, and was the stitch used by the Woodland Indians. It is used entirely by the Blackfoot, Sarsi, Cree, Flathead, Shoshoni, Assiniboin and some Crow, the Gros Ventre and the eastern Sioux who used floral patterns.

The western Sioux, in fact, most of the Plains Indians, used a stitch called the Lazy Stitch. The Lazy Stitch is used for geometric patterns in which the painstaking Overlaid Stitch was unnecessary. The Cheyenne, Arapaho, some Crow, and the Sioux used this stitch. Diagram 2 shows the Lazy Stitch where a number of beads, here five, are strung upon a thread after the thread has been fastened on the buckskin. Make a stitch at the end of the row of beads, attaching the thread to the material. Next string the same number of beads on the thread, and bring it back parallel to the first row and make another stitch. See Diagram 2A which shows what the rows will be like. Diagram 2B shows the beads pulled tight and how they look finished, with a slight arch. Like the Overlaid Stitch this one also is not sewed through the buckskin but is sewn just under the surface. In an all-over pattern, the rows of parallel ridges make it easy to recognize this type of beadwork as from the Plains. When this type of beadwork is done on cloth, it needs a backing of some sort to give the cloth body and a firm base for the beading. Today, waxed linen thread or nylon thread and a stout needle can be used, but originally the Indians used sinew and an awl. A perforation was made with an awl at the beginning edge, and another perforation was made to admit the sinew at the end of the row of beads. As in the Overlaid Stitch, the perforation does not pass through to the under side of the skin but runs horizontally just below the surface, so that underneath no stitches show. This stitch is less firm than the Overlaid Stitch, and the beads may pull out sooner, but with this method, the Sioux often covered the complete top of moccasins or a dress yoke with solid beading. In overall appearance the Lazy Stitch is somewhat reminiscent

# SIOUX BEADWORK DESIGNS

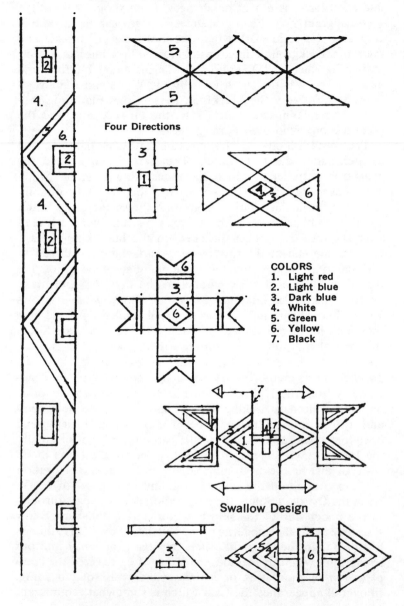

**Four Directions**

**COLORS**
1. Light red
2. Light blue
3. Dark blue
4. White
5. Green
6. Yellow
7. Black

**Swallow Design**

of quill work, with the rows of parallel ridges (Diagram 2C); however, the sewing method is different from quill work.

## BEAD LOOM

In early times, the western Sioux women did not weave either quills or beads. Weaving was an eastern art practiced by the Woodland Indians and some of the eastern Sioux. The weaving frame used by these early weavers was a bow, with several warp strings strung on it in the position of the bowstring and with perforated pieces of birchbark to be used as spreaders. Eventually an oblong wooden frame took the place of the bow and found its way to the Plains tribes in later years. Bead looms were mostly used for sale and trade items, because it was an easier and quicker method than the stitching of beads, and it was adaptable to the geometric designs of the Plains Indians. Headbands, armbands, garters, neckbands, and belts are among the items made on the bead loom. Sometimes strips are woven to be sewn on a garment.

Bead looms can be purchased at most hobby stores, or they can be made. A very simple loom can be made quickly from a cardboard box, or the same design can be made from wood. Any sturdy cardboard box about 5 or 6 inches by 8 or 10 inches will do. It should be 1½ or 2 inches deep. On each side, from one end of the box, measure 2 inches toward the center (see Diagram 1, a, vertical dotted lines). At this point cut straight down from the top edge of the box to the bottom along the dotted line, then cut around the bottom of the box to the other end and back to the other side, as shown on dotted line (Diagram 1). Set aside the part of the box you have just cut away for later use. On the end of the box where you first measured off 2 inches, find the center of this space, 1 inch from the cut edge, and halfway between the bottom and top of the box, and make a small hole, barely large enough to push a pencil through. Do the same on the other side (Diagram 1, b). Next, in the center of the end of the box (Diagram 1, c) punch another hole. This can be a little larger than the side holes. Above this center hole Diagram 1, c, at the top rim of the box end, cut two slanting notches about 1 or 1½ inches apart as shown in Diagram 1, d.

# BEAD LOOM

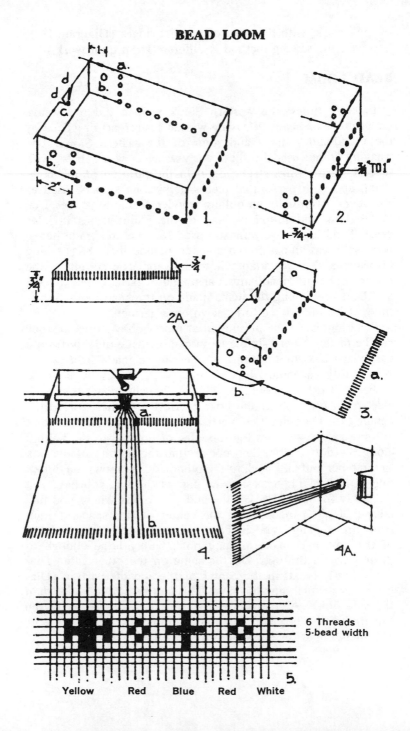

6 Threads
5-bead width

Yellow    Red    Blue    Red    White

The part that was cut from the box and set aside should now be cut ¾ inch in from the corner, and ¾ to 1 inch high, depending upon the original depth of the box (see Diagram 2). On the top edge of this end measure a line ⅛ of an inch from the edge, then make dots along this line ¹⁄₁₆ inch apart. Cut straight in from the dots to the line (See Diagram 2A). Do the same to the end of the box which has the holes cut (see Diagram 3, *a*). Make a line ⅛ inch in from the edge, then make dots along this line ¹⁄₁₆ of an inch apart (you can follow the markings on a ruler), then cut straight in from the dots to the line. Now place the ¾-inch end of the box (Diagram 2A) as shown in Diagram 3. Use glue, tape, or paper clips to hold this ¾-inch end against the side (Diagram 3, *b*).

Push a pencil through the holes in the standing sides of the box. You can use any round stick about the size of a pencil. Wind rubber bands around the pencil on the outside of the box, where the pencil sticks through. Wind the band tight and push the rubbers tight against the side of the box; this will keep the pencil from turning when the loom is threaded.

If you are making a wooden box loom, a fine-toothed comb could be fastened to the edges of the box in place of the notched edges (as in Diagram 3, *a*), or a fine wire spring can be pulled across the end to be used in place of the notches to hold the thread.

Before threading the loom you should decide on the pattern you want and how wide it should be. Use an odd number of beads in width, as this gives you a center bead for the geometric designs. There will always be one more thread on the loom than row of beads. Five beads will take 6 threads, 7 beads, 8 threads. Use graph paper to draw a design. Some hobby stores have beadwork graph paper which is scaled to bead size; otherwise, use plain graph paper, but remember the squares will be larger than the beads. Nevertheless it will show you how the design will look, and it will give you the bead spaces. Diagram 5 shows a 6-thread, 5-bead width design drawn out. The right side is the end, and the beads in those first two rows will be white; in fact, the background is white. The third row will have two white beads, a red bead, and two more white. The fourth row will have one white bead, one red, one white, one red, and one white, and on to the next row.

233

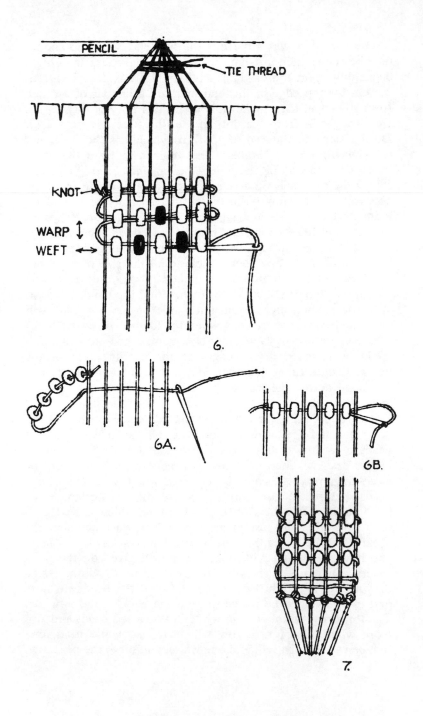

PENCIL

TIE THREAD

KNOT

WARP ↕
WEFT ↔

6.

6A.

6B.

7.

Use colored pencil to mark the colors in the spaces, so as you transfer the pattern to the loom you will begin to see the beads on the loom take on the form of the design you have drawn and colored. When you finish the double crossbar of yellow, and the next two rows of white beads, start backward with the red square, two more white rows, the blue cross, and continue. When you have finished, the yellow will be the center, and you will have a wrist band that can be sewed onto a tape and snapped around your wrist, or sewed onto an old leather strap. The bands can be made as long as you like by simply rolling the finished beading around the pencil. One long strip can be beaded for a belt, or several smaller strips can be sewn together and onto a leather strip or belt.

For threading the loom, see Diagrams 4 and 6. Decide how long your bead band will be—5 to 6 inches will make a wrist band—then allow 6 to 8 inches more length. These long lengths which you thread onto the loom are called warp threads. If your bracelet will be 5 inches long, then allow another 6 inches, or a total of 11 inches. Cut six 11-inch lengths of waxed linen or nylon thread. Put the threads together evenly at the end and tie them to the center of the pencil. Be sure they are tied firmly. Then bring the threads over the notched side of the box (Diagram 4, a), one thread to one notch, side by side. Bring the threads down across the box to the outer edge (Diagram 4, b), through the notches around the box (see Diagram 4A), pull the threads through the hole in the end center under the two notches, then wrap the extra length of thread around the notches until it holds. When cutting your length of thread you may need more than 6 inches extra length to go under the loom and be caught through the notches. Be sure to measure this before cutting your thread.

Hold the loom so it faces you, as in Diagram 4; you work back from the pencil end toward yourself. Thread the bead needle and tie the end of the thread to the left warp thread, then bring the needle and thread out to the right under the loom thread. Run the needle through the required number of beads, 5 as shown in Diagrams 6 and 6A. Space the beads under the warp threads as shown in Diagram 6B, hold them there with your left forefinger, then run the needle from the right, over the right warp thread, and through the first bead.

Continue running the needle through the other four beads, keeping the thread, or weft, on top of the warp threads. Now go underneath, add the next row of beads, and continue as before, being sure to follow your design.

You will note on Diagram 6 that there is only one row of white beads, instead of the two rows shown on the graph paper of Diagram 5. The next row has the red bead in the middle and the next row shows two red beads, as the pattern shows. As you bead, you will pull the weft thread tight and push the beads, or rows, close together. If your band is getting longer than the warp threads on top of the loom, loosen the threads from around the end notch, loosen the rubber bands on the pencil, and twist the finished beading around the pencil. Anchor the pencil tightly again with the rubber bands, wrap the threads around the end notch, and continue beading.

When you have finished the design, run the weft thread in and out of the warp threads as shown in Diagram 7 and tie it around the strands as shown.

If the band is sewn onto a tape or ribbon, the thread ends can be turned back and tucked under the end as the band is sewn on the ribbon. Leave space on the ends of the ribbon for hooks and you have a bracelet. Or you can add a tie to each end for a headband.

Beads can be bought at most hobby shops or craft stores. The most typical Indian bead colors are white, red, light blue, dark blue, black, green, and yellow, although you can use any colors that suit you. White is used a great deal for background with the designs in color. The Sioux use a blue background often.

The beadworker often named her design according to what it looked like to her when she finished. Sometimes, when looking it over, it might remind her of some natural object, so she named the design, and it wasn't necessarily symbolic, except to her. Sometimes the design evolved out of the need to cover up a seam or a flaw in the skin, perhaps from an arrow mark, or a mistake in tanning, or even a mistake in beading. Rather than undo a great deal of beading because of a mistake, the beadworker would simply incorporate the mistake into the design and go on from there. Being creative

# BEAD FLOWERS AND BEAD CHAINS

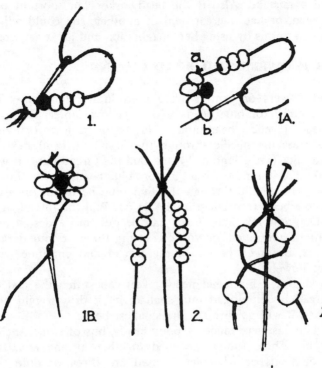

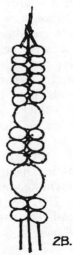

*(See page 238)*

and adaptable, it was no problem for her to adjust a design around a mistake. Also if the beadworker ran short of one color bead, or had a great deal of another, she could adjust her design to this by using her imagination and great art sense.

## BEAD FLOWERS AND BEAD CHAINS

Bead flowers or centers were used in floral designs. To make a flower of blue beads with a yellow center, thread 1 blue bead, 1 yellow bead, and 3 blue beads on linen or nylon thread. Pass the needle through the first blue bead next to the end knot (see Diagram 1) and pull the thread tight. It will look like 1A at *a*; now thread 3 more blue beads on the thread and pull the needle through the first blue bead put on after the yellow bead (see Diagram 1A at *b*). Pull the thread tight as in Diagram 1B. The flower can be put into a design and the pattern continued, or you can string three or four darker blue, red, or green beads on the thread and continue with another flower.

In place of a fine bead needle, you can stiffen the end of the thread by dipping it into shellac; let it dry straight and hard, and it will go through the smallest bead.

Bead chains were made of pony beads, bits of stone, shells, and bone. Three thongs are tied together at one end, the beads or shells or whatever is used are threaded onto the two side thongs, with the middle one left empty. The three thongs are then braided. Sometimes the three thongs are run through a larger bead or piece of bone, and the braiding continued for a necklace. Today you can use three lengths of nylon thread, tied together at one end, with bead strung on two threads as in Diagram 2. Stick a pin through the knot and into a thick pad or magazine to hold it tight when you braid the chain. Make the threads long enough and leave bead needles on the ends of the two threads so you can add beads as needed. Braid the beads around the middle thong or thread as in Diagram 2A. You can add large beads, metal pieces, anything you like in between the braided sections (see Diagram 2B). As you braid hold the thread between your thumb and the first finger of your left hand, and keep the middle thread in a straight line. Pull the other two threads,

# IMITATION INDIAN BEADS

*(See page 240)*

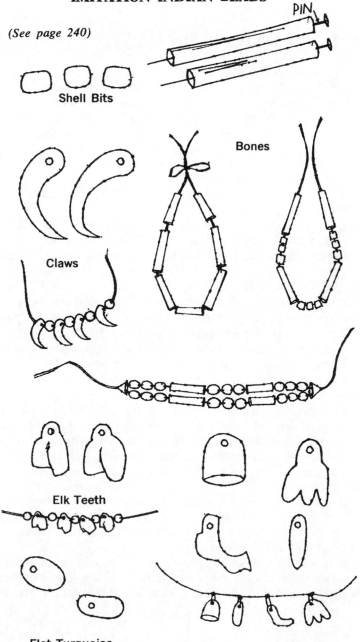

PIN

Shell Bits

Bones

Claws

Elk Teeth

Flat Turquoise

Dew Claws

with a bead on each side between cross-overs, closely together in a double row.

## IMITATION INDIAN BEADS

Indian necklaces were made of all sorts of things—claws, bones, animal teeth, stones, shells, strung separately or in combinations, on thongs, either in strands or sometimes intricately tied together. Sometimes you can buy boar teeth, and if these are polished, a hole drilled through them, and the end painted red with nail polish or enamel, when strung on a shoelace, with a colored bead between each tooth, they are much like the ancient Indian necklaces.

A basic recipe for molding all types of beads calls for the following ingredients:

Heat ¾ cups of salt in the oven until hot. This can be heated in aluminum paper or a small throw-away pan.

Put the heated salt and 1 cup of flour into an old saucepan.

Add 1 cup of water and mix well.

Put the saucepan on the stove over slow heat. Stir the mixture constantly, scraping it up from the bottom of the pan.

When it has thickened to a crumbly, dry-looking dough texture, scrape it from the pan onto a sheet of heavy aluminum foil or an old plate or tray and allow to cool slightly.

When it is cool enough to handle, knead it as you would bread dough.

You can color the dough by adding a bit of dye powder or a mere drop of food coloring or watercolor paint. If you want different colored beads, divide the dough into as many lumps as you want colors. Flatten one piece and roll it over just a pinch of the dye powder, then knead it some more until the color is even.

If you use watercolor paint it has to be mixed in the water before the dough is cooked. For this reason dye powder is easier to use. Cooking the dough makes the beads less apt to break and is the best way.

If it is impossible to cook the dough, you can mix the flour and salt together, but this method takes much less water, so you must add it a drop at a time until the dough can be kneaded. Too much water, with this method, will make the dough so sticky you can hardly work with it. Be careful.

To make shell bits take a bit from the lump and roll it between your palms. You can flatten the sides for square-looking bits, or round it like beads, or push it into odd shapes like shells. Run a large hatpin or a nail through the part which will have a thong run through it.

You'll probably need several nails of different sizes to make holes in the beads. For claws, shape the dough into claws to be strung with beads, and color them brown or black.

You can shape elks' teeth, which are used as decorations on dresses, with fringe, on bags and pouches, and as necklaces. Leave the elks' teeth the natural color of the dough.

Roll long cylindrical beads of natural color for bone necklaces and collars. Be sure to put a long pin or nail through these for a stringing hole. Add colored beads to make a long necklace or collar.

Dew claws were originally made out of hoofs and were shiny jet-black. They were shaped out of layers of hoofs into flat ornaments, a hole punched in them and tied with a thong. These can be molded out of dough and dyed black. Don't forget to put a nail or pin through them to make a hole for stringing.

For silver-looking beads or metal type ornaments, roll the dough in tiny pieces of aluminum foil. When thoroughly dry these must be shellacked to keep the foil from peeling off.

To flatten the dough for flatter pieces, roll a bit of it on a flat surface, using a smooth round bottle as a rolling pin. The flat pieces can then be cut in patterns.

Add some turquoise dye to a bit of dough and make flat-looking turquoise beads to be strung on a thong. You can make flat, rounded bits of coral beads by experimenting with dye and shapes. String these with the turquoise and shell bits.

After the beads are colored and cut, put them on a tray or some aluminum foil to dry. This will take a day or two, possibly more, depending upon the weather. In hot sun or warm air, they will dry more quickly.

It is best not to try to make these beads in rainy weather, as salt collects moisture. Even after the beads are dry, they may be affected by damp air. If you shellac all of the beads

## TYPICAL DESIGNS

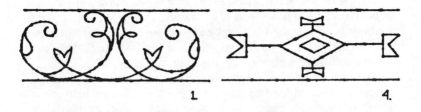

1.

4.

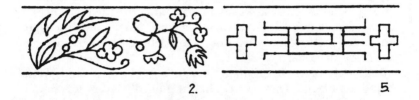

2.

5.

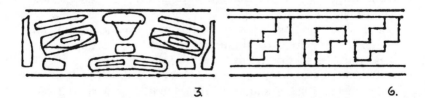

3.

6.

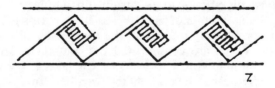

7

# DESIGNS FOR WEAVING, BEADING, OR PAINTING

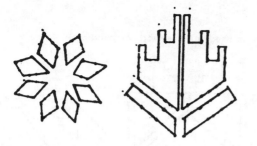

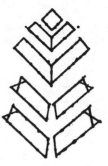

Geometric—Woodland tribes

Floral—Woodland tribes

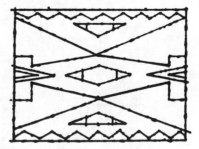

Sioux—painted design

# SIOUX OR DAKOTA DESIGNS

(These can be used for beadwork or painting.)

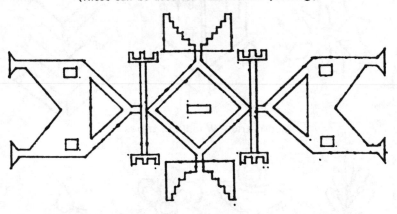

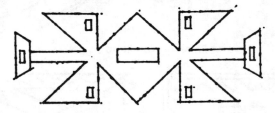

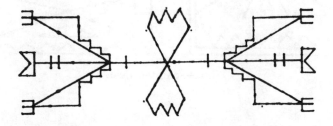

# SOUTHWEST DESERT TRIBE DESIGNS

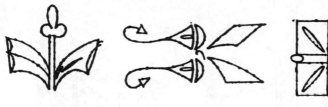

These can be put on bowls, bags, or used
in any manner of design.

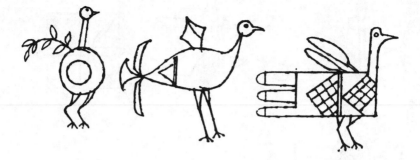

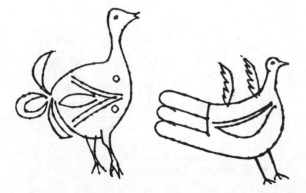

Bird Designs: To paint on pottery or wooden bowls
(These could also be put on clothing today.)

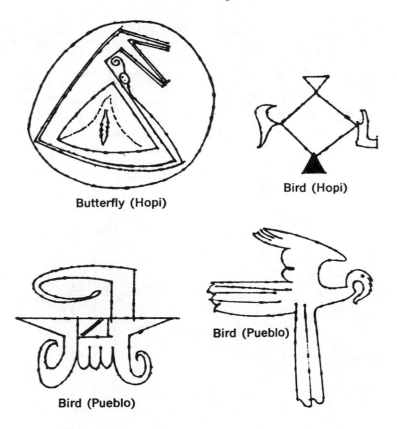

Butterfly (Hopi)

Bird (Hopi)

Bird (Pueblo)

Bird (Pueblo)

after they are dry, they will have a waterproof coat and last much longer.

## TYPICAL DESIGNS

Diagram 1, a design of the Woodland tribes based on curves, appears in a number of variations in bead embroidery, painted on skin, or etched on birchbark. Diagram 2 is also from this area, a semirealistic representation of plants and flowers, based on the ancient curving lines and the floral style

# Thunderbird Designs

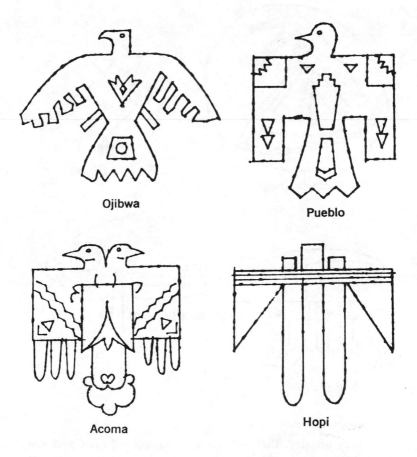

Ojibwa

Pueblo

Acoma

Hopi

introduced to the Indians by the French in the seventeenth and eighteenth centuries. While each flower may be quite true to nature, many different kinds of fruits or flowers often appear to be from one plant.

Diagram 3 shows a design typical of the Northwest Coast people. The special characteristics of this style are the curving lines, not moving in regular geometric forms but enclosing parts of the animal designs, which are so typical together

# DECORATION FOR SANTO DOMINGO
## PUEBLO POTTERY

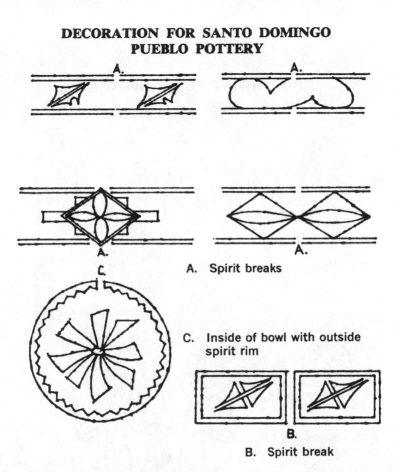

A. Spirit breaks

C. Inside of bowl with outside spirit rim

B. Spirit break

with the animals. These designs are particularly suited to the totem pole.

Diagram 4 shows a design typical of the Plains Indians, where the triangle is the most widespread and characteristic design element. It is used alone or in simple combinations, in quill work, and for the last one hundred years in beadwork. Diagram 5 is a square element of tracks and the four directions. The Blackfoot use the square design almost exclusively.

The Southwest design, Diagram 6, shows predominately

# NORTHWEST COAST DESIGNS

## (Haida Tattoo)

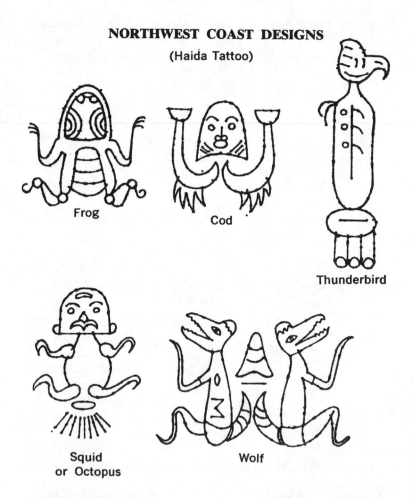

Frog

Cod

Thunderbird

Squid
or Octopus

Wolf

angular forms. Right angles are more common than other forms; however, the variety of art techniques and design styles is so rich and varied that it is almost impossible to completely characterize the art of this area. The angular design in Diagram 7 is also from this area.

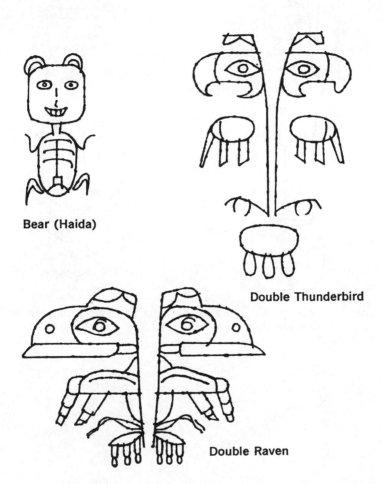

Bear (Haida)

Double Thunderbird

Double Raven

## The Spirit Path

The gap in encircling lines on jars or bowls, commonly known as the "exit trail of life," "ceremonial path," or "spirit path" is constantly used in Santo Domingo decoration. The ancient belief persists that every pot is the abiding place of a spirit which is manifested by the resonance of the vessel

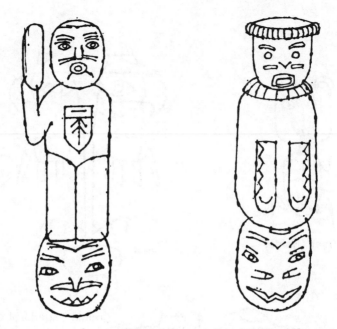

These are carved according to the crest or totem of the owner of the house and represent men standing on the head of an animal.

when tapped, and that to curb its freedom of exit and return by painting completely encircling lines is to endanger the vessel which may be broken through the efforts of the spirit to pass these barriers. Breaks in lines occur in more than 90 percent of all Santo Domingo pottery.

# PART VI

# WAR PAINT AND COUNTING COUP

*(Crafts begin on page 275)*

Before the arrival of the white man, there was little organized warfare between the various Indian tribes, and the main reason for the fighting between these tribes was the difference in dialects or languages. Another reason was the stealing of women, and later of horses.

The Northwest Coast tribes seemed to have had a military organization for war. Competition and rivalry regarding the accumulation of wealth were causes of war among many of these tribes, or injury to a member of a tribe by another tribe could result in conflict.

The California tribes were among the most peace-loving of all the natives of North America. Their hostilities were mostly between kinship groups or villages because of trespassing on tribal lands. When these tribes did fight it was mostly surprise attacks. Still some would challenge another village to a prearranged fight. In this type of warfare not many lives would be lost, and they were often stopped when a single member of either tribe was killed. In warfare the one who seized the plunder kept it.

The Pueblo people were also peaceful, but they did have their war chief, or priest, who ranked with the civil priest in executive authority, and these two were responsible for the decisions of the tribe. In some of the Pueblo tribes, the war priest led the fighting forces, in others it was his lieutenant. The war priest and the warriors formed a group ready to cope with any type of trouble. Fear of witchcraft was the cause of some battles or hostilities. If one tribe felt evil or supernatural powers had been sent against them they would

255

**MEDICINE BAG**
Painted rawhide medicine bag once belonged to Chief Joseph of the Nez Perce.

go to war to rid the village of this evil. Robbery was not a general cause of war as neighbors among the desert tribes had little to steal.

The Plains and Woodland tribes had more organized warfare. However it was not on a large scale, and not very common before the arrival of the white man. Small parties of five to fifty men would engage in conflict with one another. The largest band making up a war party was probably that of the Iroquois, who had a war band of about one thousand men. Later the white man's demand for furs and other trade goods created a general economic competition which the Indian had not known.

## INDIAN WARFARE

Indian warfare cannot easily be generalized, as each tribe had its own set of rules and customs of warfare. There were usually three kinds of warfare—defensive, aggressive, and unauthorized.

Many tribes used warfare as a means of acquiring prestige for an individual. In many tribes a young man could not marry or even be classed as an adult until he went on the warpath.

War parties of any size had their scouts and sentries, and the men were divided into divisions or squadrons. The Indian used his natural ability for living off the land and his knowledge of birds and animals to communicate with the members of his war party by imitating the sounds of the birds and animals. The Indian could go for long periods without food or water, making him an even more formidable foe.

The Omaha believed that the thunderbird ruled the battlefield and that he either preserved life or caused it to be lost. When the Omaha Plains Indian suffered a wrong, such as a member of a family being killed by another tribe, or a woman stolen, or horses taken, he could not take it upon himself to declare war as a personal revenge, but had to follow certain rules, which were that he must take his grievance to the

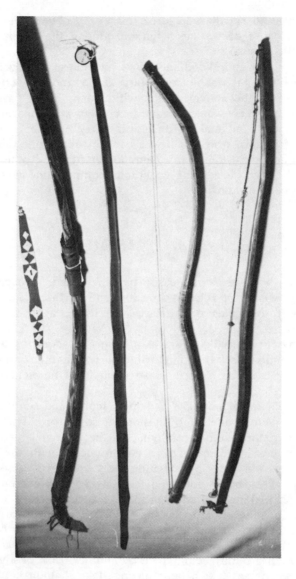

**BOWS**
Left, child's ceremonial beaded bow probably from a Sioux tribe.
Cheyenne bow with wrapped center on the wood.
Tribe unknown. Bow of wood.
Sioux bow.
Curved type bow from the Kiowa tribe.

"Keeper of the Sacred Pack" and ask for a feast of the War Bundle. If the Keeper of the Sacred Pack consented, there was a ceremony and the war chief was told what he must do to be successful in making war. He was given tribal charms such as stuffed birds, taken from the War Bundle, which would give magical aid. The Omaha war party might consist of anywhere from eight to a hundred warriors. All were volunteers who went because of some previous sorrow or wrong, either real or fancied. Once a man vowed to go on the warpath he must live according to rules until it was time to leave for the battle.

The Omaha war captain was called "Nudonhonga" and it was his duty to direct the movement of the troops, to drill them and give them the necessary instructions. He alone was responsible for the success of the war party. He divided his warriors into four sections, and the scouts made the fifth group. Each section was assigned special duties along with the fighting. The first group were the hunters who were to secure the game for all the warriors as they moved. The second group were the moccasin carriers, whose duty it was to obtain and carry extra moccasins for the men, so they could have new footwear as their moccasins wore out on the journey. The third were the kettle keepers and carriers. It was the duty of this group to look after the utensils and cook the food while on the warpath. The fourth group were those who carried their basic food supply from the village, and whose duty it was to find water. This group also made the fire. The last or fifth group were the scouts.

The scouts were always men of high rank and the most trustworthy of the tribe. These scout warriors had the privilege of smoking the sacred war pipe. They must never show cowardice and had to vow that their lives belonged to the tribe. A scout must be truthful in his reports about battle conditions, and was expected to risk or even give his life for the protection of his tribe or fellow members of the war party, if necessary.

The war captain was a man of honor and it was up to him to use his ability and judgment in behalf of his men. He had to seek safety when they were in danger, and should he seek safety for himself in time of danger it would mean a life of disgrace thereafter.

Ceremonies were a part of war, before and after. Women often took part in these, and in the celebrations of victory. There were also ceremonies for dead relatives or friends. Among the Navaho there were times when the men could not go to war unless the women decided they should.

The Plains tribes had a set of graded war honors. Counting coup (see explanation on pages 295-99) meant more than killing a man. Slaying an enemy, scalping, stealing horses, each had its own honors. If anyone lied about his war honors he could be challenged by any person who had been on the war party with him.

The Cheyenne had several military societies, and a young man could join any one of them, but usually would join the one his father belonged to. The war societies not only served in time of war, but as tribal police forces. Each society had its own set of rules and duties, such as protecting the movement of the camp from one place to another and enforcing the rules of hunting so the buffalo wouldn't be scared away before the tribal hunt. Only very brave young men could belong to the elite society of the Contraries. These were actors of a sort as well as warriors, and played the part of clowns when necessary. They said "no" when they meant "yes," when they went away they really meant to come forward. When they turned left, they should have gone right, and they would sit shivering on a hot day and go without their blanket on a zero day. Their antics took the pressure off the camp and amused the people in times of war, hunger, or any other disaster. They made the people laugh and forget their woes. They also took chances on the warpath that the others did not, doing what seemed to be foolish things, often to save someone, or to divert the attention of the enemy.

Some tribes had a society that was arranged in order of the age of the members. As a member grew older he moved up a step. In this way there was a warrior society for all the young men. There were times when a young boy did not want to become a warrior, or a member of any warrior society. These young men were known as "berdache," and there was no scorn connected with their decision. At times there might be a bit of awe at the condition, which the Indians did not believe was of the young man's doing.

Captives were many times adopted into the tribe. If a son had been killed or had died, a young warrior might be taken into the family. At other times, a captive might be killed, but with much ceremony. The Indian warrior knew that if he was captured, he would probably be tortured and killed, but from his early training as a warrior he knew this and was trained to die bravely. If a captive was taken into a family, he was made to dance a number of times around the campfire, given a new name, usually that of a slain relative of the family, and taken to the home of the family who would adopt him. Women and children were usually taken into the tribe.

It was the duty of every warrior to capture or kill as many of the enemy as possible. However, a greater honor was to walk up to an enemy, slap his face, then walk away without killing him. This was considered the greatest honor of war.

In the Woodland tribes, if a man surrendered to an enemy tribe he was considered dead to his own. If he was adopted into the enemy tribe it was with a ceremony of rebirth; thus he could marry in his new tribe, but was compelled to give up all ties with his old tribe, and pledge his loyalty to his new family and tribe. He was expected to live up to his new name and even go on the warpath against his own people if need be. There are few records of anyone who took a new name and a new tribe ever becoming a traitor to it. Many became leading members of the new tribe and their most stalwart warriors. The new family gave the adopted man gifts and educated him in their ways. The Iroquois have been known to take whole villages captive, and by the close of the seventeenth century many of the Iroquois tribes were either captives or descendants of captives.

Scalps were taken from a dead enemy to serve as trophy, but this was not a general Indian custom before the arrival of the white man. Early white settlers would pay a bounty on dead Indians and the scalp was one way of collecting this bounty. In the 1700's, payment was as much as $60 for every scalp. By the mid-eighteenth century $134 was paid for Indian male scalps and $50 each for females and children.

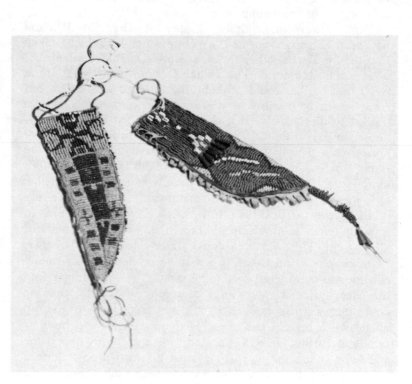

**KNIFE SHEATHS**—Sioux
Both are beaded in blue, red, and yellow.

# SIGNALS

Every Indian boy was taught to track birds and animals and to recognize their call. They knew that birds had seasonal calls and that they differed from spring to autumn. They used the calls of birds and animals as warning signals to their tribe, or as other signals.

Some Indians acted as spies, and they grew very adept at literally disappearing from under the very nose of the enemy when being pursued. Many carried false feet of the bear, wolf, horse, buffalo, or deer, leading their pursuers to believe that only an animal had gone along the trail.

Indians used fire to signal; they built a small fire, then smothered it with damp grass. A blanket was then thrown over this smoldering fire and by quickly removing the blanket, rounded clouds of smoke were sent upward. By again replacing the blanket and withdrawing it, more smoke would be produced and then released. Usually two or more persons would hold the blanket.

At times several fires were built a few yards apart in order to send up parallel columns of smoke. Such multiple fires were used by many of the tribes of the Southwest. The Apache used three columns of smoke when they wanted to signal an alarm, or if danger was near they might build several fires. The density of the smoke was produced by using pine, scrub cedar, or other desert evergreen to which leaves and grass were mixed.

Night signals were sent by making a brisk fire, then smothering it for a moment. This would produce a series of dots and dashes. Torches were also used at night to send signals or codes.

Blanket signals were used by most of the tribes. If the end of the blanket was waved downward several times it meant to stop or halt. A folded blanket waved to the right and left, in front of the body, asked just how the enemy had been captured. To ask how many men or animals were near, some tribes would wave the blanket in front of the body. Running

**MEDICINE MAN HEADDRESS**—Plains
Made of buffalo horn, fur, and horse tail.

in a circle, holding the blanket over the head meant something had been found. Peace was often conveyed by the blanket being grasped by two corners, then waved above the head, and then thrown upward and allowed to fall to the ground. Should a chief open his blanket and hang it in front of his body, it mean the camp was surrendered. A folded blanket held high above the head meant surrender.

## THE SIGNIFICANCE OF FEATHERS

Feathers showed just how brave the warrior had been in battle. An eagle feather was very important, but the spreading eagle bonnet one sees so often worn by Indians was really worn only by a few of the Plains tribes, and then only by a chief or some greatly honored warrior, and generally for ceremonies only.

The most prized feather was the plume of the eagle, the long, finely formed feather with a black tip. A perfect tail feather was often worth one pony. Smaller feathers were used to decorate clothing and other items. The Pueblo Indians prized the down of the eagle, as it was used in their ceremonial clothes. The light airy feather was a symbol of the intermediate region between things of the spirit world and the earth. Hopi prayer sticks also were adorned with the eagle feather and crested with down.

The way a feather was worn by the warrior indicated the honors he had won. Among the Omaha, a warrior of the first grade was entitled to wear the white-tipped feather from the tail of the golden eagle fastened straight upward. Those who held second-grade honors wore a white-tipped tail feather of the golden eagle fastened to the scalp lock in such a manner that it projected horizontally from the side of the head. Those holding third-grade honors wore the arrow thrust through the scalp lock, often with a feather attached. Fifth honors wore a suspended eagle feather from the scalp lock, and sixth honors did not wear feathers, but did act as master of ceremony at the feast accompanying the meeting of the company of warriors.

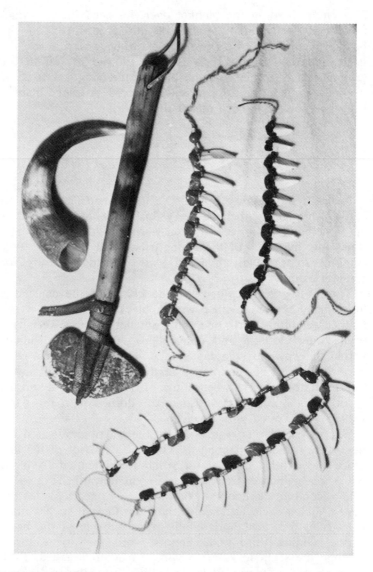

**INDIAN ITEMS**
Teeth necklace and armbands were made of boar's teeth, polished
and strung on a leather thong.
Polished sheep horn.
Tomahawk is made of a stone tied with leather thongs to a piece
of wood and then tightly bound.

Those holding first, second, and third honors could also wear the deer-tail roach. This was made from deer tails fastened together so as to form a roach and dyed red. In the roach was placed a feather to lean forward, one hanging over the base of the scalp lock, and a third standing upright.

## WAR SHIELDS

Most of the Indian tribes carried war shields made of buffalo hide. These were believed to have magical power and were usually painted in accordance with the totem, or vision dream of the owner. It was considered one of the most valued possessions, and to carry one into battle was considered something of a distinction, as the shield bearer was always conspicuous and the most likely to be shot at. It also was especially desirable and quite a feat to capture an enemy shield. The shield was a help in battle, though, because it could stop an arrow and some bullets. The medicine, or mystical, power of the shield was contained in the designs painted on it, along with the other decorations. The design was drawn on the front of the shield and on the soft buckskin cover which laced over it. Animals, birds, symbols, and other objects could be painted, with many of these the result of the vision dream of the owner. A bear might mean the owner would have the strength of a bear. A deer meant swiftness. The tortoise who lived a long life was added protection, as its long life was transferred to the owner of the shield. Clouds and rain meant abundance and good hunting. Eagles gave the bearer the swiftness and cunning of the eagle. Some of the shields were small, but they had the same power as the large ones. Shields were made in secret; some were about 17 inches in diameter, others varied from one foot to 26 inches.

To make the shield, a piece was cut from the neck or breast of a fresh hide, about twice as large as the shield was to be when finished. The hide was shrunk by heating or steaming it until it was almost twice the original thickness. Decoration was done with special ceremonies, conducted by

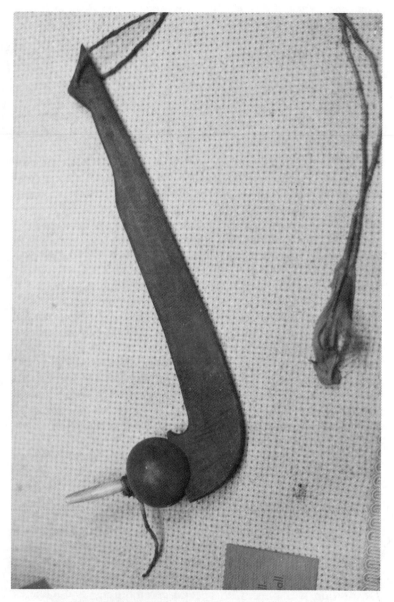

BALL HEADED WAR CLUB—Woodland tribes
A ball head with a bone spike.

the medicine man and experienced warriors. The cover was painted first and this was kept in place until the warrior went into battle, when at the last minute the cover was pulled off, and in this way the full power of the shield was exposed to the enemy. The front of the shield was painted after the cover was made and the decorations were attached to it. A sling of soft skin was fastened to the upper edge and this was used to sling the shield from the left shoulder of the warrior, so that his left hand was free for grasping the bow. The making of the shield was completed with song and ceremony. Then the warrior entered the sweat pledge; after his purification, the finished shield was taken to his tipi or dwelling where it was hung in a place of honor. It hung inside on bad stormy days, and at night, but on nice days it was always hung outside the lodge at the rear, to ward off any danger that might be lurking about.

## WEAPONS

Lances and coup sticks were carried by many of the Plains tribes and they were very important in ceremonies, as well as being part of the insignia of some of the warrior societies. The lance and the coup stick were very similar except for the flint or metal point on the lance. Unlike the lance, the coup stick was never used to kill an enemy.

The Kaitsenko Society was made up of the bravest of Kiowa warriors, as were other societies among other tribes. They carried a crooked lance wrapped with otter skin, and they wore a broad sash of buckskin at the waist or about their necks. The sashes were quite long, and in battle a warrior would dismount, drive his lance through the sash into the ground, and there he would stand fighting until he was killed, or until some of his companions freed him. No one could free himself after having done this or the dishonor would be worse than death.

Lances were usually decorated with otter, mink, beaver, and weasel skin, plus feathers. Each feather had its own special meaning to the one who carried the lance. When the

## WAR CLUBS AND AXES
Right, stone war club with a wooden handle.
Large stone club with blue and white inlay. Handle is white raw-
hide with silver beads.
Small club is of stone and wrapped with horsehair rope.
Stone club with bits of downy feather on wrapped rawhide handle.
Later period axe is made of red catlinite.

point was made of flint, because it was related to thunder and lightning, it became a symbol that power would strike the enemy before he was aware of danger.

War clubs were an important part of a warrior's equipment, and were made by all tribes in various forms, from wood, stone, bone, and horn. They could be decorated or plain. Like the shield, each war club was especially made to give it medicine, or mystical power.

Bows and arrows were carried by all Indian braves. The Iroquois carried bows and arrows but used them only from ambush as they preferred hand-to-hand combat with war clubs. They carried a wooden shield, and at times wore a kind of armor made of sticks laced together with buckskins. A few of the northwestern tribes also had a sort of armor. Fire arrows were used among some tribes. The ends of long arrows were wrapped, then dipped in tallow or oil. When these were lighted and blazed across the sky they looked like meteors. After the arrival of the white man, the Indians then dipped their arrows in gummed pitch and smeared them with gunpowder.

George Washington, after the Revolutionary War, thought of adding the bow and arrow as part of the armament of the thirteen colonies. He had been present at Braddock's defeat and had seen what a bow and arrow could do. While the English soldier had to reload with powder and shoot through the muzzle, the Indians could shoot at least half a dozen arrows. Sometimes the English soldier's flint would fail to produce a spark or the powder was wet. The Indians did not have this problem. Against the breech-load gun, however, the bow and arrow was not as fast and proved inferior.

## WAR COSTUME

Usually the Indian went into battle wearing only a breech-cloth, moccasins, and leggings. His body might be painted with symbols of protection and power, as was his face. For this he used colors of red, black, or white. Even the warrior's horse was sometimes painted. Black usually meant death,

**HORN WAR CLUB**
Made from buffalo horn with rawhide painted red around the center and a rawhide wrapped handle.

red was power and life, blue was the sky, yellow was joy and victory. White was usually peace. In battle, the totem, or vision dream animal, was often painted on the face and on the war horse. The chest was painted with a series of lightning lines. The face and body were sometimes painted different colors, with spots. The paint used for this had magical power and was kept in special containers.

The war shirt was one of the most important parts of the Indian costume and was made with great ceremony. Decorated with hair or fur and heavily beaded, it was believed to have great medicine. It had the power to protect the wearer, but could be worn only for special occasions and by warriors who had distinguished themselves in battle or were in some capacity of authority. The war shirt was often painted. The Dakota and Cheyenne war shirts were trimmed with hair, while the Blackfoot and the Crow usually decorated their shirts with weasel fur. Because of their hair decorations, believed to be that of enemies, the shirts of the Dakota and the Cheyenne were often called "scalp shirts." This was not always true, as often the hair was from the man's own head, or from his wife's head, or even from his horse's mane or tail. Each lock sewed on meant a coup won by capturing a horse, taking prisoners, getting wounded, saving a life in battle, or killing an enemy. As a rule the war shirt was not worn in battle, but only at the victory dance.

The advent of the horse produced a major change in the life of the Indian. It became one of the main reasons for war. Parties would go out to steal horses, and this often led to conflict. In the period of a few short years, the Indian became mounted and his way of life changed. Before, he had to hunt, fight his battles, and travel on foot. The Spanish brought the first horses the Indians had seen. At first they were fearful of the horse and thought the rider and animal were one. The Hopi considered the animal sacred and spread scarves on the ground for it to walk upon. The Dakota called it "mystery dog." The Indians quickly adapted to the horse and rode bareback or with a sort of saddle made of a pad of skin. Their bridles were thongs looped around the horse's lower jaw. The Indian would keep a long neck rope dragging so he could

273

**WAR SHIRT—Cheyenne**
Buckskin shirt is ornamented with Ute scalps and narrowly fringed around the bottom and sleeve edges. The lower half is dyed yellow and the upper portion, blue. The neck flap is yellow and the neck banded in red and laced with thong. Bands are beaded in white and dark blue.

grasp the rope should he become unseated. Indians broke wild horses by their own special method. They would spend days becoming familiar to the horse, or they would use a method whereby the horse would almost become hypnotized by use of a blanket. An Indian-gentled horse was highly prized among white men, because he was tough but easily managed. The Indian mounted his horse from the right side instead of the left as the cowboy did. The old calvalryman and those who carried swords had mounted on the left, so this custom was handed down to the cowboy. But the Indians, not bound by custom, did it the way that seemed easy.

Pinto ponies and gray horses were favored by the Indian because they blended with the landscape and also took war paint better. The horses were often highly decorated and sometimes medicine bundles were tied in their manes when going into battle.

## FEATHERED WAR BONNET

The making of a war bonnet was a special event. The man who was to receive the bonnet called together the chief men of his tribe and invited them to a feast, after the feathers and material for the bonnet had been gathered. For a man to be entitled to wear a war bonnet he had to accumulate honors; then he had to secure the necessary eagle feathers. Originally the war bonnet was worn only on special occasions and had a special significance to the owner. While many tribes wore feathered headbands and used feathers for decoration, only the Plains tribes wore the large eagle-feather headdresses in early times. The war bonnet's value was not in its spectacular looks, but more in its medicine or sacred power which protected the wearer in battle. A man could only wear a war bonnet with the consent of his fellow warriors.

After the feast was over, each man prepared a feather for the bonnet. As each feather was handed to the owner, he told of the honor which entitled him to it. It was then handed to the man making the bonnet and put in place. A bonnet contained from thirty to fifty feathers and with the storytelling and ceremony it sometimes took several sessions and weeks

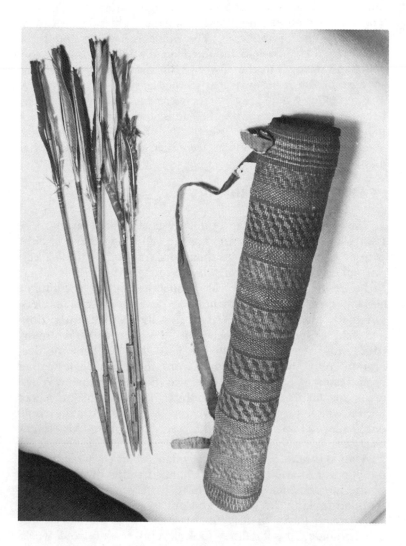

QUIVER AND ARROWS—Northwest Coast tribe unknown

to complete a war bonnet. First a skullcap of soft buckskin was made. This was the foundation to which the feathers were attached. To the skullcap a long strip of buckskin was fastened, called a trail. Before the day of horses, the trail came only to the waist, but later they were so long that when a warrior dismounted, the trail with its feathers would drag on the ground. Sometimes two trails were added, parallel from the cap to the ground because the owner had won so many honors that two trails were needed to hold all the feathers. After the feathers were prepared and in place, the bonnet was decorated with a band of quill or beadwork and strips of white weasel fur. As the weasel is skillful and alert in evading the hunter, this power was believed to come to the bonnet owner through the weasel fur decorations. Actually the completed war bonnet represented a group of warriors, with each feather being a man, and the horsehair strands at the feather tip represented his scalp lock. The peeled shaft of a long feather, to which was tied three or four fluffy feathers at its tip, was fastened to the skullcap so that it stood out in the center of the circle of bonnet feathers. This was called the "plume" and represented the bonnet owner. Sometimes a very great warrior, or a medicine man, had the privilege of wearing horns on his bonnet as a symbol of power and strength. When buffalo horns were used, they were hollowed out or split to make them light, and then were highly polished.

The wide open plains was perfect for the wearing of these huge feathered headdresses, as it was also perfect for the use of the horse, and these two seemed to go together to form the usual picture of the American Indian—a man on horseback wearing the great eagle-feather war bonnet. It is believed that this type of headdress spread from the Sioux to other tribes. There was a variety of bonnets, although most were of the "swept back" type with the feathers on the cap flowing toward the back, as worn by the central and southern Plains tribes. To the northwest the Blackfoot made their bonnets with "straight-up" feathers. This type did not have a cap; the feathers were fastened straight up from a wide headband. Another variety, found mostly among the eastern Apache, is made with the features sloping out evenly all the way around. The trails, either single or double, are found on

277

# FEATHERED WAR BONNET

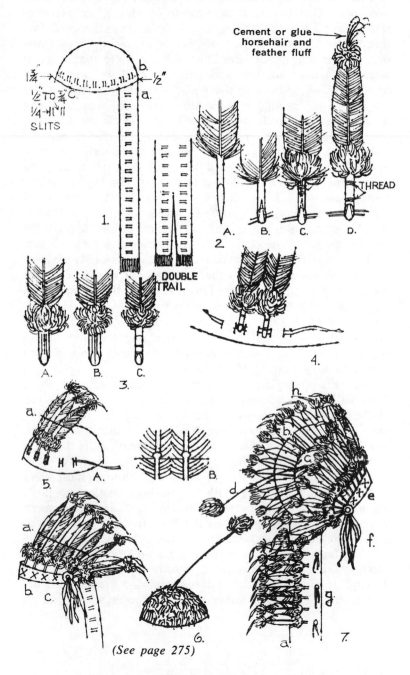

Cement or glue horsehair and feather fluff

THREAD

1.

DOUBLE TRAIL

2.

A.    B.    C.    D.

3.

A.    B.    C.

4.

5.

A.    A.    B.

6.

7.

a.    b.    c.    d.    e.    f.    g.    h.

1¾"
½"
½ TO ¾"
¼"
SLITS

*(See page 275)*

most Plains Indian war bonnets, but many bonnets are made without trails.

Within the last hundred years the skin cap at times has been replaced by a commercial felt hat with the brim cut off. The top of the hat is then covered with small feathers or fur, or both in combination. The trail if not made of skin was later made of red wool, 8 to 12 inches wide and of varying lengths. It can be to the waist, to the ankles, and either single in width or double. The double trail is usually split for the lower half of its length.

When making a bonnet today, white turkey or goose feathers with the tips dyed dark brown or black can be used in place of eagle feathers. These can be found in millinery supply houses or hobby shops. You'll need about 25 to 30 feathers for the bonnet proper, and about 20 more if you add the long strip or trail. You'll also need an old felt hat and 8 to 10 inches of red flannel or similar material. If you buy this at a fabric store, ⅛ yard will be enough. Fit the crown of the hat over your head as in Diagram 1 and cut it so that it is close-fitting and comes well down on the forehead. Fold the hat from the middle front to the middle back, then measuring 1¾ inches up from the edge of the hat in front, draw a line around the side from this point to ½ inch at the back. Make another line around the other side, so that a line runs around the edge of the hat from 1¾ inches in the front to ½ inch at the back. Above this line cut small vertical slits in the felt hat, the slits to be about ¼ of an inch long and spaced evenly ¼ inch apart (see Diagram 1a). Leave a ½- to ¾-inch space between pairs of slits. With a pencil and tape, measure around the hat, and mark where the slits will be. In this way when you cut the slits, you'll be sure they are spaced evenly around the hat edge. If you have a trail on your bonnet, cut slits horizontally down the middle of this in the same manner as the hat (see Diagram 1a). On this, the pairs of slits should be 1 inch apart instead of the ½ to ¾ inch, as on the hat. Sew the trail to the back edge of the hat. Bind the long edge of the trail with contrasting colored ribbon, or just hem it along the edge. Later you can add small feathers along the edge, or bits of thong or beading. If you like, the bottom of the trail can be fringed. Make a small hole on each side of the hat, just above the edge. Tie a lace to each side and use this for tying the bonnet under your chin to hold it in place.

Next the feathers must be prepared. You can sew them, or use good household cement. On each large feather, the quill end is cut at an angle, after being softened in hot water (see Diagram 2A). This pointed cut end is then inserted back into the quill as in Diagram 2B. Now bind two or three small fluffy feathers to the shaft of the large feather, as in Diagram 2C. After they have been sewed or glued in place, cut a piece of red flannel or material about 2 inches long and 1 inch wide. Wrap this around the feather shaft so it covers the quill end as in Diagram 2D. This can be sewn or glued; then wrap the red material at the top and bottom with yellow or white thread. Cut a small strand of horsehair or red dyed twine, wind a thread around it to hold it together, and cement to the upper tip of the long feather. Before the cement dries, press a bit of fluff or small feather to the tip as shown in Diagram 2D. The feather is now ready to be used.

There is another method for preparing the quill end of the feather as shown in Diagram 3. Cut a piece of leather about ¼ inch wide and 3 inches long. Fold this over the quill end of the feather as in Diagram 3A and sew or glue to the feather shaft, being careful to leave the bottom loop, where it is folded over, open as in Diagram 3B. This loop at the bottom should be from ⅛ to ¼ inch. This is done after the small fluffy feathers have been affixed to the shaft of the long feather, as shown in Diagram 2C. Now bind the red flannel around the feather shaft as described above in Diagram 2D and wrap it with thread. Finish the feather tip with horsehair and fluff as described before for Diagram 2D.

After all of the feathers have been made ready, lay them out on a table or other flat surface, putting the largest in the center, the next in size to the left and right of center, and continuing from largest to the smallest around each side of the hat. If all the feathers you have are of equal size, you will not have to do this.When placing feathers for the trail, the largest feather goes at the top nearest the head and on down to the bottom.

To lace the feathers onto the hat, begin at the center front and work around one side, then go back to the center and work around the other side. Poke a shoelace or leather thong through the slit at the front of the hat from the inside, then through the quill end loop of the largest feather and then push the lace through the slit ¼ inch away, drawing the feather down tight. The next feather in size is laced on in the same way until all the feathers on one side are in place. One half of the shoelace should be hanging inside the hat, and this is to be used to lace the other side with feathers, in the same way as described above (see Diagram 4).

When the feathers are all laced onto the hat and trail, an additional thread must be put through the feathers about mid-way. This lacing gives the bonnet its shape and holds the feathers upright. Use an awl, ice pick, or darning needle to make a hole through the shaft on the under side of each feather about midway up the feather (see Diagrams 5A, *a* and 5A, *c*). Then with waxed linen thread or nylon thread sew through this hole, around the under side of the shaft and through the hole again (see Diagram 5B). Allow about 1 inch of thread between the feathers and then sew the next feather in the same way. Start this upper lacing thread at the back of the war bonnet or hat, and continue all the way around. The bonnet is then shaped by adjusting the distance between feathers, and the ends of the thread are tied at the back. The trail feathers are adjusted in the same way, starting at the bottom and sewing to the top of the hat near the top center.

The "plume," see Diagram 6, represents the bonnet owner and is made by stripping the shaft of a long feather, or in place of this, a wire can be wrapped with ribbon. To either of these a bunch of fluffy feathers is tied. Tie the bottom end with a flannel lacing loop as described in Diagram 3. Fasten this to the center top of the hat. The hat can be covered with feathers or fur or a combination of both. Sew or glue the bits of fur and feathers to the hat, completely covering it.

Finish the bonnet with a beaded headband around the front half, or a ribbon, embroidered band, or contrasting color band can be used. At the sides of the band place round orna-ments with bits of long fur or feathers as in Diagram 5C, *b*. Use old ermine tails, rabbit fur, or strips of imitation fur in place of the weasel skins used by the Indians. These should

281

# QUIVER AND BOW CASE

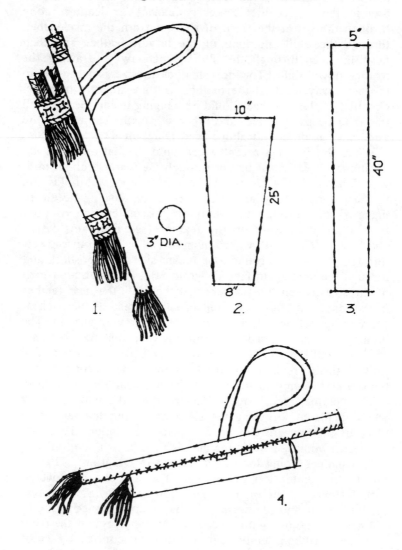

5″

10″

3″ DIA.

25″

8″

40″

1.

2.

3.

4.

cover the place where the chin ties are put on the hat. Bits of ribbons, beading, or jingle-type ornaments can be sewn along the edge of the trail.

Diagram 7 shows the finished war bonnet: *a* to *c* shows the middle feather shaft lacing along the trail; *b* shows the lacing around the hat; *d* is the owner "plume," *e* is the decorated headband with circle or button ending, and *f* is the fur strips; *g* is the decorated edge of the trail, ribbon-bound and tied with bits of cloth and thong; *h* is the fluff and horsehair tip of the bonnet feathers. Your war bonnet is ready to wear.

## QUIVER AND BOW CASE

The quiver, or arrow and bow cases were usually decorated to go with the other war equipment. These hung to the back of the lodge, near the shield, and usually within easy reach. Some cases were elaborately decorated with beading and fringe and were made of buckskin. Some quivers were of fur, trimmed with red material.

Diagram 1 shows a quiver and bow case with the shoulder strap. This is of buckskin, beaded and fringed.

These cases can be made today of heavy felt, imitation leather, or suede or painted canvas, if it is stiff enough. The size will depend upon the length of your bow and arrows. The measurements here are merely given as an example. After you have the size you need, cut your material in relation to patterns of Diagrams 2 and 3. Sew a round piece to 2*a* at the bottom of the arrow case, then sew the case along the side. Sew the bow case along the side (Diagram 3) lengthwise. If you make a paper or muslin pattern first, you'll be sure it will fit your arrows and bow when you cut into more expensive material. Place the stitched sides of the two cases together and sew (see Diagram 4). Cut a shoulder strap that accords in width and length to your own measurements. It should go over the right shoulder and under the left arm. Place this where it is most comfortable and so that the quiver hangs in the right position for quick handling of the arrows. Stitch the shoulder straps in with the quiver and bow case as shown on the *x* line in Diagram 4. Add fringe and decorate with beads, paint, fur, or bits of red yarn or material.

# BOWS AND ARROWS

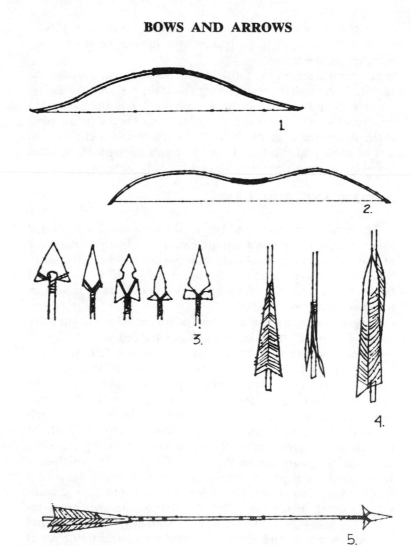

## BOWS AND ARROWS

Bows and arrows are probably the best known of Indian equipment, and were the most important, until guns became available. The protection and survival of the tribe depended upon the bow and arrow. The bow was even superior to muzzle-loading guns because many arrows could be fired in a fight at close quarters in the time it took to load and fire a gun once. The repeating rifles, of course, changed this. The Eastern Indians used a longer bow, but those of the Plains were shorter, and this short length is where the Indian bow differs from the English bows. The Indians generally preferred a short, flat, broad bow, and short, heavy, well-feathered arrows. Arrowheads varied, according to the area and the game that was hunted. Long, sharp, lance-like arrows of flint or steel were used for killing large game, while small, blunt-headed wood arrows were used for birds and small game.

Bows were made of wood, wood backed with sinew, and of buffalo, elk, and mountain sheep horn. Some of the Plains tribes gathered their wood for bows in the very early spring while the sap was still down. This insured that the wood would season with little danger of shrinkage and splitting. When cut and trimmed, the green bow stave was covered with bear grease and hung high up in the tipi so the smoke of the fire but not the flames could reach it. When the wood was properly seasoned, it was shaped and rubbed smooth with a piece of sandstone. This usually took some time to do well. Bowstrings were made of sinew or vegetable fibers. The string was tied to notches at one end of the bow, and the noosed end was slipped over the notch at the opposite end. Usually bows were flat when unstrung, but some were made curved. The curves were made by greasing the part, holding it over a fire until hot, then bending the wood with the foot held in place until the wood cooled and the curve was permanent. Sinew was applied with hot glue to the flat back of the bow which had been roughened (see Diagrams 1 and 2).

Usually each man made his own arrows, and they were more intricate to make than the bow. Seldom were two arrows of the same length and each man could recognize his own arrows. Every arrow had an owner mark on it to identify which arrows killed the game. Arrow wood was also cut in winter, slim branches or sticks about the size of a little finger, straight and smooth. After being cut to the desired length, they were wrapped tightly with rawhide or elk skin, in bundles of twenty or so. These bundles were hung high in the tipi in the smoke from the fire. After several weeks, the bundles were taken down, and the bark taken off the sticks, which were then scraped, straightened, and smoothed. This was a time-consuming task, as every crooked place had to be greased and heated until the wood was hot enough to be bent. Then the wood had to be held firmly until it cooled. Often the sticks were drawn through a stone or deer's horn in which holes had been made, as a means of straightening the arrow stick. The sticks were finally twirled between sandstone to polish them and finish off the final shaping. The arrowhead was then fastened in a notch in the shaft with a binding of sinew and glue. Originally the arrowheads were of flint, bone, shell, wood, and later metal. Sinew arrow points were made of the hard sinew along the top of the buffalo's neck. These points were used in hunting buffalo, because when the hard sinew arrow point struck a rib it would go round it, while a flint or other type of arrowhead would break the bone. War arrowheads were made in such a way that they split the shaft and would stay in the wound when the shaft was pulled out. As the last step, the arrow was feathered with two or three trimmed feathers of the eagle or some other bird. The feathers were glued and bound in place with sinew. Diagram 3 shows different types of arrowheads and their binding. Diagram 4 shows the feathered shaft.

Although each man could recognized his own work, he also put ownership marks on his arrows. Diagram 5 shows the marks, round marks usually in red or black. These are painted on and are not to be confused with the burned marks sometimes seen on arrows which are the marks from grooved heat straighteners. The straighteners were made of stone, ivory, bone, or any hard object with a small hole through which heated and greased arrow shaft was pulled in order to straighten any warped or crooked areas.

# WAR SHIELDS

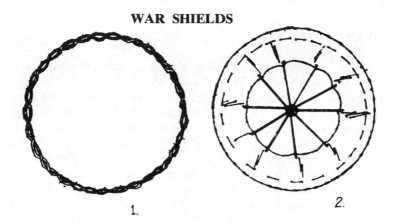

1.

2.

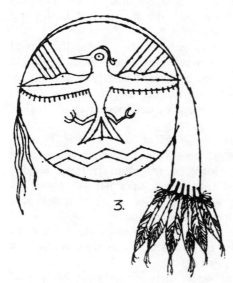

3.

*(See page 288)*

## WAR SHIELDS

War shields were made from the breast of the bull buffalo. The skin was smoked and allowed to contract to the desired thickness. It was then shaped and decorated. Some tribes gave the shield a convex surface by staking the hide, when damp, over a mound of earth. The shield was one of the most valuable possessions of the warrior. It was not only his protection in battle, it was also his medicine, or spirit power. The decorations on the shield usually had meaning, perhaps showing the animal who protected the warrior, or the design could be from his vision dream, or it might be a family shield handed down from father to son, and, because it had protected previous members of a family, had built up great medicine, and was especially valued. Most shields had a cover that was pulled off just as the warrior went into battle. This, too, had special symbols painted on it, but its main purpose was to protect the medicine or magic of the shield, so that the emblems on the shield would not be seen until the moment of battle and would therefore be more powerful.

The war shield hung at the back of the tipi, at the top of the lining. On nice days the man's shield and other medicine articles were hung on a tripod outside. The tripod was sometimes made of lances stuck into the ground behind the lodge. The shield and other things were turned periodically so they always faced the sun.

A modern adaptation of a war shield can be made by making a hoop of twisted wire, or a barrel hoop, and covering this with canvas, heavy cloth, or imitation leather. Shields used by the horsemen of the Plains were usually about 18 inches across, as this size was more effective from horseback. Foot warriors usually carried larger shields about 23 or 24 inches across. The larger shields were used in the Southwest. The Woodland Indians did not use shields, as they could be a hindrance in the forests.

Decide on the size you want, then make your hoop that size (Diagram 1). Next cut the material to fit the hoop plus 4 to 6 inches more, which is turned under and caught (see Diagram 2). Paint a design on the shield, a symbol of your

4.

5.

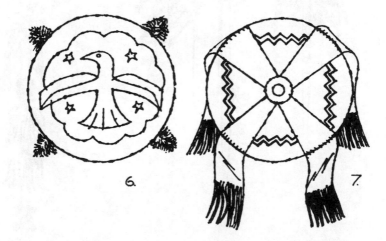

6.

7.

own or one of those shown; then around the top edge sew a length of red material, with feathers sewn on one end and bits of fur, like tails, on the other side. Usually the red piece goes around and hangs evenly down on both sides, sometimes only on one side (see Diagram 3). The eagle decoration represents protection. Here it is shown in blue with yellow sun rays

# COUP STICKS AND LANCE

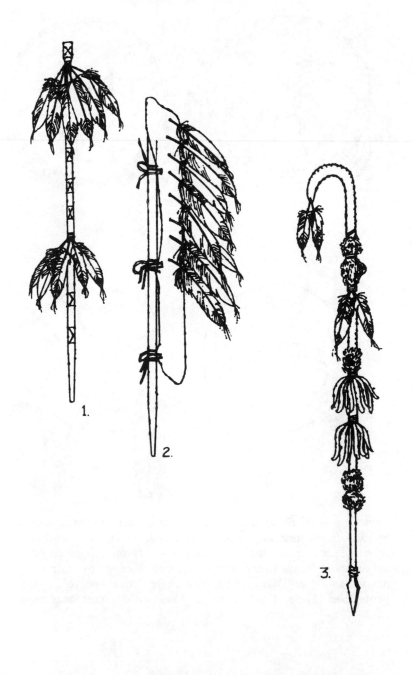

behind it, and a red lightning symbol below showing the death-dealing power conferred on the owner of the shield.

Diagrams 4, 5, 6, and 7 show how shields are decorated. Diagram 4 is possibly Nez Perce as they were the Indians who bred the war pony with the spots which mark this horse so beautifully—the Appaloosa. The horse on the shield is shown decorated with feathers, and feathers decorate the shield. The background color is yellow for the dawn. A series of arrow points in red band the rim. Diagram 5 shows the rain pattern, blue on a white background. Below is a yellow star, from which hang eagle feathers. A band of buckskin around the edge ends in fringe at the bottom. Diagram 6 is an eagle pattern in dark blue on a white ground. The four stars are of different colors, yellow for the dawn, red for day, green for the sky, and black for night. A light blue cloud-effect bands the shield, and four tufts of downy feathers decorate it. Diagram 7 represents the four directions of the universe in colors of red for east, black for south, yellow for west, and blue for north. Lightning connects the four points, indicating the awesome power of the shield. Strips of fringed and colored buckskin extend from the four directions pattern on the shield.

The shield was excellent protection against arrows, and could even deflect musket balls, but it offered little protection against guns.

## COUP STICKS AND LANCE

Coup (pronounced "coo") sticks were part of the equipment of every warrior. They were slender, decorated sticks with which an Indian counted coup in battle. Coup meant striking or touching an enemy, and the highest honor went to the warrior who was able to touch a living enemy.

A coup stick is from 4 to 5 feet long, and some stand about a foot or two above the head of the owner. The coup stick and the lance were very similar except the coup stick did not have the flint or steel head, and could not inflict wounds. It was used only for touching the enemy in battle and some-times was used in dances of the Plains Indians.

Coup sticks were decorated with feathers, fur, and beading, as was the lance. To the Pawnee, a bunch of owl feathers represented the North Star which watches over people at night. Owls watched over the camp and warned the people of enemies prowling near. Crow feathers were attached, as crows are always the first to find food and helped the people find buffalo. The thunderbird was believed to bring thunderstorms which many times saved the camp when enemies were about to attack, so swan feathers were used to represent the thunderbird. If a lance was being made, flint was used at the end, because this stone was believed to be found where lightning strikes.

A coup stick is made like a lance except that it does not have a point. To make a coup stick, you'll need a slender stick about ¾ inch thick. Paint it, carve it, or burn a design on it. You can wrap it with tape and bits of bright felt. Feathers and fur can be added by taping or wrapping them onto the stick.

In Diagram 1 the coup stick is decorated with bands of beading and feathers. In Diagram 2, the coup stick is the banner type. This type of stick with more feathers was also used as an Indian flag or banner and was sometimes carried into battle. Red or colored flannel or buckskin was tied to one end of the stick, and then at intervals along its length to about a foot from the bottom. To this was added strings of feathers, either just sewn to the material or attached by the quill as they are for the war bonnet.

In Diagram 3 a dog soldier's lance has a rather special use. Almost all Plains tribes had a society that had names that meant "brave dog," "crazy dog" and such, and because of this they became known as dog soldiers to the settlers and soldiers who respected their bravery and fighting qualities. These were always the bravest warriors, and in many tribes they carried a crooked lance. With this, the warrior also wore a broad sash, or neck scarf, and if battle went against him he would dismount, drive the lance through the sash, and stand there fighting, until killed or until a fellow member withdrew the lance and allowed him to escape. These lances were usually decorated with beaver, mink, otter and weasel skins, together with feathers. A similar crooked end lance without the spear point, as shown in Diagram 3, was used by the dog soldiers as a coup stick.

# WAR CLUBS

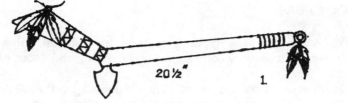

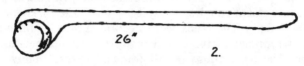

20½"

1.

26"

2.

2A.

18"

3.

18"

4.

5"

18"

5.

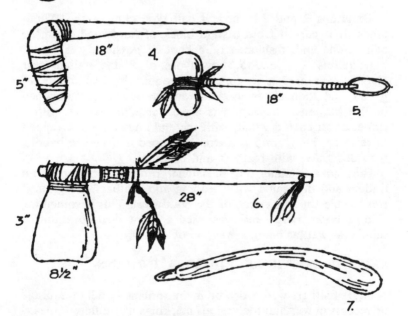

28"

6.

3"

8½"

7.

*(See page 294)*

## WAR CLUBS

War clubs of many types were used by different tribes. They were made of wood, stone, bone, horn, and later of metal.

Diagram 1 shows a type of club influenced by the white man's gun. It is made of hardwood shaped like a gun butt. Flint or metal blades, or spikes were often fastened at the lower edges. The clubs were decorated with nailheads, beading, wrappings of fur or red material, and feathers and horsehair. The decorations on all war clubs were highly personal, depending upon the individual taste. The power medicine or magic of the owner especially was contained within the club. Sometimes the war club appeared to be very plain, but prayer and vision had gone into the making of it. The gun-shaped club was used by both the Plains and Woodland groups.

Diagrams 2 and 2A show a ball type club of the Woodlands. It is carved from a solid block of hardwood, with the ball at one end, fashioned of a knot, if possible.

Diagrams 3, 4 and 5 show types of Plains Indians war clubs. Diagram 3 is a stone and wooden handle bound together and then all encased in rawhide which is dampened until it hardens. Diagram 4 is a wooden club handle, with a stone, or all carved wood, with the end encased and wrapped in rawhide. Diagram 5 is a stone wrapped and tied to handle, then decorated with feathers and beading.

Diagram 6 is a later type of hatchet, probably obtained from traders and decorated with beading and feathers. Diagram 7 is a Pueblo throwing stick of the Southwest. This is something "like a boomerang" and was used a great deal for hunting rabbits as well as being a weapon of war.

## EXPLOIT FEATHERS—HIDATSA INDIANS

Eagle feathers were worn by many Indians to tell of courage or success in war and the various markings had different meanings. Among the Hidatsa Plains Indians feathers had a special meaning which was different from the other tribes.

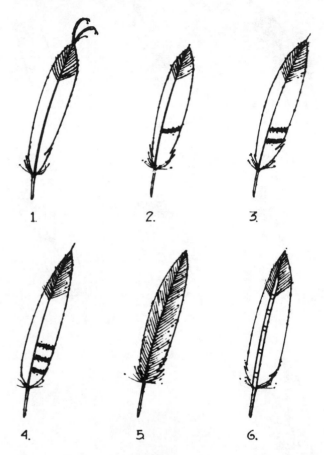

If a tuft of down or several strands of horsehair dyed red, was attached to the tip of a feather, it meant that the wearer had killed an enemy and that he was the first to touch or strike him with the coup stick (Diagram 1).

A feather with one red bar painted on the lower half of the feather shows the wearer to have been the second to strike the fallen enemy with a coup stick (Diagram 2).

Diagram 3 shows a feather with two red bars painted on

295

# EXPLOIT FEATHERS—SIOUX INDIANS

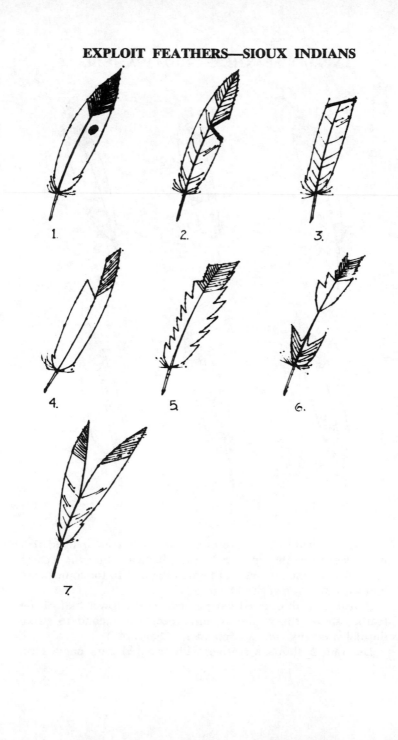

1.

2.

3.

4.

5

6.

7.

the lower half which indicated the wearer was the third person to strike the body.

Three red bars painted on the lower half of a feather signified that the wearer was the fourth to strike the fallen enemy (Diagram 4). Beyond this point honors are not counted.

A red feather denotes that the wearer was wounded in an encounter with the enemy (Diagram 5).

Diagram 6 shows a feather worn by one who has killed a woman belonging to a hostile tribe. For this to be an honor it was possibly a woman who was well guarded, or a medicine woman of great medicine or magic, or a woman of great importance in the hostile tribe. This special feather is decorated with a narrow strip of rawhide which has been wrapped end to end with porcupine quills dyed red, and one or two dyed white to break the monotony of the red. This narrow decorated strip is attached to the inner surface of the rib of the quill by very thin fibers of sinew. Sometimes the porcupine quills are applied directly to the rib of the feathers.

## EXPLOIT FEATHERS—SIOUX INDIANS

Every warrior among the Sioux Plains Indians was entitled to wear feathers marked and painted to show his bravery and to indicate his past deeds, much like the insignia and decorations of a soldier. Personal bravery was highly prized and these feathers were marks of distinction.

Diagram 1 shows a feather painted with one red dot, indicating that the wearer has killed an enemy.

Diagram 2, with a notch edged in red, indicates the wearer has cut the throat of an enemy and taken his scalp.

Diagram 3, showing the feather cut off across the top and edged in red, denotes the wearer has cut an enemy's throat.

Diagram 4, with part of the feather tip cut away, means the wearer was the third to touch the body of the enemy.

Diagram 5 shows a feather which has been notched along its sides, indicating that the wearer was the fourth to touch the enemy.

Diagram 6, which has the middle portion of the feather stripped away, indicates the wearer to be the fifth to touch the fallen enemy.

Diagram 7, the split feather, indicates the wearer has been wounded in many places by the enemy.

## EXPLOIT MARKS ON ROBES, BLANKETS, OR PERSONS

These are usually in red or blue and are mostly painted on robes, blankets, or boat paddles. Frequently a warrior might paint them on his thighs, but only for festive occasions or dancing.

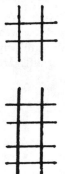

The wearer has successfully defended himself against the enemy by throwing up a ridge of earth or sand to protect his body.

The wearer has upon two different occasions defended himself by hiding his body within low earthworks.
A doubling of the first sign.

When found on body, leggings, blankets, boots, or other property, this means that the warrior has distinguished himself by capturing a horse belonging to an enemy tribe.

The warrior was first to strike an enemy with his coup stick.

The second to strike an enemy.

Third person to strike an enemy.

298

The fourth to strike an enemy.

According to the Arikara, the fourth to strike an enemy.

The wearer had four encounters.

# PART VII

# *DRUMS, RATTLES, AND STAMPING FEET*

*(Crafts begin on page 320)*

Music was a natural part of daily Indian life and expressed all of their emotions. Indians didn't write down their music, but learned and remembered it. Many of the songs were sacred and were used in ceremonials as prayers. There were songs for work and play, lullabies, game songs and children's songs, and just the song of a happy person. Many of the songs were considered personal possessions, especially those that came to a man in dream visions and were supposed to have medicine power. These songs were owned, but could be sold or given away; otherwise no one else had the right to them.

## INDIAN MUSIC

The music of the Indian is composed of three elements, rhythm, melody, and harmony. Rhythm has always been in the consciousness of man, in the throb of the pulse, the break of the waves, the hoof beats of animals. All life is rhythmic. Melody is a succession of sounds of different pitch; the laughter of children, the call of birds, the cry of an animal, and the wind—a melody of nature. From the emotional responses of man, song becomes the cry of the heart, and the transfiguration of the spoken word. Harmony is the combination of different sounds, the blending, blurring overtones of nature that melt many songs into one. This all developed and evolved into music, the unfolding of man's comprehension of the universe, the very essence of life. Music is the reflex of the soul's

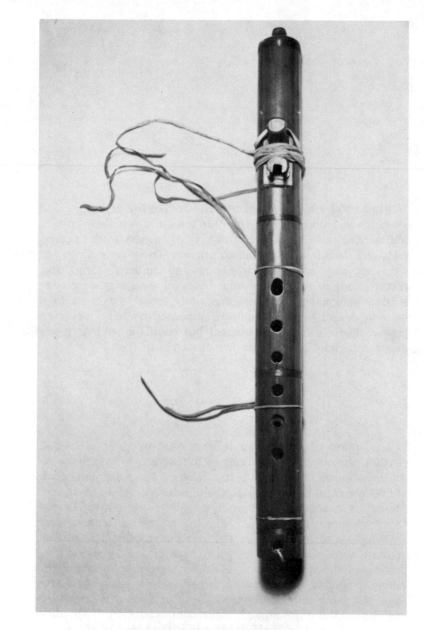

**PLAINS INDIAN FLUTE**
Wooden with a vent-control device.

impressions, and song, the language that expresses thoughts, emotions, and aspirations which are not able to be expressed in a less spiritual form. Indian life was so linked with nature that their art and music was an expression of this.

The Indians of the plains and woodland lakes, who sang in the open air in all kinds of weather, had developed voices ranging from falsetto tenor to a deep bass. The songs often begin with a high quavering tone, then descend, ending with a low note that fades away. The beating of drums and rattles accompany the singers.

The Pueblo Indians have strong, clear voices, but the notes of their ceremonies are deep and solemn. Women of the Zuñi have high flute-like voices. Hopi women have veiled tones, with long drawn-out slurring phrases, making their songs somewhat suggestive of the endless desert. The Navaho and Apache chant with low nasal tones, but their dance songs are strong with a somewhat lusty vigor.

Singing was believed to have magical power and would put the singer in harmony with the essential essence of all things. This was another reason why singing was so much a part of Indian life.

Indians often had little meter in their songs, the whole problem of form is inextricably complicated with movement and melody. The Indian would many times make his verse conform to his dance, which probably accounts for the liberal use of meaningless syllables such as eh, ah, yi, ye, ya. There seem to be no specific form or classification. Indian rhythms arise from the center of self-preservation rather than of self-consciousness, or the music is produced for the person rather than for any effect that will be produced on another. Indian verse is usually sung or chanted, and there is difficulty in fitting Indian rhythm to European music. This is surpassed only by the difficulty of getting Indian music arranged in European notations.

The song of the Indian was often to accomplish specific results which he felt were beyond his power as an individual. Thus there were songs for certain seasons of the year, for ancestors, to honor the chief or the warrior, to heal the sick, to pray for rain and for good hunting. Indians also sang according to impulse and emotions.

Songs of the Northwest Coast are usually slow in tempo and are accompanied by a drum. The principal function of music in this area is religious, and men and women owned their own songs as property which could be inherited or sold. There were no professionals, but music was taught and then rehearsed, and those who made musical errors were punished.

The Basin–Plateau tribes had music that was very simple. Their singing was smooth and the range small, and many songs had no accompaniment. Their rattles were rawhide filled with pebbles, and they had a musical rasp which was a notched stick about two feet long that was rubbed back and forth with a smaller stick. These rasps later spread to the Plains tribes.

The music of the California area had a somewhat higher pitch. Their instruments included drums, musical rasps, rattles, split stick clappers, and baskets which were beaten or scraped. Whistles and flutes were also used. In the nineteenth century the tambourine was introduced into this area.

The Plains tribes sing with great loudness, with strong accents and long tones. Songs usually begin and end with a drumbeat or rattles. Flutes were found in this area, but were played mostly by young men courting their lady love, and were not used in ceremonies. Plains music is mostly functional and often connected with dancing. Music was part of the male activities such as religious ritual, cult societies, warfare, and military and other ceremonies. Music was used for entertainment, social dancing, games, and storytelling. Women sang lullabies to their children. There were no professional musicians and the songs were owned, sold, or inherited. Individuals owned songs and societies also owned their songs. A ghost could give a person a song, or one could be learned in a dream or a vision. A bird, or someone else singing could be the reason for a song. Among some tribes, it was believed one could not have power without a song. All medicine men had their own songs. A good warrior went into battle with his song, and during battle would sing the song as protection. Warriors even composed their own death song, especially if they were captured and must die at the hands of their captors. In this case, a warrior died singing his death song.

The people of the desert have three musical styles. In the Pueblo style, the vocal technique resembles that of the Plains except many of the Pueblo Kachina songs begin on a very low note. They usually have rhythm accompaniment. The Pima Papago music combines that of the Pueblo and the California style. The songs are smooth and relaxed, but seldom exceed an octave in range. Rhythm patterns are simple. The Navaho ritual music has been learned from the Pueblo. The vocal technique is much like the Pueblos and the Plains Indian, and the melodies cover a wide range. Their instruments included several types of drums: the double-headed drum, single-headed hand drum, pottery drum, and a foot drum consisting of a plank over a pit. Baskets are beaten, and musical rasps are used. Rattles made from gourds filled with pebbles or seeds are used by almost all tribes, in ordinary dances and as sacred objects in ritual and religious festivals.

A young Navaho singer paid tuition to an older singer who would teach the text and music of the long ceremonial songs, as well as the accompaniment. This required much time and effort. Chants were so important that if a medicine man, during a curing ceremony, while dancing around a person, heard one of the singers make a mistake, the complete ceremony must be started again from the beginning.

In the east true Indian music was hard to describe, because of the early influence of white man's music.

## MUSICAL INSTRUMENTS

The drum was used in connection with most Indian songs and dances. Some drums were merely a round hollowed log with one or both ends covered with dried skin or rawhide. These could be beaten with a stick or with the hands and were also referred to as tom-toms. There was a single-headed drum and a double-headed drum, as well as a drum so large that several persons played it. The Woodland people used a water drum. The rawhide head of a drum was tightened by holding it before the fire, and the head of the water drum was tightened by wetting it with the water filling the drum. Drums were usually round, but in the northwest part of California a square drum was used.

**MUSICAL RATTLES**
Made of rawhide and used in ceremonies and dancing.

Rattles were probably next most important to Indian music. These were made from horns, turtle shells, rawhide, and gourds. Actually anything that made a noise could be used as a rattle.

Whistles made from the wingbone of a bird and pottery whistles had their place in the music of the Indians. Flutes were made and used mostly by the young men in their courting. Bells were popular in ceremonies and dancing, and it is believed that Indians were familiar with bells before the arrival of Columbus.

The bull roarer produced a whizzing or roaring sound, and was said to make the sound of the thunderbird who caused the thunder and lightning. This was sometimes used in games, and at times called the rain-making instrument.

The morache, or rasp, was a ceremonial scraping stick, also called guayos. It was a notched stick which was scraped with another stick and sometimes used with a gourd.

The musical bow was the only stringed instrument in early times, and only a few tribes used it. A tone was produced with this by stroking a thong stretched on a bow.

## DANCING

Social dancing was not very important to the Indians, but ceremonial dancing was almost a way of praying. Some dances were ceremonials with the purpose of influencing the supernatural powers or to repay a vow. Others were associated with nature, or held before a battle, or after one as a victory dance. There were special dances for good hunting and fishing, for abundant crops, for rain, and to cure the sick. There was some social dancing, as well as comic dancing and stories told by dancing. Many of the dances, like the songs, could be owned by one person and only the owner could perform the dance. Often several people took part in the dancing, such as a social organization or a clan, and in this case only the men danced. There were dances in which the dancer wore the disguise of an animal. In this case, the dancer was given the special power of the animal. Many ritual dances were performed, such as the Snake Dance, Sun Dance, and Ghost Dance.

Many Indian dances, as well as the accompanying songs, were inherited. Both songs and dances had to be performed correctly, as it was believed misfortune would befall the dancer or tribe if a mistake was made, and in some cases the dancer or singer was punished.

Some dances had to be learned according to strict rules, while others allowed the dancer freedom for his own expression and invention. Even then a dancer must stay within certain limits, so his dance as well as the story he was telling could be understood. Dances varied from tribe to tribe and one given the same intertribal name might be entirely different from one tribe to another.

Masks, when used in a dance, were mostly of a religious nature, even when worn by the clowns. By dancing, the clowns, or, as they were sometimes called, the "delight makers," would relieve the seriousness of the dance, or even a situation in a village. The clowns would be mischievous, but they also were believed to have the power to contact the gods of rain and bring abundance into the village.

Indian dancers saw, felt, and heard the story they were dancing, and it was seldom that an audience did not understand what the story was about. The good dancers were also good actors, and the dancer's body was an instrument for storytelling. Dances to cure illness were sometimes violent in order to scare away the evil causing the illness.

Women usually danced in a circle or facing each other in a line with little movement, mostly just moving from side to side, with some movement toward the front. In social dances, with both men and women, a circle was formed, with the men on the outside, moving in the direction of the sun, and the women on the inside, facing the men and moving away from the sun.

The Iroquois believed that those who had powerful dreams could become shamans and could cure sickness, especially if they were connected with the false faces. The false faces were horrible heads without bodies who would appear to people in the forest and bewitch them into sickness. These people could only be cured by members of the False Face Society who had

310

the power to break the evil spell by a religious dance ceremony in which they themselves would wear wooden masks carved in the likeness of the false faces. These evil spirits hide in the dark corners of the forest, in the hollow of trees, and among the rocks and crevices. The False Face Society was formed as protection against these evil spirits. The dancers dressed in ragged clothing and carried tortoiseshell rattles.

To rid the person of the spirit of illness, the False Face Society would put on a frightening performance at the home of the sick person, in the hopes of scaring away the evil and its illness. Dancing around the sick person in a circle and shaking their rattles over him, they sang strange songs. After they had circled around twice, they sat down facing a fire. Then the leader stood up and walked around the circle once, carrying a sacred bag from which he scattered wood ashes over the head of each dancer. He then gave a signal and all the dancers got up and danced around the circle again. After a bit they formed a single line and danced away. If the dance was not performed correctly, the illness would not be cured and misfortune would affect the dancers.

The false face the dancer wore was not to hide anything, but was more of a cleansing mask to frighten the evil spirits. Small masks were sometimes made in the image of the large one, to be used as charms. The Iroquois regarded the masks as portraits of the supernatural. The large masks were cut from a living tree. The outline of the mask would be carved in the trunk of a living tree, then as the tree grew it was believed the mask would take on the qualities of the tree. If the tree died before the mask was finished and used, the tree was cut down and the mask destroyed. Otherwise when the time was near for the ceremony, which was held at certain times in the year, the tree was cut down and the mask completed. If while the tree was growing the mask had grown into a strange distorted shape, it was even more special.

When a mask was carved, a ceremony was held in which the spirit would manifest itself to the carver so that the mask could be finished with great care. The image of the mask was not worshipped, only what it signified. If a mask was cut out at noon it was painted black; at afternoon it was painted red;

and if carved in the morning, and finished in the afternoon, it was painted red and black and referred to as the whirlwind.

The Apache had a dance mistakenly called the Devil Dance, as the dancers were really masked clowns and their weird dancing was to scare away evil spirits and to convey blessings on all who watched. Some of the blessing was to bring rain and plenty to the tribe. This is a dance of good winning over evil. The devil, portrayed by one dancer, subdues a warrior dancer, then the medicine man or clown enters and revives him and chases away the devil. The medicine man or clown is dressed in a colorful costume with a long skirt and leggings and moccasins. His body is painted black and at times he has designs on his arms and chest. He wears a black hood over his head and a huge headdress, and carries two spirit sticks or wands. The devil's body is painted black and he wears only a breechcloth and a black hood over his head and face. He carries two eagle feathers. The warrior is dressed in a breechcloth and moccasins and he has an eagle feather in his hair. He sometimes wears bells about his ankles. The dance has many variations, but it always ends with the good chasing the evil or devil.

Every two years the Hopi of Arizona have a ceremony called the Snake Dance. This ceremony is held in connection with the Antelope Fraternity for rain to fall and crops to be abundant, as it is believed the snakes have power over the clouds, just as the Great Plumed Serpent has control over the waters of the underworld. All the mysterious rites of the Hopi are performed in underground kivas. In this ceremony the altars are set up and floors are painted with special designs. About the middle of August preparation is made to catch the snakes. Each member of the society paints himself with symbolic designs, and four days before the dance, he takes his rattle, snake whip, wands, and snake bag, and along with others goes on the snake hunt. The first day they go to the north, the next to the east, the third day to the south, and the last to the west. When a snake is found it is put into the snake bag and sprinkled with sacred meal. Two types of snakes are searched for—the bull snake and the whip snake. At sunset the men return to the kiva. While the men are in the kiva, they take the snakes out of the bag and put them into snake jugs. Later the snakes are taken out of the jars, washed, then placed upon the painting in the center of the kiva floor. The snakes must be dry before the dance can take place, so they are left in the care of small boys who are allowed to play with them. The Snake Dance must take place as the sun goes down, so it is danced in the late afternoon. The Snake and Antelope priests enter their own kivas where they paint themselves, put on kilt, leg rattle, bandoleer, and make themselves ready for the dance. Ceremonial songs are begun as the Antelopes, led by their priest, emerge from their kiva and form a line in front of the snake kiva. After a short time, the Snake dancers come from their kiva, each holding his meal bag and snake wand, and each dressed in kilt, leg rattles, red moccasins, and ankle fringe. A necklace of shells completes the çostume.

The Antelope group move to the plaza and perform their dance, then the Snake clan face the Antelope and sing in low humming tones. As the Snake priest approaches, he takes a snake and places it in his mouth so that its head points to the right. The rest of the Snake dancers do the same, then the Antelope dancers are given snakes. After all the snakes have been carried about, with dancing, a circle is formed and the snakes thrown into the circle. Then the women come into the circle and toss sacred meal over the snakes. At a second signal, the Snake priest rushes into the circle and picks up as many snakes as possible and rushes toward the four cardinal points of the universe, east, west, south, north, from which the snakes were gathered. The snakes are set free on the mesa and the priests return to the kivas, take off their ceremonial clothes, then go to the south side of the camp where the women have food ready.

An important dance of the Plains tribes was the Sun Dance ceremony. This was performed by the Arapaho, Cheyenne, Siksika, and Cree, who were of Algonkin stock; the Dakota, Mandan, Assiniboin, Crow, Ponca, and Omaha of Siouan stock; the Pawnee of Caddoan stock; and the Kiowa, Shoshoni, and Ute of Shoshonean stock. In this ceremony the Indian considered he offered the Great Spirit his strongest training, the ability to endure physical pain, plus fulfillment of a vow made during battle, or when someone of his family was ill. Voluntary

313

suffering had deep significance, and this was one dance which was misunderstood by the white man and widely protested.

Although the Sun Dance had a common origin, it varied among the tribes taking part in it. It was held in summer, but could also be held in autumn. The length of the ceremony was usually four days, but might be eight. One of the most common pleas was to avert lightning, which was so fierce on the prairie.

The place the dance was held changed from year to year among some tribes. A month before the dance was to take place, the Dakota medicine man would pray for fair weather. He would sing, burn sweet grass, offer pipes to the sky, earth, and the four cardinal points. The men who were to take part in the dance would start to gather, along with their families, at the place designated. The Sun Dance leader was usually one who had returned successfully from the warpath, and had a reputation above reproach. It was his duty to furnish the sacred pole and the buffalo fat in which the pole was embedded. He was also expected to offer the Sun Dance pipe and the buffalo skull used in the ceremony. The Sun Dance pipe was decorated by one of the most skilled women in bead and quill work, and it was a great honor to be chosen. There was no prescribed pattern, except that the decoration did not cover the entire stem. There were usually ten decorated sticks placed in the ground, and each had a gift of tobacco tied at the top.

If a man taking part in the dance made the vow of cutting his flesh, he was allowed to offer a pipe also. Preparations for the Sun Dance required four young men who were to take part in the ceremony to select the tree from which the sacred pole would be made. They had to be unmarried and of great integrity. Twenty or more men were then selected to carry back the pole and erect it in the Sun Dance circle of the camp.

There were several Begging Dances held before the Sun Dance, and in these several men and women carrying a drum went from tipi to tipi singing until food was given.

Those taking part in the Sun Dance went through much preparation including a visit to the vapor or sweat lodge; then their bodies were painted according to their own choice. The young men taking part in this dance wore their hair long and loose but had one lock tied at the back of the head to which was fastened an upright white downy eagle feather. Four small sticks about 8 inches long were fastened to the hair also and these were decorated with quill work, beads, and tassels. A dancer was not allowed to touch his head during the dance and these scratching sticks were for that purpose. Only a breechcloth was worn during the dance, as the dancers did not even wear moccasins. A whistle hung from the neck by a cord. This was made from the wingbone of an eagle and wound with porcupine quill and tipped with a downy white eagle feather. The whistle was decorated by the same woman who decorated the pipe.

The dancers danced around the sacred pole, after having their skin cut and wooden pegs put through the cuts, just under the skin. Rawhide thongs were attached to these and they were then tied to the sacred pole. The dancer had to dance about until the skin was torn loose. Sometimes a dancer would tie a buffalo skull in the same manner to his skin and dance until he had pulled loose from it. In return for this, the Great Spirit was to offer his special blessings to the dancer.

During the second day of the dance, men were allowed brief intermissions, but they were not allowed food or water. After the dance was over, the dancers spent some time in the vapor lodge before taking water. Their first drink was merely a sip. A large bowl of water was placed near a bunch of sweet grass, the dancer would dip the grass into the water and place it to his lips. He was then given bits of cooked buffalo meat and later a meal in his own lodge. The scars left from the dance were considered honors and if a warrior had many such scars, it indicated to others that he had danced in the Sun Dance several times. Much singing and beating of drums always accompanied this dancing.

The Ghost Dance ritual derived its name from the Indians' belief that they would be united with their dead and all would be as it was before the coming of the white man to their lands. This is a fairly recent ceremony, originating in 1870 when a Paiute Indian went into a trance and preached that the deceased were to be returned to the earth and the ancient life would be restored, that the animals would again roam the land in vast numbers and the rivers would flow full and clear. He preached peace among all the people.

This dance did not gain much recognition among the Plains

people until 1889 when another young Paiute, called Wovoka or Jack Wilson, ill with fever, believed he had died but was sent back by the Great Spirit to give the Indians a message. He told them that if they would sing and dance as he directed, they would get the land back. He was still ill when an eclipse of the sun took place on New Year's Day in 1889. This seemed an omen and caused great excitement among the tribes. It was the sign they had been waiting for. The buffalo was disappearing, and they were a weary people, being pushed onto reservations and into strange ways of life, looking for signs and symbols of help from the Great Spirit. Now the sign had come and the idea spread like prairie fire across the plains. It is almost impossible to state the area involved and the number of people, but it was estimated that at least thirty-five tribes were involved and at least 60,000 persons. Some of the tribes were the Paiute, Shoshoni, Arapaho, Cheyenne, Caddo, Pawnee, Comanche, and the Dakota, or Sioux.

Wovoka preached peace and said the Indian must always do right and harm no one. He combined Indian beliefs with Christian teachings, and preached that an Indian Christ would appear who would right all wrongs, and that the land would again belong to the Indian as in ancient times.

The various tribes had different names for the Ghost Dance. The Paiute called it *Nanigukwa* or "dance in a circle." This *nuka* or circle dance distinguished it from the other dances of the tribe, which had only up-and-down steps and not the circular movement. The Shoshoni called it *Tana'rayun*, or *Tamana 'rayara*, meaning "everybody dragging," suggesting the manner in which the dancers moved about in a circle holding hands. The Comanche called it *A'p-aneka'ra*, or "the Father's dance," or the "dance with joined hands." The Kiowa called it *Manposo'ti guan*, or "dance with clasped hands." They also called it *Guan a'dalka-i* "dance craziness." The Caddo knew it as *A'a kaki'mbawi'ut*, or "the prayer of all to the Father." The Sioux and Arapaho and others of the prairie tribes called it Ghost Dance or Spirit Dance, from the Sioux *Wana'ghi wa'-chipi* and the Arapaho *Thigu'nawat*, because everything connected with this dance related to the coming of the spirits of the dead from the spirit world. Ghost Dance is the name by which it came to be known among the white men.

316

The dance itself differed from tribe to tribe, but generally dancing was to the beat of a drum, and some members carried ghost sticks, or sacred wands. Sometimes a woman of the tribe would hold out four sacred arrows toward the sun; these arrows were without points, but on some occasions they were shot skyward. When they landed, they were gathered up and tied to a circle made of bent twigs tied together and called a gaming wheel. The wheel and arrows were then tied to a tree. All of this was done with appropriate prayers. The dancers stood, first behind each other with hands on the shoulders of the person ahead. The dancers chanted as they moved about, forming a circle. As they chanted they called to the Great Spirit, repeating the names of dead loved ones. They took up handfuls of dust and rubbed it over their faces and arms, and, raising their eyes to the sky, would cry out. The ceremony lasted about fifteen minutes. Then all would sit down and when they arose again would enlarge the circle by holding hands and moving in a circle following the sun. They would dance faster and faster, their bodies swaying, and every now and then one would fall, to be jerked to his feet back into position, until he was no longer able to stand. Some of the dancers would break away from the circle and dance alone.

It was believed that an ill person would become well if he took part in the dance, so old people on canes hopped about with the dancers. Many dancers kept going until they fell exhausted in an almost hypnotic state. No one took notice of those who fell, unless to pull them out of the circle. Men and women, children and elders could dance in the Ghost Dance; if a woman with a baby showed signs of falling, then a friend or someone near would catch her so no harm came to the child she held.

The Sioux believed that Wovoka was the Messiah that the "black robes," as they called the missionary priests, had told them about. Now the Son of God had returned to punish the white men for their sins against the Indians. It was believed that by the coming spring of the next year (1891), the white man would disappear from the land and once again it would belong to the Indians. However, the Ghost Dance ended in tragedy when on December 12, 1890, orders went through to arrest the Sioux chief, Sitting Bull, the leader of the Ghost

Dance. Three days after the arrest he was shot and killed as he left his cabin. The shock of this put an end to the Ghost Dance and the belief that the sacred Ghost Dance and the ghost shirt would stop the white man's bullets. Disheartened, the Indians started to drift back to the reservations.

Among those who turned back to the reservation was chief Big Foot and his band of about 350 men, women, and children, including about 100 warriors who had taken part in the Ghost Dance. This Sioux chief and his band had been ordered back to the reservation by the government agency and were under its protection when they camped on the Wounded Knee River near the agency. On the morning of December 29th, armed troops completely surrounded the encampment in order to take the warriors into custody. The warriors had previously surrendered most of their guns and arms, so they were in no position to fight. The band of women and children, all wearing their magic ghost shirts, stood helplessly about as the soldiers ripped through their tipis hunting for warriors. Big Foot threw some dirt into the air, whether as a prayer to the Great Spirit or as a sign to his people was never known, because the next moment the soldiers opened fire. The warriors rushed forth to defend the women and children, using anything at hand to protect their families. In a few minutes the battle was over, with 200 Indians dead or dying, most of them women and children, and 20 soldiers killed. The bodies of the dead and wounded Indians were scattered along a distance of two miles. A blizzard followed, and many of the injured Indians froze to death. With this massacre died the last hope of the Sioux nation and of all the Indians who had looked to Wovoka as their prophet or messiah, to lead them back to the splendor and freedom of ancient days.

The ghost shirt was the most important item of the Ghost Dance. It was not worn by all the tribes. The Cheyenne would not allow their people to wear it, as they felt that to wear the ghost shirt was to make it an item of war. It was Black Elk, a young Sioux, who had a vision in which the Great Spirit spoke and gave to him the ghost shirt. It was believed that properly made and decorated, the ghost shirt had a wonderful magic which would make the wearer invincible to the bullets or weapons of the white man. During the dance, the shirt was

# DRUMS

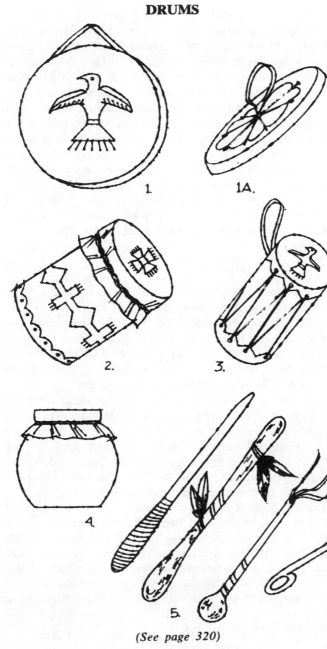

1.  1A.

2.  3.

4.  5.

*(See page 320)*

worn on the outside, and as an inner garment at all other times. The shape, fringing, and feather adornments were almost the same in every case, but variations existed in the painting of the design. Some were very simple, others had elaborate symbols of the sun, moon, stars, and other designs of Indian mythology. At times the visions of the dance trance were painted on a ghost shirt. The feathers attached to the ghost shirt were always those of the eagle, and the thread used to sew the buckskin shirts was always the old method sinew. Fringe and other parts of the garment were sometimes painted red to represent the messiah. Animal skins were scarce by 1890, so some of the shirts were made of unbleached muslin, but regardless of the material, all were cut alike. This was the first time that all the Indian women were allowed to wear the eagle feather, which was attached to the ghost shirt.

## DRUMS

There are three main types of drum used by the different tribes. Probably the most commonly used is the small hand drum, which usually has only one head, but can have two. There is also a large two-headed drum, usually made of wood, and a water drum which is keg-shaped with a single removable head. This drum contains an inch or two of water in the bottom which adds to the resonance of the drum.

The hand drum is easily carried and is used if the drummer or dancer moves about a great deal (see Diagram 1). This is made by stretching a piece of hide over a circular band from 10 to 15 inches in diameter. The thongs which keep the skin pulled tight over the sides are crossed in back and form a handle (see Diagram 1A). The front of these drums can be decorated with paintings, or they may be left plain.

Diagram 2 shows a large two-headed drum, usually made by hollowing out a section of log and stretching a skin over each end. These vary in size from 1 foot to 3 feet in height, and from 1 to 2½ feet in diameter. Kegs and even washtubs are used. In the southwestern pueblos the big drum is held and beaten, usually by a single player as he stands before it. The Plains tribes and the eastern tribes place the drum on the

320

# WATER DRUM

*(See page 322)*

ground and it is struck by several seated men. Sometimes the drum is supported by stakes, or held by others. Diagram 2 shows the skin tacked over the bottom and tied around the top. Diagram 3 shows the skin stretched over each end and laced together with thongs.

Usually the heads of the drums are painted with a decorative symbol, many times something seen in a dream vision by the owner. Sometimes the drums are plain, and at times, the underside of the hand drum, with one head, is painted.

Some of the southwest tribes made a one-headed drum of pottery (see Diagram 4). The skin is pulled tight over the top of a pottery jar and tied around the top. The Northwest Coast Indians often use a long wooden box as a drum, it is beaten by the heels of men seated on it.

Commercial drums can be used to make an Indian drum. The heads can be painted with your favorite design, and streamers, feathers, or bits of fur can be added around the edge, or tied to the side. This type of adaptation can look very authentic.

Drumsticks are made of slender sticks with one end padded. either with rags wrapped around the stick or with bits of skin mixed with soft material tied to a stick. Some sticks are fur-covered and decorated with feathers. In the Southwest, a stick with a bare end bent in a complete circle is used. See Diagram 5 for various types.

Drumbeats are usually in combination of slow and fast, weak and strong.

## WATER DRUM

This drum is about 18 to 20 inches in height. Originally it was made from a hollowed log and later from a small barrel or keg, opened at one end with a rawhide skin pulled tight over the top and tied with a hoop around the barrel. A hole is made in the side of the barrel so the water can be emptied. Before the drum is used, the head is removed and water is placed in the opening. The head is then dampened and re-placed, with the hoop holding it tight. The water in the bottom adds greatly to the resonance of the drum. This drum is most common in the north-central section of the country.

## RATTLES

Rattles differed widely, depending upon what tribe was using them. They were made from gourds, buffalo horn, raw-hide, birchbark, shells, metal, almost anything that could be shaken to the rhythm of dancers, drumming, or singing.

In later years, when the tin can found its way to the settle-ments, rattles were made from the cans as well as from bits of cans that were cut and rolled in the shape of cone jinglers. (See Part V for an explanation of how to make tin cone jing-lers.)

Make the cone jinglers any size from 1 inch to 3 inches, de-pending upon how you plan to use them. They can be attached to a cord or small piece of leather and the leather strip at-tached to a wooden handle, as in Diagram 1. For this the tin jinglers should be small; from three to four strips can be attached to the handle. The leather strips, after being tacked or glued to the handle, hang loose, except at each end where they are held. The handle can be wrapped in leather strips and a wrist strap added. The top can be decorated with small fluffy feathers for color. Diagram 1A shows another method for attaching tin cone jinglers. These are hung directly on the

# RATTLES

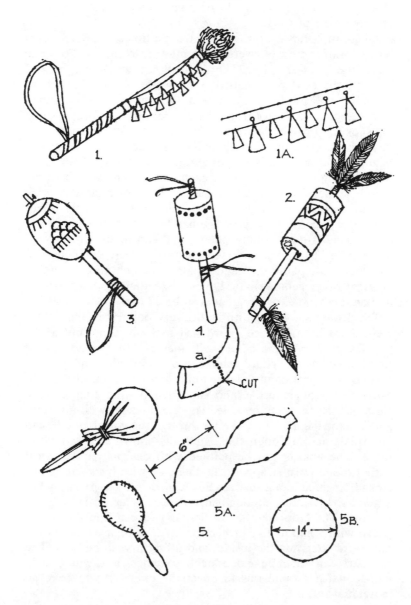

1.

1A.

2.

3.

4.

a.

CUT

5A.

6"

5.

5B.

14"

wooden handle by small bits of cord. These can be tacked or glued, and the jinglers should be larger than those used in the previous type of rattle.

Diagram 2 shows a rattle made from a tin can. In later years on the prairie, tin cans were often made into rattles. To make this rattle holes are pierced through the center of the top and bottom, the contents emptied, then water is run through to clean out the can. Let the can sit in the sun to dry inside, then insert a stick or dowel from the lumberyard. Before pushing the stick up through the top of the can, put a few small pebbles through the top opening to make the rattle, and push the handle stick or dowel on through the can. Anchor the handle in the can with a small nail at each end of the can where the handle comes through. About 2 or 3 inches of handle or stick should protrude through the top of the can. Small rubber washers can be pushed up on the handle against the end of the can to hold it more solidly, then a nail can be driven through the handle just below this (see Diagram 2, *a*). Paint the can with flat white paint, then add a pattern of lightning, triangles, or some other geometric design. Add feathers to the top, and one on the handle, or streamers can be added.

Diagram 3 shows a gourd rattle, very popular in the Southwest. Actually any dried gourd will make a rattle, but a few pebbles or dried peas added will increase the sound. Cut a small hole in the gourd, shake out the seeds, and with a twisted wire, scoop out the dried pith and any additional seeds. Put a few pebbles inside, and run a small stick, long enough for a handle, through the hole. This can be held with a washer glued to the handle where it goes through the gourd, or you can put small nails through the handle as shown in the tin-can rattle. The gourds can be painted with designs, and finished with a thong wrist strap with feathers, or with buckskin fringe tacked or glued along the handle. A 5- or 6-inch-gourd makes a good-sized rattle, although any size, smaller or larger, can be used. The Hopi like flat rattles. If you can find a crooked gourd with a handle-like projection this can be used by cutting the gourd, cleaning the inside, and filling it with pebbles. The cut part can then be glued back together, a rawhide strip glued or tied around this to cover the cut, and you have an individual rattle.

324

Diagram 4 is a rattle made of horn. Originally buffalo horn was used on the Plains, but steer horn is used today. Cut a portion off the wide end of the horn (see Diagram 4, *a*). Make two wooden disks to plug the openings and fasten them in place with round-headed tacks or glue. Before fastening the last plug into the horn, put a few pebbles inside. Bore a small hole in the wooden plugs for the handle to fit through. If the horn has been polished it will have a lovely shine. Fasten a small feather or streamers to the rattle.

Rawhide rattles (Diagram 5) can be made in two ways. Soak the hide, then cut it in either of the two patterns shown. For 5A, after cutting the pattern sew the two pieces together halfway around, then fill with wet sand and clay, or just wet sand. Finish sewing, leaving the end open for a handle later. Put the wet sand-filled rawhide in the sun to dry. Be sure it is packed as tight as possible. When dry, the rawhide will be hard. Knock out the sand, put in a few pebbles, insert a handle, and tie with a wet thong. Let the thong dry and the rattle is ready to use. To make 5B, place a ball of wet sand and clay in the middle of the round piece after it has been soaked and cut. Pull the rawhide into a pouch-like bundle around the wet sand. Insert the handle and tie it lightly so the handle can be pulled out. After the rawhide has dried in the sun, pull out the handle, which should have been just barely inserted, gently knock out the sand, put a few pebbles inside, put the handle back in, and, as the rawhide is stiff, you may have to wrap extra wet rawhide around the handle where it fits into the ball. Tie this with a wet thong and let it dry. A feather or colored streamer can be tied at the handle.

Greeting Song - Woodland

Baby Song - Pueblo

Work Song - Pueblo

Plains Love Song

Baby Song - Desert Southwest

Love Song - Flains

Baby Song - Sioux

a wa wa   wa   inina isti mama   wa wa

wa inina   isti mama a wa   wa wa inina isti

mama a   wa wa a   inina istimama

Be still - inina
Sleep - istimama
Baby - wa wa

* THE MUSICAL NOTES AND TIMING,
for this music, were taken down
from individual humming or drum
beats, and are as accurate as
possible.

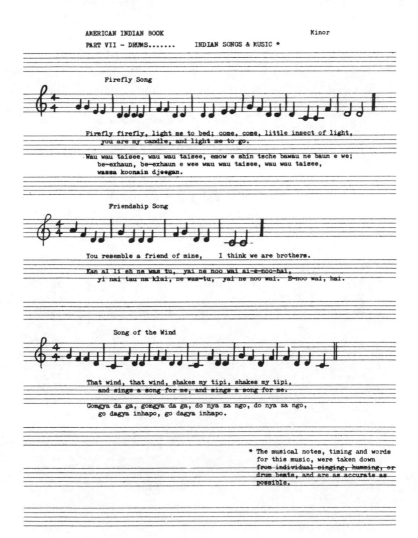

**Firefly Song**

Firefly firefly, light me to bed; come, come, little insect of light,
you are my candle, and light me to go.

Wau wau taisee, wau wau taisee, emow e shin tsche bawau ne baun e we;
be-exhaun, be-exhaun e wee wau wau taisee, wau wau taisee,
wassa koonain djeegan.

**Friendship Song**

You resemble a friend of mine,    I think we are brothers.

Kan al li eh ne was tu,  yai ne noo wai ai-e-noo-hai,
yi nai tau na klai, ne was-tu,  yai ne noo wai. E-noo wai, hai.

**Song of the Wind**

That wind, that wind, shakes my tipi, shakes my tipi,
and sings a song for me, and sings a song for me.

Gomgya da ga, gomgya da ga, do nya za ngo, do nya za ngo,
go dagya inhapo, go dagya inhapo.

* The musical notes, timing and words
for this music, were taken down
from individual singing, humming, or
drum beats, and are as accurate as
possible.

Lullaby – Plains

Dance – Plains

Game Song – Plains

Lullaby – Seminole

War Song

* The musical notes, and timing
  for this music, were taken down
  from individual humming or drum
  beats, and are as accurate as
  possible.

PART VIII

# GAMES, SPORTS, AND STORIES

*(Crafts begin on page 345)*

The American Indians loved the competition of games, and most of their games fell into two categories, those of chance and those of dexterity. Games of pure skill and calculation, such as chess, were not known until contact with the white man. A few games were believed to have magical effects. Some games were played only during festivals or religious occasions. Some were children's and women's games, and many were gambling games.

## GAMES AND SPORTS

Games of chance were of two types: those games in which implements, such as dice, were thrown at random to determine a number or numbers, the sum of the count being kept by means of sticks, pebbles, or bits of bone; and those in which one or more players guessed in which of two or more places something was concealed, with success or failure resulting in the gain or loss of counters.

Games of dexterity included archery, sliding javelins or darts upon the ground, shooting at moving targets such as a netted wheel or ring, ball games in several forms, and racing games including horse racing.

In games of chance, a man might gamble away much of his personal property, including a good horse, with the throw of the dice. Certain forms of throwing dice or sticks was played by some 130 tribes belonging to thirty linguistic groups.

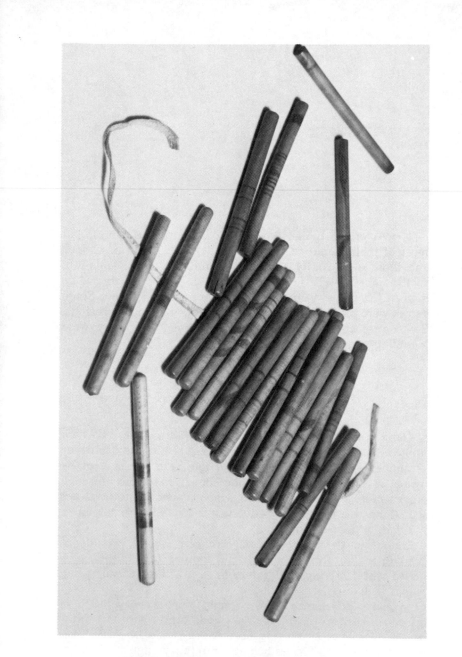

**STICK GAME**
Used in many Indian games and as counters.

The rules of the game varied according to the tribe, as did the so-called dice used, but the essential implements consisted of the dice and the instruments for keeping count. The dice varied according to color or markings and could be made of split cane, wooden staves, blocks, beaver or woodchuck teeth, walnut shells, plum or peach stones, grains of corn, bone, shells, brass, or pottery disks. The dice were either thrown by hand or tossed in a basket or bowl. The basket or bowl game was generally played by the women, though not always. Scores for the hand or basket–bowl game were kept by counting sticks, which were passed from hand to hand. Sometimes the count was kept or cut on a piece of wood. Counting sticks were made from wood, bone, or pottery.

A game somewhat like "Button, button, who's got the button" was played using two small objects. One was marked with a string around the middle, the other was plain. The idea was to guess in which hand the unmarked object was held.

Another guessing game was the moccasin or hidden ball. In this a small object was placed in a moccasin and the player had to guess in which moccasin it would be found.

Games of dexterity were usually accompanied by heavy wagers, and these were played with arrows, or darts and spears thrown at a given mark.

Snow snake was a man's game. It was played with a long flattened stick or pole usually ten feet long; for the younger boys, the stick they started with was about six feet long. The forward and slightly upward curve of the snow snake stick was like the runner of a sled, and sometimes resembled the head of a snake. The rear of the stick was slightly notched, making a place for the fingers when throwing the stick. The "snake" or stick was thrown along the surface of the snow or in a straight shallow groove which had been made hollow by dragging a log through the snow. The players tried for distance and the "snake" that was thrown the farthest won a point for the thrower. Sometimes pegs were set up and the "snake" had to reach beyond these. The game took great skill.

The game of hoop and pole was played throughout North America. This had some variations, but mainly consisted of shooting an arrow or throwing a spear at a hoop or ring. The counts were determined by the way the dart fell in reference to the target. The implements for this were the hoop, or target; the darts, or poles; and the counters. A common and much used form of hoop was one of twined net resembling a spider web. Some tribes had small rings covered with beads of different colors set at equal distances around the inside of the hoop. Each color, usually made from beading, equaled a certain count if one could place an arrow or dart near the colored small bead. Hoops were made of sapling lashed with rawhide. The Hopi made a hoop of cornhusk. The darts could be arrows shot from a bow or thrown by hand. Long poles were also used. This game could be played by two or by a group.

Indian ball games were the type in which the ball was tossed with a racket. Shinny was usually a woman's game and was played with wooden billets tied together and tossed with sticks. There were ball races in which a ball or stick was kicked about. Other forms of ball included a type of football, hand and football, tossed ball, and juggling a hot ball.

Hot ball was a game of training for young men. An elder man of the tribe would take a stone ball and put it into the fire. When it was hot he removed it and tossed it as far as possible; a young man had to find the ball and run as far as he could with it, before he was forced to drop it because of the heat. Types of balls varied from wood, bladder netted with sinew and bone or stone balls. Ball races seemed to have been most popular among the Indians of the Southwest.

Lacrosse is the best known of the Indian games, the name coming from the "crosse" or racket-like sticks carried by the player. The French colonists likened these to a bishop's crozier. Lacrosse is one of the oldest and fastest games known, and the one game that was adopted by the white man. The object of this game was that each player tried to get the ball and carry it to the opponents' goalpost. The game was played on a field from 500 feet to a mile and a half in length. It had two posts set several hundred feet apart at each end of the field. The ball could be thrown or carried in the racket, but at no time could it be touched with the hand. This game was excellent training for war as it developed teamwork and gave practice in fast running and in warding off blows from an adversary. Preparation for a big game were carried on for as long as a month before the game. A part of the training was bathing, exercise, and diet. Some of the training was governed by religious beliefs and superstition. The Cherokee players could not eat frogs' legs before a game, as they were brittle and break easily, and this was something no player wanted to be associated with. It was felt that the eating of frogs' legs might somehow confer their breaking properties to the player. However the player would often rub their legs with those of a turtle because the turtle is strong and sure. The players could not eat rabbit because a rabbit is timid and will lose its wits when pursued by its enemies. Dances and ceremonies were held before a game to bring good luck to the team and to assure success.

Shinny was a favorite with many tribes. The game was played with a small ball, and a stick three or four feet long and curved at one end. Two goalposts or stakes were set three feet apart at the end of the field. The ball was placed in a shallow pit in the center of the field and the team lined up just inside the goalposts. At a given signal, both teams would rush to the hole to get the ball and drive it into their opponents' goal. The ball could not be touched by any part of the body. Women usually played this game, and any number could play, but there were times when teams of men played against the women, or there were mixed teams.

Double ball was mostly played by the women, except in southern California, where men also played it. Most of the time this was called "woman's ball." Two balls were used, or similar objects attached to each other by a thong, with a curved stick by which the balls were thrown. The balls, equal in weight, varied in shape and material but were usually made of sand or clay covered with buckskin. Teams played on an open field which could be of any length, with goalposts at each end. The goalposts were six feet apart and had a cross arm about the same distance from the ground. A goal was made when the balls or billets were hung across the arm of the posts. The sticks were about three feet long, smoothed off and tapered gradually from an inch in diameter at the handle end to a half inch at the other end. The teams faced each other at a distance of about twenty feet. An umpire would toss the ball and each team would try to catch it on the stick they

**CHEYENNE DOLL**
About 14 inches high with real hair and bound in buckskin.
Dress is decorated in white and yellow beads with cowrie shells;
the belt includes metal pieces. Doll's legs are buckskin with beads
of white and red trim.

held, then toss it to another member of the team. The one with the most catches, in a given period, or the team which kept the ball the longest, won the game.

The game of toss and catch was played in some form from Alaska to Mexico. The Indians of North America used a thin bone awl on which they caught hollow bones. The bones were loosely strung on a buckskin thong and tied to the end of the awl. The object was to catch the string of bones on the awl.

Ball juggling was tossing two or more balls into the air at the same time and not letting them fall to the ground, or catching them before they did. Many young Indian boys were very good at this game.

Horse racing was always one of the favorite sports, especially among the Plains Indians, who were among the world's best horsemen. An Indian rider could seemingly disappear from either side of his horse, while the horse was running at top speed. Competition and feats of horsemanship were part of a young boy's life. Swimming, running, and jumping were a part of the games played, and winning brought honors, even to the very young. There were games for both summer and winter, and for two, or contests for teams. The boys played at marking trail and at hiding from each other, just as the little girls played at housekeeping and at moving camp. Skill at beadwork became competitive among the young girls, as did cooking, tanning, and putting up the tipi. Almost every game an Indian child played was preparation for adulthood. Competition, dexterity, endurance, all were stressed in the games, but along with this went humor and jokes and stories of amusing incidents.

## STORIES AND LEGENDS

On winter evenings, when the dark dropped down early and the chill wind blew around the tipi when the families were warm inside with the flickering flames from the firepit lighting the designs of the tipi lining, and the children were snug in their fur-covered beds, and the elders were resting

## CHILD'S SHIELD
Such a toy was given to a boy so he might learn the uses of bow and arrow and the importance of the shield. This 10-inch example is made of cloth and bound in red with red-tipped feathers around it.

against the comfortable backrests, then the legends would be told to the children.

Many of the legends were simple stories about the animals of the forests, the prairie, and the desert. Others were more complicated, encompassing all forms of Indian life and explaining many things. Every young boy wanted to be a storyteller when he grew up, as they were much respected among the Indians. While these were not games in the general sense, still the children repeated the stories to each other and often acted out the legends they had heard, so that they became a part of their play and their games.

The following Iroquois legend tells "How the chipmunk got his stripe."

When the world was young all of the animals were called together to decide whether there should be night and darkness all of the time, or if it would be better to have the day and sunlight. This was a very important question and a violent discussion took place; many wished for daylight only, and others wanted darkness and night all of the time.

The chipmunk wanted equal dark and light, or night and day, and he prayed to the gods with a song he sang: "The light will come, the night will come, the light will come, the night will come."

He kept repeating his prayer song. In the meantime the bear sang, "Night is best, we must have darkness for all of the time, for rest, rest."

As the chipmunk was singing and dancing around faster than the bear, the day began to dawn. When the other animals who wanted darkness and were singing with the bear saw this, they were angry. The bear turned to grab the chipmunk, but the chipmunk escaped, or almost. As he jumped into the hole in the hollow tree, the bear again grabbed for him, but only the huge paw of the bear grazed the back of the chipmunk as he disappeared into his home in the tree. To this day you can see the black mark where the bear's paw touched the chipmunk. And since that time the night comes, and the light comes, in equal parts.

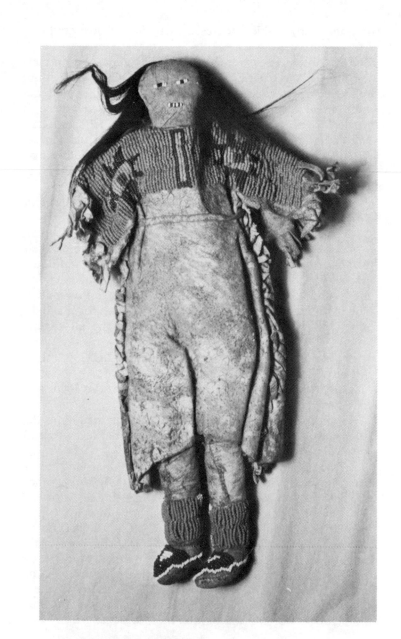

**PLAINS TRIBE DOLL**
Buckskin dress with a blue yoke beaded in a red design.

Another legend of the Woodland people tells of the Northern Lights and what they mean. If the Northern Lights were white it was believed that frost would very soon follow; if yellow, there would be sickness and much trouble to the nation; if the lights were red, very red, it indicated war and harm to many innocent people. However, if the Northern Lights flashed all colors, especially in the springtime, it was the best possible sign of all and assured good crops for the coming season.

The scent of the skunk is regarded as powerful medicine, or magic, and there is a legend as to how this came about.

Many moons ago the skunk was large, but then suddenly he began to grow smaller, probably due to the evil influence of other animals who were jealous of his beautiful striped coat. But as he became smaller, he began to worry. "How can I take care of myself, how can I hunt, if I lose my strength." He thought and thought and decided that he would make a strong hunting medicine that would give him even more skill than he had when he was big. He hunted and hunted to find all the plants he would need to make his great medicine. He finally found four that were very strong. He took these home and ground them up into fine powder, singing and praying as he did so. When his medicine was ready he placed it in a little pouch which he carried wherever he went. Finally he decided to test this medicine against the biggest and strongest thing he could find.

He took some powder out of his pouch—only a pinch was needed. He put it in water and drank it; then, to make more powerful medicine, he sang, "Who is going out hunting? I, for I go out to hunt." The skunk then shot at the oak tree, not with an arrow, but with this medicine, a foul-smelling liquid, and the tree shrank away, growing smaller and smaller until it was nothing but a small twig. This is the same medicine the skunk carries today.

The legend of the redbird tells how helpfulness is rewarded, but it also points out how cunning can overcome an enemy, as the racoon did.

341

**PLATEAU DOLL**
Boy doll with a beaded hat and a piece of red cloth around and
down the front. A large metal cross is suspended around the neck.

Once long ago, a racoon, passing a wolf, made some insulting remarks. Finally the wolf became angry and turned to chase the racoon. The racoon ran to a tree beside the river and climbed up. He stretched out on a limb overhanging the water. The wolf saw the reflection of the racoon in the water, and thinking it was really the racoon, jumped in. He was nearly drowned before he could scramble out, and he was all wet and exhausted. He lay down on the bank to dry and fell asleep. While he was sleeping the racoon came down and plastered the wolf's eyes with mud.

When the wolf awoke he found he could not open his eyes and he began to cry. A little brown bird passing by heard the wolf and asked him why he was crying.

The wolf told his story and said, "If you will get my eyes open, I'll show you where you might find some lovely red paint, so you can paint yourself and be like a bright flower among the leaves of the trees." The little brown bird was delighted and agreed to help the wolf. He began to peck at the hardened mud over the wolf's eyes. Very carefully the little brown bird worked; it took a long time, but at last the wolf could see. Then as he'd promised, he took the little brown bird to a great rock with streaks of red running through it, and he helped the little bird paint each feather until he was no longer brown but a gay, happy red color. Today, the redbird is this same red color.

The Sioux have a charming legend about the rainbow and its beautiful colors.

Many moons ago, on a bright summer day, all the flowers were out playing; some were nodding their bright heads in the breeze and others were scattering their gay colors through the grass.

The Great Spirit heard one of the older flowers saying, "We are happy now, but I wonder where we will go when winter comes and we must depart. I do wish it could be different."

"Yes," said another, "we do our share to make the earth beautiful, and to bring happiness to those who see us. I

343

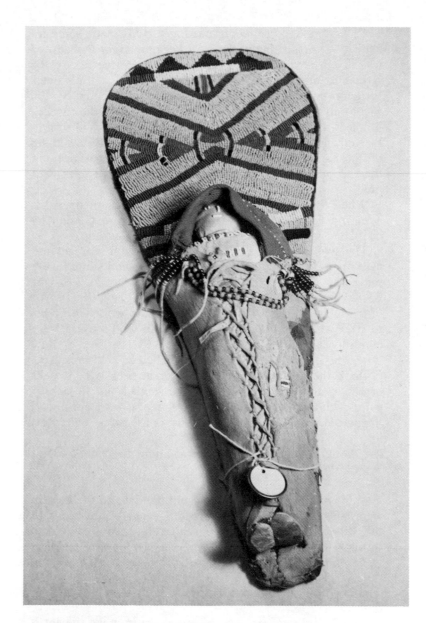

CHILD'S TOY—Shoshoni tribe
Doll in a 14-inch cradleboard and beaded in blue, white, and yellow.

believe we should have a Happy Hunting Ground of our own that we could go to when we must leave the earth."

The Great Spirit heard this and thought about it. He finally decided that when winter came the flowers should not have to completely disappear. When he told the flowers of his plan they were all happy. Now, after a refreshing rain, when you look up into the sky you see all of the pretty flowers of the past year making a beautiful colored rainbow across the bowl of the sky.

According to the Sioux, we can thank a little dog for keeping the world from ending.

For thousands of years, an old Indian woman has been sitting in the moonlight decorating a large bag with porcupine quills. Near her a fire is burning brightly, and a kettle of herbs is boiling. Nearby sits a small black dog, watching her. When the old Indian woman puts down her work to stir the herbs in the kettle, or add more wood to the fire, the little dog quickly unravels her quill work. As fast as she sews and decorates, the dog unravels it. If the old Indian woman ever completes her work the world will come to an instant end, because she will put the world in her bag and carry it off.

## BASKET GAMBLE

This is a form of Indian dice and is played in some manner by almost all Indian tribes.

It is played with six plum or peach pits, marked on one side with a big dot, and a flat type basket, as shown in Diagrams 1 and 2. Counters are also needed to keep score. Usually everyone had their own counters made of twigs or thin pieces of wood and painted or decorated. These were from 6 to 12 inches long. Today, colored toothpicks can be used.

Two to twelve people, or even more, can play Basket Gamble as long as the number is even. Decide if you'll play as two teams, or individually. The players sit on the ground facing each other. The player who makes the throw holds the basket in front of him, close to the ground. The basket is

# BASKET GAMBLE

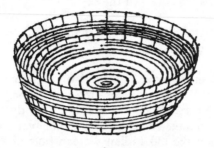

1

2

held in both hands, one on each side of the basket. The basket, with the marked pits inside, is given a shake upward, causing the pits to leap into the air; at the same time the basket is moved smartly down against the ground, and the stones or pits fall back into it. The pits are not thrown high, but the movement of the basket is quick, and it is brought down hard on the ground, so that the sound of this slap against the earth can easily be heard. The pits which land with the marked side up are counted and the count sticks are placed in front and to one side of the player. With teams, an official count keeper sometimes is appointed to keep the score. After each play the basket is passed across to the player opposite.

Sometimes the players make wagers with each other as to the outcome of the game. Before starting to play, determine how many tosses by each player constitutes a game. For example if eight people play, four to each side, you might decide that each player will have eight tosses as a total. In other words, the basket will be passed around until each player has had eight turns. The side with the greatest total score wins the game. Among the Indians personal items, even

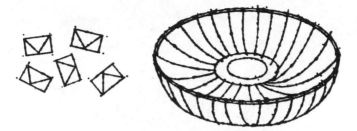

prized horses, were sometimes put up as bets. Other versions were played with painted pebbles and wooden bowls. In some games, eight peach stones were used. In more complicated versions, each stone was painted differently on the one side and the stones counted for different amounts, if they fell painted-side up.

In playing this game you can use any shallow basket, pan, or bowl. Wash and dry the peach or plum pits, then mark them on one side. India ink is good for marking as it doesn't come off once it is dry. You can mark the pits with dots, bands, triangles, squares, or your initial if you like, just as long as you leave one side blank. In keeping score use toothpick counter sticks, nails, or coins.

## ZUÑI BASKET GAME

In this game five wooden blocks are used, 1 by 1½ inches and about ¼ inch thick. One side of a block is painted, the other side is left plain. A basket 10¼ inches (or thereabouts) is used. The idea of the game is to throw the wooden blocks up from the basket and to catch them again in the basket. Points are counted from the side that lands upright in the basket.

The count is: All five painted with design = 10 points. Five plain = 5. Four plain = 4. Three plain = 3. Two plain = 2. One plain = 1. The object of the game is to get 10 points.

# BASKET AND BALL GAME

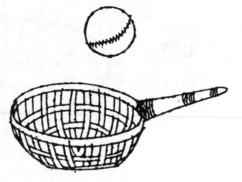

## BASKET AND BALL GAME

This is a game that was played by the women. Players stand about 50 feet apart and throw a 4-inch ball filled with buckskin and hair. The ball is also made of buckskin. Each player holds a basket and as the ball is tossed back and forth, each tries to catch it in the basket. At no time may players touch the ball with their hands.

To play this game today a basket with a handle can be used and a rubber ball or tennis ball.

## HOOP AND POLE GAME

Many tribes played a form of hoop and pole, a sort of elaborate dart game.

Diagram 1 shows a type of hoop and pole game made more difficult with inside colored beads to be hit for certain points or score. The ring or hoop is a wrapped sapling, with small colored beads or stones, sewn on the inside at approximately equal intervals. The hoop is about 4 inches in diameter. The inside beads are rather small, about ¾ to 1 inch and it takes much skill to hit them with the pole. The hoop was usually tied, hanging, from a tree limb, or from a lance or spear stuck into the ground. For a player's pole to hit a group of colored beads attached to the inside of the four-inch wrapped loop

# HOOP AND POLE GAME

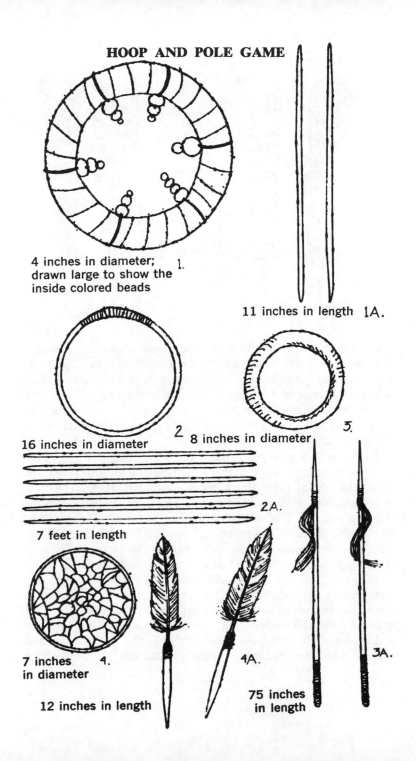

4 inches in diameter; drawn large to show the inside colored beads   1.

11 inches in length   1A.

16 inches in diameter   2.

8 inches in diameter   3.

7 feet in length   2A.

7 inches in diameter   4.

12 inches in length

4A.

75 inches in length

3A.

# CORNCOB AND RING GAME

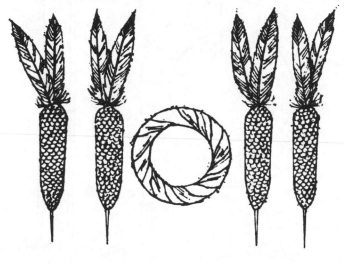

was quite a feat. In the diagram the beads which score as one if they are hit, are blue next to the ring, then red. The two-score is yellow and blue. The five-score is green and red. The ten-score is yellow and green. The fifteen-score is blue and green. The twenty-score beads are colored red next to the ring, and white. The game is usually played by two men with poles or sticks, 11 inches in length.

Diagram 2 is a larger hoop made of saplings tied together to form the circle, 16 inches in diameter. The long poles are 7 feet in length. Five or six people play this game. The ring is rolled and all throw their poles. The one whose pole stops the ring owns it. The others then shoot in turn, and the owner of the ring takes all the poles that miss and shoots them at the ring, winning those that he puts through it. If two men stop the ring or hoop on the first throw, they divide the poles.

Diagram 3 is still another hoop game. This is a ring approximately 8 inches in diameter, covered with buckskin sewed on the inner side with thong, and painted white. Two painted poles, 75 inches long, are used. Both ends are painted red, and the center of the pole is white. The tips are pointed and each has four buckskin thongs painted red, attached about

# TOSS AND CATCH

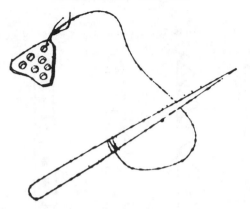

15 inches from the end. The ring or hoop is rolled by an umpire at some distance in front of, and horizontal to, the two players who try to throw their poles inside the rolling hoop in such a way that the buckskin thongs curl around the hoop and stop it. The one whose pole falls with the hoop caught between the buckskin thongs of his pole, wins the game.

Diagram 4 is a small hoop, 7 inches in diameter, made of bent twig and covered with a net of yucca fiber. Two feather darts 12 inches in length are used. The darts consist of pins of hardwood about 4 inches long to which single feathers, twisted spirally, are bound with fiber. This is used somewhat like a plain dart board.

The game illustrated on page 350 uses a ring of wrapped cornhusks. Make the ring about 4 or 5 inches in diameter. Take four corncobs, add a sharp object to one end and feathers to the other.

Place the ring on the ground about 10 feet away from the player, then try to hit the center of the ring.

The object of the toss and catch game is to catch the stick in a hole of the bone. The stick is about 12 inches long. Instead of bone with holes bored, a small wooden piece can be used. Sometimes rings are laced on the thong and the rings must be caught on the stick. Scoring depends upon how many times one bets this can be done.

# STICK SLIDE GAME

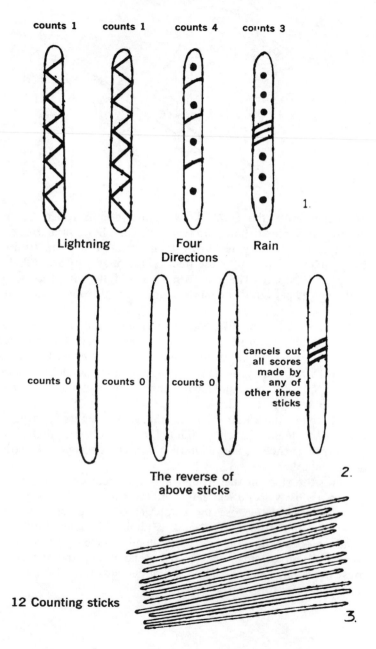

counts 1  counts 1  counts 4  counts 3

Lightning  Four Directions  Rain

1.

counts 0  counts 0  counts 0  cancels out all scores made by any of other three sticks

The reverse of above sticks

2.

12 Counting sticks

3.

## STICK SLIDE GAME

This is generally a woman's game, although anyone can play. Four straight bones or sticks were made from buffalo ribs, about 7 or 8 inches long, ¼ inch thick, and about ¾ of an inch wide, tapering to blunt points at both ends.

Today these could be made from rib bones, cut from plastic or whittled from wood. Wood could be marked with a wood-burning pencil or India ink.

Diagram 1 shows how the sticks are marked on one side. Two are marked with zigzag lines to represent lightning and these sticks are named Lightning. One stick is called Four Directions, and is divided into four parts by a line drawn across the stick. In each of these four divisions a round dot is made. The fourth bone or stick is marked with three lines across the middle of the stick, and on on each side of the center, three dots are made. This stick is called Rain.

Diagram 2 shows the reverse of the above sticks. The two Lightning sticks, and the Four Direction stick, are blank on the reverse side. The one Rain stick has three lines drawn across the middle on the reverse side.

Usually these markings are painted in red, blue, or black. The game can be played by two women or a group of women sitting across from each other. When two lines of women, facing each other, play the game, they play against the woman sitting opposite. Twelve counting sticks are used as counters and are placed on the ground between the players.

Sometimes the sticks are slid to determine who plays first. To play, the four sticks or bones are grasped in the right or left hand, holding the sticks vertically with the ends resting on the ground. With a slight sliding motion the player scatters the bones or sticks on the ground in front of her. The sides which fall uppermost show the count, or the failure to count.

The person making a successful throw takes from the heap of counting sticks the number called for by the points of the throw, one stick for each point. As long as the throw counts, the player continues to throw, but if the throw has no count then the play goes to the player opposite. When the counting sticks have all been taken from the pile on the ground be-

353

tween them, the successful thrower begins to take from her opponent the number of sticks called for by her throw. Twelve points must be made before the 12 counters come into the possession of one player. The game can become drawn out. In fact counters can be kept by the players and the game discontinued and started up, where everyone left off, on the next day.

Points are as follows: When a Lightning stick falls with the zigzag showing, this counts 1. Either Lightning stick counts 1. The Four Direction stick counts 4. The Rain stick counts 3. The two Lightning sticks and the Four Direction stick, when reversed to blank, count as zero. The reverse of the Rain stick, which shows the three marks across the center, cancels out any counts that might be made with the other sticks. As an example, if the Four Directions falls upright, counting 4, and one Lightning, counting 1 a blank, then the reverse of Rain, with the three cross marks in the middle, your score of 4 and 1, or 5, is canceled and your score for this throw is zero.

Toothpicks can be used as counting sticks (Diagram 3).

## HO'KIAMONNE: A ZUÑI GAME

Ho'kiamonne is a favorite game of the Zuñis. It was one offered to the gods of war at the winter solstice. The game was frequently played for rain; when played in this connection, sacred meal was sprinkled on the ground before the ball was tossed. The first one to win, offers thanks to the gods.

The implements of this game are a ball of yucca ribbons and two slender sticks, each sharpened at one end and passed through a piece of corncob having two hawk plumes inserted in the other end. The yucca ball was placed on the ground and the sticks thrown at it from a short distance. The object: to penetrate the ball. If the first player strikes the ball, the stick is allowed to remain in place until the other player plays. If both sticks strike the ball, the game is a draw. If the second stick fails to strike, it remains where it falls and the first player removes his sticks from the ball and throws again. The one who strikes the ball the greatest number of times wins.

You can make this game by using a ball of yarn or foam.

354

# HO'KIAMONNE: A ZUÑI GAME

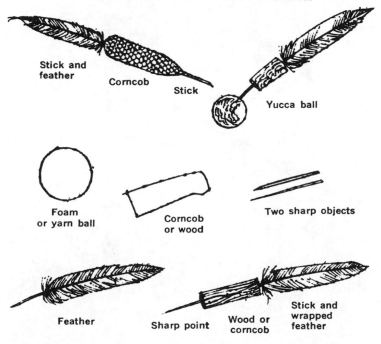

Stick and feather    Corncob    Stick    Yucca ball

Foam or yarn ball    Corncob or wood    Two sharp objects

Feather    Sharp point    Wood or corncob    Stick and wrapped feather

You can use corncobs or wood and add the sharpened sticks and feathers to toss at the ball. Wrap feathers around the stick at blunt end of the corncob or wood.

## BULL ROARER STICKS

These were used by the children as noisemakers and by the medicine men to drive away evil with the noise they make. No two ever sound alike, possibly because each is made according to individual specifications. A Bull Roarer consists of a stick for a handle, a length of thong tied to it, and at the other end of the thong a thin, flat, rectangular piece of wood, usually painted with some symbolic design. When held by the handle-stick and whirled around the head, a whizzing or moaning noise is made. Diagram 1 shows the handle notched where

# BULL ROARER STICKS

the thong or cord is tied on and the flat whizzer painted with the design of cross-arrows. Diagram 2 shows how this could be made from an old broom handle which has a metal ring in the end for hanging. Use the metal ring to attach the thong rather than drilling a hole through the pole or notching it. The whizzer piece of wood has also been notched at the upper corners, and this one is painted with a symbolic design of a flying bird.

The whizzer can be cut or painted in any way you like. The handle can be as short as 8 inches or as long as 30 inches. Modern wood-burning pencils can be used to trace a design on them, or they can be painted or left plain. These sticks are completely individual, so experiment until you make one that has the right feel and makes exactly the noise you like; then decorate it with initials, a figure, or anything that has meaning for you. You'll have a Bull Roarer that is truly yours.

# WHIP TOPS

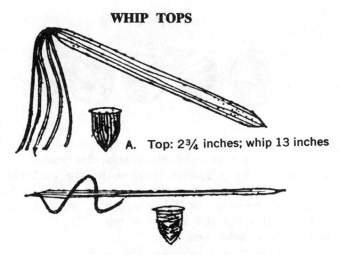

**A.** Top: 2¾ inches; whip 13 inches

**B.** Top: 2½ inches; whip 22½ inches

## TOPS

The top was one of the most widespread of Indian children's playthings. The whip top was common among the children. This was made of wood, horn, stone, or clay, and was sometimes painted or decorated with symbols.

## SPINNING TOPS OR WHIRLIGIGS

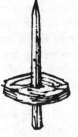  

**C.** Wood: 4 inches    **D.** Wood: 5 inches    **E.** Nut or wood: 3¾ inches

357

# STONE GAME

A. This top is of solid black horn 2¾ inches in length, accompanied by a 13-inch whip with four buckskin lashes and a wooden handle painted red. The top can be made out of wood, and the whip out of leather with a wooden stick.

B. Wooden top and whip; the top is 2½ inches and the whip is 22½ inches long.

The spinning top or whirligig was also used by the children.

C. This is 4 inches long with the disk, which is also 4 inches. This top was made from wood.

D. This top is 5 inches long and was carved from a piece of wood.

E. This was made from a nut 3¾ inches long; it could be carved from a piece of wood.

The stone game is played by two people. Five stones are used; it is best if they are round pebbles about ⅝ of an inch large. The first player selects a stone to be his. The stones should be a bit different in color, although this is not necessary. The player tosses the stone in the air. While the stone is in the air, the player tries to snatch up one or more of the remaining four stones before the one tossed in the air falls to the ground. If all are picked up, the game is won. If all are not picked up, the player tries again, but this time it is more difficult. The stone is tossed up as before, but the remaining stones must be shoved under an arch formed by the thumb and middle finger, with the first finger crossed over the middle one. Another way to play this is for the player to select one stone, which he calls his opponent's, that he will pick up first.

# BUZZER

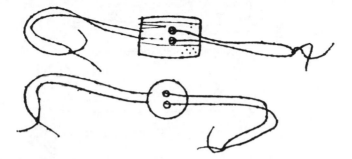

Buzzers can be made from wood or large buttons. Place a string through holes in the center of the wood or button. The ends are tied to form a loop on each side. Hold the loops in each hand and twist the cord; the disk will spin, making a humming sound. The wood may be painted with designs if desired.

## SHINNY

*The Sticks:*

The sticks shown are as follows:

> ARAPAHO—40 inches long. This was painted red and blue and curved slightly at the end. The ball was of rawhide.
> CHEYENNE—35 inches long. This was curved and expanded at the end. The stick had a picture of an elk and an eagle painted in red or black on the yellow stick with green ends. The ball was made of rawhide.
> NAVAHO—32 inches long. This was painted various shades, or to the owner's choice. The stick was somewhat curved. The ball was made of rawhide.
> PAWNEE—34 inches. long. The stick was painted red and had green bands. The ball was made of rawhide.

# SHINNY STICKS AND BALLS

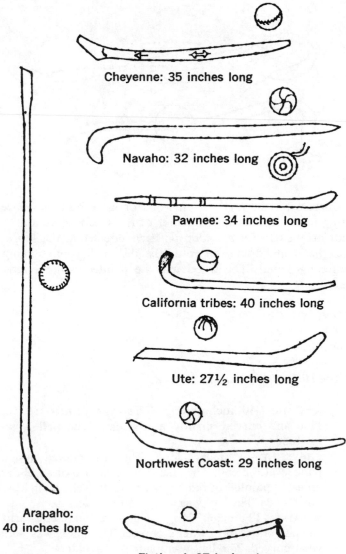

Cheyenne: 35 inches long

Navaho: 32 inches long

Pawnee: 34 inches long

California tribes: 40 inches long

Ute: 27½ inches long

Northwest Coast: 29 inches long

Arapaho:
40 inches long

Flathead: 27 inches long

CALIFORNIA TRIBES—40 inches long. The stick was painted red at the ends. The ball was made of rawhide.
UTE—27½ inches long with a long, broad, curved end. Natural in color; a rawhide ball was used.
NORTHWEST COAST—29 inches long. This has a flattened end. The color was natural; at times just a flattened stick or club was used and it was not made especially for the game. The ball was of rawhide.
FLATHEAD—27 inches long. This was flattened at one end and had a knob for a handle at the other end. The ball was of rawhide.

*The Game:*

This was a favorite game of the Indians. The rules varied among the tribes, but generally the game was played with curved sticks and a ball. The sticks and ball size differed among the tribes. Two posts or stakes were set about three feet apart at the end of a field. The field varied in length according to the tribe playing. Any number could play on a team.

The ball was placed in a shallow pit in the center of the field by someone who was chosen to be the umpire. The players lined up facing each other just inside the goalposts, which were tree limbs or old tipi poles or stakes, stuck upright into the ground and 3 feet apart. When the umpire gave the signal, both teams, or some members chosen from each team, would rush to the hole and try to secure the ball. The team who succeeded in getting the ball then tried to drive it toward the opponents' goal. The ball could not be touched with the hand or foot or any part of the body.

Another form of shinny was played by two teams forming parallel lines, somewhat in the manner of a foot race. They would be spaced about a hundred feet apart. The ground for this game had to be very smooth, as the players would try to drive the ball from one to another, or the first to where the second man stood, the second to the third, and so on. If the ball failed to hit its mark the first time, another try was made until it reached the man it was aimed toward. The smallest number of strokes on a side wins the game.

# LACROSSE STICKS

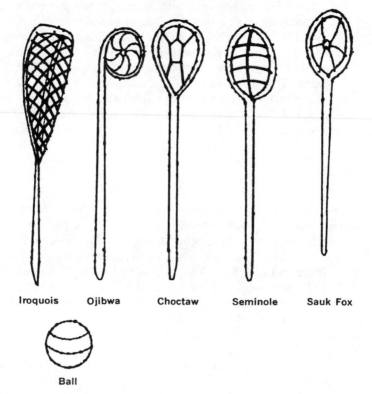

Iroquois  Ojibwa  Choctaw  Seminole  Sauk Fox

Ball

## LACROSSE

This is one of the best known Indian games and was played in one form or another among many tribes. The "crosse," or racket-like stick, for which the game is named, varied among different groups.

The object of the game is to run rapidly and to pass the ball, and to stop a player of the opposite team. Play was rough and there were some injuries. Some tribes would prepare months in advance for the game. Teams trained; bathing, exercises, and diet were prescribed by custom, and a man almost never broke his training program. Much of this was governed by religious beliefs and superstitions.

The game was usually played on a field about 500 feet to a mile and a half long. At each end were goals consisting of two posts set several feet apart. The object of the game was for one team to drive a wooden or buckskin ball between their opponents' goalposts. At no time could the ball be touched by hand; it could only be thrown or carried in the racket.

**SIOUX DOLL**
Buckskin doll with a buckskin dress trimmed with red, blue, and a few white beads. The leggings are beaded in blue and red. The doll wears a headband and has real hair; red yarn is tied around its middle.

# PART IX

## *INDIAN LANGUAGE*

The Indian had a language that really spoke pictures; their names were often those of birds, animals, stars, sun, wind, anything in nature. They might have a name given to them from a deed or an honor or some event that happened to them.

The way the Indian spoke at times seemed strange, for their placement of words was not the same as in English. They usually counted from one to ten, then started over again. The names they gave their months were descriptive; most times the name told what was happening in that period of the year.

The Indians had their own prayers, but the white man translated the Indian language into the prayers of the white man. The most common was the Lord's Prayer.

As the Indian had no written language the spelling of the words varied as the way the Indian pronounced a word sounded different to various people. Therefore, one name or word might have several spellings, so it is always difficult to be exact. Moreover, the Indian language has undergone changes since the first time the word was written down, so there are variant forms of many words, as different from one another as old English is from modern. As they have been throughout the book, the names and other Indian words in this chapter are spelled the way they are most commonly found.

## PICK YOURSELF AN INDIAN NAME

Why not pick yourself an Indian name, or give one to someone else? The names are listed according to the section of the country the tribe lived in and the language it spoke.

Unless otherwise indicated, the vowels are pronounced as follows: *a* as in father, *e* as in they, *i* as in marine, *o* as in note, and *u* as in flute. The vowels *ai* like *i* in fire, and *au* as *ow* in now. The consonants are pronounced the same as in English.

*EASTERN WOODLAND TRIBES—Principal languages Iroquoian, Siouan of Hokan-Sioux, and Algonkin*

DELAWARE—Algonkin family
| | |
|---|---|
| Arrow | *Al'lunth* |
| Bird | *Cho'le na* |
| Bluebird | *Chi ma'lus* |
| Cricket | *Ze'lo ze los* |
| Flower | *Wod'twēs* |
| Handsome | *Wu lis'so* |
| Medicine Man | *Quecksa'piet* |

NARRAGANSETT—Algonkin family
| | |
|---|---|
| Fawn | *Moo'quin* |
| Rain | *Sokan'on* |

POWHATAN—Algonkin family
| | |
|---|---|
| Fawn | *Nona'tawn* |
| Friend | *Ne'tab* |

OJIBWA—Algonkin family
| | |
|---|---|
| Bird | *Pe na she* |
| Butterfly | *Men'en gaw* |
| Dancer | *Na'mid* |
| Daybreak | *Bib'a ban* |
| Dreamer | *En a ban'dang* |
| Eagle | *Mig a ze* |
| Fire | *Ish ko da* |
| Lightning | *Wa wa'sa mo* |
| Little Star | *A nou gons'* |
| Moon | *Te be ke sis* |
| Owl | *Koo koo ku'ho* |
| Robin | *Pee cha* |
| Star | *A nang'* |
| Sun | *Ke sis* |

| Thunder | *Ah ne me ke* |
| Wind | *No din* |

**MOHAWK—Iroquoian family**

| Fire | *Oche'erle* |
| Moon | *Kelau'quaw* |
| Sun | *Kara'glwa* |
| Wind | *Ta'orlunde* |

**ONEIDAS—Iroquoian family**

| Earth | *Ohun Jea* |
| Sun | *Wah neda* |

**MENOMINI—Algonkin family**

| Approaching Day | *Pita'nowe* |
| Autumn | *Ta'kwa kwao* |
| Beaver Woman | *Nama'kukiu* |
| Bird Woman | *Petau Mitamo* |
| Dawn | *Pew'waba* |
| Good One | *Wio'ska sit* |
| Gray Squirrel | *Tamo* |
| Honey | *Moso'poma* |
| Humming Bird | *Nana'taka* |
| Little One | *Kino ka* |
| Moon Woman | *Kes'hiu qkau* |
| Rain | *Kime'wan* |
| Red Fox | *Wa ko* |
| Sky | *Ke'so* |
| Small Thunder | *Anama'kit* |
| Sweet | *Se'wan* |
| True Eagle | *Mia'kineu* |
| Truth Teller | *Namo'tan* |
| Wild Pigeon | *Om ini* |
| Winter | *Po'noe* |
| Woman | *Mita'mu* |
| Young Eagle | *Kine she* |

**IROQUOIS—Iroquois family**

| Bear | *Ya'o gah* |
| Beautiful Mountain | *On'on tuo* |
| Bright Flower | *A wen'ont* |

| Crow | *Ga′ga* |
| Day | *An′da* |
| Early Day | *A wen de′s* |
| Earth | *O eh′da* |
| Flying Messenger | *Daka rih′hon tye* |
| Muskrat | *No′ji* |
| Night | *So′a* |
| Owl | *O ho′wa* |
| Robin | *Jis ko′ko* |
| Snow | *O′kah* |
| Tireless | *Da go no′we da* |
| Turtle | *Ha nuna* |
| Wind | *Ga′a* |

*SOUTHEASTERN TRIBES—Principal languages Muskho-gean, Iroquoian, Siouan of Hokan-Sioux, Tunican, Cad-doan, and Yuchan*

CREEK—Muskhogean family

| Arrow | *Ch lee* |
| Bird | *Fus wa′* |
| Day | *Nit′tah* |
| Feather | *Tah fah′* |
| Flower | *Pah pah ee* |
| Fox | *Tso la* |
| Friend | *His′see* |
| Hawk | *Ai′o* |
| Owl | *O′pah* |
| Pepper | *Ho ma* |
| Pine Tree | *Chu′li* |
| Rain | *Os kee* |
| Robin | *Is pak wa* |
| Sky | *So′tah* |
| Star | *Ko tso tsum′pa* |
| Summer | *Mis kee* |
| Sun | *Hos′ see* |
| Thunder | *Tin it kee* |
| Wind | *Ho Tallee* |
| Wolf | *Ya ha* |

**CHEROKEE**—Iroquoian of Hokan-Sioux

| | |
|---|---|
| Bear | *Ya'na* |
| Black Fox | *I na'li* |
| Butterfly | *Ka ma'ma* |
| Most Perfect | *Tsun ga'ni* |
| Noonday Sun | *Nu da ye'li* |
| Star | *Na'kwi si* |
| Worker | *Ayi'ta* |
| Young Deer | *Awini'ta* |

**CHOCTAW**—Muskhogean of Hokan-Sioux

| | |
|---|---|
| Arrow | *Os'k* |
| Bear | *Ni'ta* |
| Beautiful | *Aiuk'li* |
| Beaver | *Kin'ta* |
| Beloved | *Holo'ka* |
| Bird | *Hu'shi* |
| Blackberry | *Bis'sa* |
| Black Eyes | *Ni'shkin lusa* |
| Black Squirrel | *Fani'lusa* |
| Blue Eyes | *Okta'lonli* |
| Brave Man | *Hatak'nakni* |
| Careful | *A'hah ah ni* |
| Cedar | *Cham'puli* |
| Chatterbox | *Anumpu'li shali* |
| Day | *Ni'tak* |
| Daylight | *Onna* |
| Eagle | *Ta la'ko* |
| Earth | *Yak'ni* |
| Echo | *Hoba'chi* |
| First-born | *Ti'kba atta* |
| Fox | *Chu'la* |
| Fragrant | *Bala'ma* |
| Good-Humored | *Yuk'pa* |
| Graceful | *Amaka'li* |
| Gray Eagle | *Tala'ko* |
| Gray Eyes | *Okys' onli* |
| Gray Squirrel | *Fani'tasho* |
| Great Wind | *Ma'li chi'tp* |
| Happy | *Yuk'pa* |

371

| | |
|---|---|
| Healer | *Atta'chi* |
| Helper | *A pe la'chi* |
| He Wolf | *Nas'hoba makni* |
| Honey | *Cha'mou lachi* |
| Jester | *Yopu'la* |
| Large Eyes | *Okchi'lali* |
| Lucky | *Imo'la* |
| Night | *Ni'nak* |
| Owl | *O'pa* |
| Peach | *Tok'kon oe tokon* |
| Pine | *Ti'ak* |
| Pure | *Achu'kma* |
| Rain | *Um ba* |
| Rainbow | *Hinak'bite puli* |
| Robin | *Bish'koko* |
| Runner | *Bale'li* |
| She Wolf | *Nasho'ba tek* |
| Small Bluebird | *Okchan'lush* |
| Small (little) Rabbit | *Ku'chas sha* |
| Small Redheaded Woodpecker | *Chil'antak* |
| South Wind | *Oka mali mali* |
| Star | *Fich'ik* |
| Strong Wind | *Mali'kallo* |
| Sunbeam | *Hashto'mi tombi* |
| Sunflower | *Has'hi* |
| Sunrise | *Hashi kucha* |
| Sunset | *Hash okatu* |
| Sweet One | *Akoma'chi* |
| Swift | *Cha'li* |
| Thunder | *Hi'lo ha* |
| To Blow Like Wind | *Mali'* |
| Waterfowl | *Oka hushi* |
| Whirlwind | *Apanu'kfila* |
| Wild Plum | *Tok'kon lushi* |
| Wild Rose | *Kalti ancho* |
| Wolf | *Na sho'ba* |

SHAWNEE—Algonkin family

| | |
|---|---|
| Arrow | *La nah we* |
| Autumn | *Pep one wee* |

| Bear | M'kwah |
|---|---|
| Chief | O'kee mah |
| Day | Kee'sa kee |
| Eagle | Pel ae thee |
| Feather | Meek o nob |
| Flower | Papa kee wa |
| Friend | Nee kah nah |
| Good | O wes sah |
| Lightning | Pa puk ee |
| Snow | Ko nah |
| Summer | Pee ah wee |
| Wolf | M'wae wah |

*PLAINS TRIBES—Principal languages, Caddoan, Siouan, Algonkin, Athapascan, and Uto-Aztecan*

COMANCHE—Uto-Aztecan family
| Arrow | Pa'ark |
|---|---|
| Friend | Hoartch |
| Star | Ta arch |

HIDATSA—Siouan of Hokan-Sioux family
| Golden Eagle | Mai shu' |
|---|---|
| Rose | Mit ska'pa |
| Snowbird | Mad'adaka |
| Young Woman | Mia kaza |

KIOWA—Athapascan family
| Arrow | Ze'bat |
|---|---|
| Beaver | P'o |
| Black Bird | Ta ko'ta couche |
| Brave Man | Nah'tam |
| Flying Squirrel | Cha'hon de ton |
| Keeps His Name | Da'tekan |
| Knife | K'a |
| Medicine Day | Daki'ada |
| No Moccasins | Dohe'nte |
| Otter | A'pen |
| Sleeping Wolf | Gu'i ka'ts |
| Sun Spring | Pai ton |
| Wolf Lying Down | Gu'i kate |
| Yellow Bull | Pa'gu sk'o |

373

PAWNEE—Caddoan family

| | |
|---|---|
| Buffalo | *Tarha* |
| Crow | *Kaka* |
| Earth | *Hura* |
| Friend | *Ir'ari* |
| Mad Chief | *Saritsaris* |
| Moon | *Ko'ru* |
| Sits Among | *Kaku* |
| Sun | *Saku* |
| Walking Women | *Riwi tsapat* |
| White Fox | *Kiwaku* |

OSAGE—Siouan of Hokan-Sioux

| | |
|---|---|
| Fawn | *Ni'abi* |
| Imperial Eagle | *Hon'ga* |
| Younger Sister | *We'he* |

CHEYENNE—Algonkin family

| | |
|---|---|
| Bear | *Nahqui* |
| Bird | *Wi'kis* |
| Friend | *Hoah* |
| Rain | *Hoco* |
| Raven | *Okoka* |
| Robin | *Mai'shi* |
| Sky | *Voha* |
| Star | *Oto ke* |
| Wind | *H'hah* |
| Worker | *I hi'kona* |

ARAPAHOE—Algonkin family

| | |
|---|---|
| Bear | *Whoth* |
| Friend | *Na ter ha ah* |
| Rain | *As son ick* |
| Raven | *Ouo* |
| Sky | *On nah* |
| Star | *Ah thah* |

MANDAN—Siouan family

| | |
|---|---|
| Bear | *Mato* |
| Friend | *Manuka* |
| Rain | *Ye* |

| | |
|---|---|
| Raven | *Keka* |
| Star | *Ykeke* |

**BLACKFOOT**—Algonkin family

| | |
|---|---|
| Arrow | *Aps'si* |
| Berry Woman | *Mi na'ku* |
| Buffalo | *I ni'wa griz* |
| Butterfly | *Apo'ni* |
| Eagle Woman | *Pe'ta ki* |
| Earth | *Chah ko'* |
| Fire | *Is'tsi* |
| Friend | *Nap pe'* |
| Grizzly Bear | *Kyai'u* |
| Moon | *Ko ko mi'kye* |
| Mountain Lion | *O mah ka tai'yu* |
| Night | *Ko'ko* |
| Pretty Head | *A na'tp ki* |
| Running Wolf | *A pe'so muc ca* |
| Star | *Ko'ka to si* |
| Sun | *Na to'si* |
| Sun Woman | *Na'to sa ki* |
| Water | *Oh kiu'* |
| Water Bird | *Sit'so kig* |
| Willow | *Ma nou'* |
| Wind | *Su po'* |
| Wolf | *Ma ku'ya* |

**OMAHA**—Siouan of Hokan-Sioux family

| | |
|---|---|
| Bear | *Mon'chu* |
| Black Wolf | *Shon ga'sab he* |
| Elk | *Opa* |
| Facing Wind | *Ki mon'hon* |
| Fairy Woman | *Migi'na* |
| Graceful Walker | *Mon'ke ne* |
| Gray Owl | *Wa po'ga* |
| He Is Feared | *Mon pe wa'tha* |
| New Moon | *Tai'gi* |
| Sacred Moon | *Mi a kon ca* |
| She Has Victory | *Wa'te win* |
| South Wind | *A ka'wi* |

| Sun Woman | *Mi'he wi* |
| Thunderbird | *Wa gi'om* |
| White Buffalo | *Te'thon* |
| Wind Maiden | *Ta'de win* |
| Wise One | *Wa zhin'ska* |

ASSINIBOIN—Siouan family

| Bird | *Zit' kah nah* |
| Day | *Om pai too* |
| Fire | *Pai tah* |
| Friend | *Codah* |
| Gray Fox | *Toka'na* |
| Hawk | *Chai tun* |
| Knife | *Men'ah* |
| Moon | *How wee* |
| Owl | *Hee hun* |
| Star | *Wee chah pee* |
| Sun | *Om pa wee'* |
| Thunder | *O' Tee* |
| Wind | *Tah tai'* |

DAKOTA OR SIOUX—Siouan of the Hokan-Sioux family

| Afraid | *Iko'po* |
| Antelope | *Ta'toka* |
| Bear with Loud Voice | *Mato po tan'ka* |
| Beautiful Woman | *Wi'was teka* |
| Beaver | *Cha'pa* |
| Beginning | *Toka'he* |
| Bird | *Zit ka la* |
| Black Eyes | *Ista'sha pa* |
| Blue Earth | *Maka'tp* |
| Blue Heron | *Ho k'a to* |
| Blue Jay | *Te'te ni ca* |
| Buffalo Bull | *Ta tan'ka* |
| Butterfly | *Ki'nma* |
| Cat | *I'nmu* |
| Clear Eyes | *Skoso'ta* |
| Clear-sighted | *Mde'za* |
| Covered with Snow | *Wa'akata* |
| Deer | *Tah'cha* |

| | |
|---|---|
| Dewdrop | *Chu'ma ni* |
| Earth | *Maka'* |
| Earth Woman | *Mak'a win* |
| Firefly | *Wan yecha* |
| First-born Daughter | *Wi' nona* |
| Flower | *Wana'hea* |
| Fortunate One | *Waa'nas doka* |
| Friend | *Koda or Kola* |
| Gentle | *Wawa'teca* |
| Good Fortune | *Oglu'was'te* |
| Goose | *Ma'ga* |
| Grizzly Bear | *Ma'to* |
| Hazlenut | *U'ma* |
| Helper | *Wa wo'ki te* |
| Helpmate | *Ta'wasi* |
| Hope | *Wo'ape* |
| Jester | *Iha'ha ka a* |
| Knife | *Mi'na* |
| Little Things | *Watu'tka* |
| Lost Bird | *Zitkala noni* |
| Make a Noise | *Ko'ke la* |
| Make Glad | *Pida'ua* |
| Marksman | *Wa o'ka* |
| Medicine Bear | *Ma'to wa kan* |
| Night Hawk | *Pis ko* |
| Old Buffalo | *Tagu'* |
| One Who Answers | *Was'yupte* |
| One Who Is Accomplished | *Ohi'ka* |
| One Who Shoots | *Wa ku ta* |
| Peace | *Woki'yapi* |
| Place Where the Sun Sets | *Wi yo pi ya ta* |
| Prairie Wolf | *Miya ca* |
| Prophet | *Waa'yate* |
| Red | *Luta* |
| Red Earth | *Matka'sa* |
| Red Fox | *To'ka la luta* |
| Sharp | *Na'sa* |
| Snowdrift | *Wo'gan* |
| Soft Snow | *Wahi'hi* |
| Spider | *Ikto'mi* |

| | |
|---|---|
| Spirit | *Nagi'* |
| Spring | *Mi'mi yowe* |
| Still Silent | *I ni'la* |
| Talks Until the Fire Goes Out | *Waya'sni* |
| Thunder | *Wa'kin yan* |
| To be True | *Wic'haka* |
| Trustworthy | *Zon'ta* |
| Truth | *Wow'ichake* |
| Water | *Mi'ni* |
| Whirlwind | *Tate'iyumni* |
| Wind | *Ta te'* |
| Wind Whistles | *Tete'kes'a* |
| Wisdom | *Wp'ksape* |
| Wisely | *Ik'sa, ua* |
| Worker | *Wo wa'she* |
| Yellow Bear | *Mato'zi* |
| Yellow Bird | *Zitakala zi* |

*NORTHWEST COAST TRIBES—Principal languages Algonkin, Athapascan, Hokan-Sioux, Penutian, and Salish*

NOOTKA, Salish language, somewhat related to Algonkin

| | |
|---|---|
| Crane | *Kwa'lis* |
| East Wind | *Tu'chi* |
| North Wind | *Yo'ati* |
| Red Pine | *Ma'wi* |

*BASIN–PLATEAU TRIBES—Principal languages Uto-Aztecan, Salish and Shahaptian*

YAKIMA—Shahaptian family

| | |
|---|---|
| Beaver | *Yu'ha* |
| Deer | *Ya'mash* |
| Earth | *Ti'cham* |
| Owl | *A'mash* |
| Star | *Has'lu* |
| Wolf | *Lal la'wish* |

SHOSHONI—Uto-Aztecan family

| | |
|---|---|
| Beaver | *Har nitz* |
| Long Shells | *Taw acan* |

378

| Sun | *Tai pe* |
| Water | *Pa ah* |

NEZ PERCE—Shahaptian family

| Dove | *Wi'ta lu* |
| Fox | *Ti'li pe* |
| Wind | *Ha'ti ya* |

*CALIFORNIA TRIBES—Principal languages, Uto-Aztecan, and Penutian, and Hokan Athapascan, also some Algonkin*

HUPA—Athapascan family

| Beaver | *Chwa'ai* |
| Duck | *Na to'ai* |
| Eagle | *Tis'mil* |
| Earth | *Nin nis'tan* |
| Rain | *Na ai'ua* |
| River | *Ga'ni* |
| Wind | *Tse'che* |

*MISSION INDIANS (most of Shoshonean stock, but brought together under the Catholic order of Franciscan Fathers about 1769)*

| Arrow | *To yo* |
| Big Star | *He si comah* |
| Evening | *Co ho le* |
| Moon | *Co mah* |
| Morning | *Hou nah* |
| Rain | *Lu ho lo* |
| Sky | *Woo tcha* |
| Springtime | *Tcha ke he* |
| Sun | *Tu ka* |
| Thunder | *Me me ach* |
| Wind | *To to sah* |

*DESERT TRIBES—Principal languages Uto-Aztecan, Zuñian, Tonoan, Keresan, and Athapascan*

PIMA—probably Uto-Aztecan

| Butterfly | *Yak'imali* |

| | |
|---|---|
| Coyote | *Pan'si* |
| Dust | *Kom'uhi* |
| Eagle | *Pa'haka* |
| Elder Brother | *I itai* |
| Evening | *Ho'dony* |
| Friend | *No'itch* |
| Magician | *Ma'kai* |
| Moon | *Mah'satu* |
| Star | *Ou on* |
| Wind | *Ta tu* |

ZUÑI—Zuñian family

| | |
|---|---|
| Arrow | *S'ho ai lai* |
| Bear | *Iee shai* |
| Beautiful | *E'lu* |
| Bee | *Oh'apa* |
| Blue Jay | *A'yaya* |
| Corn | *Tay'ya* |
| Day | *Yah toh* |
| Eagle | *Kee Ki lee* |
| Earth | *Ah wai ka li nai* |
| Fire | *Mah ke ai* |
| Flower | *U'teyan* |
| Friend | *Kee heh* |
| Lightning | *We lo lon na nai* |
| Little | *Tsa'na* |
| Moon | *Yah o nan nai* |
| Moss | *A'wisho* |
| Owl | *Moo hoo quee* |
| Rabbit | *Ok'shi ko* |
| Rain | *Lo na wai* |
| Rainbow | *A' mitolan* |
| Raven | *Ko ko* |
| Red | *A'hona* |
| Rose | *Mo che ko tai ah wi* |
| Sky | *Ah po yan nai* |
| Sun | *Yah to ke ah* |
| Sunflower | *Om'tsupa* |
| Thunder | *Co lo lan na ni* |
| Wind | *O to keeh* |

HOPI—Uto-Aztecan family

| | |
|---|---|
| Bluebird | *Do li'* |
| Butterfly | *Ka lug* |
| Butterfly Girl | *Po le na na* |
| Eagle Hunter | *Ma'kya* |
| Flower | *Bi ot'ka hi* |
| Flute Maiden | *Len ma'na* |
| Little Star | *So'ya zhe* |
| Morning Star | *So'sto* |
| Mountain Lion | *Nash tu i'tso* |
| Owl | *Nas'cha* |
| Strong Deer | *He's ho'no vi* |
| Sun Girl | *Taw ma na* |
| Yellow Bird | *Sik ya'tsi* |

NAVAHO—Athapascan family

| | |
|---|---|
| Bee | *Tsis na'* |
| Bird | *Tsi'dii* |
| Black Bird | *Ch'agii* |
| Butterfly | *K'aalogii* |
| Crescent Moon | *Dah yita* |
| Day | *Chee'go* |
| Dewdrop | *Doh too* |
| Down Feather | *Bit'so* |
| Friend | *Kwa'ssini* |
| Grizzly Bear | *Shash'tsoh* |
| Hawk | *D'zili* |
| Helper | *Adoo' wolii* |
| Honeybee | *Tsis'na* |
| Humming Bird | *Dah yii'thi* |
| Joy | *Il hozho* |
| Mocking Bird | *Ze'hal anii* |
| Morning Star | *So'tso* |
| Owl | *Nes iah* |
| Robin | *Tee'ihai chi'i* |
| Sky | *Ee yah* |
| Sun | *Cho ko no i* |

APACHE—Athapascan family

| | |
|---|---|
| Arrow | *Kah* |
| Bird | *Hah see* |

| | |
|---|---|
| Chief | *Nanta* |
| Friend | *Skeetzee* |
| Moon | *Clarai* |
| Sky | *S'ah* |
| Sun | *Skee mai* |
| Warrior | *Naium* |
| Wind | *Ooskaz* |
| Wolf | *Mah tzo* |

## PHRASES YOU CAN USE

IN THE ALGONKIN LANGUAGE:

| | |
|---|---|
| *Ke minno iau nuh?* | Are you well? |
| *Aupadush shawaindaugoozzeyun.* | Good luck attend you. |
| *Mitshau muggud.* | It is large. |
| *Ahwanain e-mah ai-aud?* | Who is there? |
| *Ahwanain iau we yun?* | Who are you? |
| *Waigonain wau iayun?* | What do you want? |
| *Waigonain ewinain maundun?* | What is this? |
| *Auneen akeedoyun?* | What do you say? |
| *Auneen dizheekauzoyun?* | What is your name? |
| *Auneende aindauyun?* | Where do you live? |
| *Anuneende azhauyun?* | Where are you going? |

CHEROKEE PHRASES:

| | |
|---|---|
| *Go-sto.* | I am good. |
| *Ga-lo-i-ha.* | I am trying it. |

CHIPPEWA:

| | |
|---|---|
| *Ga wau bu me nem.* | I see you. |
| *Ne wee wau ba muu.* | I wish to see him. |
| *Ne wau bu me goo zee dog.* | Perhaps I am not seen. |
| *Nen ne boau gau.* | I am wise. |
| *Nen du no gee.* | I work. |
| *Ne noon daug.* | He hears me. |
| *Ge mees.* | You gave it to me. |

NAVAHO:

| | |
|---|---|
| *Yishdiah.* | I am laughing. |
| *Yaah?* | What did you say? |

382

| | |
|---|---|
| *T'oo adishni.* | I am just joking. |
| *T'oo afini.* | You are just kidding. |
| *T'oo shoodi.* | Please. |
| *Oolkit dikwiigoo?* | What time is it? |
| *Ndiists'a.* | I understand you. |
| *Hoozhood baa shit.* | I am happy about it. |
| *Hashni'nit.* | Let me tell you something. |
| *Ooj'onli.* | May it be delightful. |
| *Adeeshniit.* | I will do it. |
| *Baa hodeeshnih.* | I will tell you about it. |
| *Ch'eeh deya.* | I am tired, or I am exhausted. |
| *Deeshaal.* | I will go. |
| *Doo nisin da.* | I do not care for it. |
| *Dooleelee.* | I wish it would be. |
| *Doo ndiists'a da.* | I cannot hear you. |
| *Haasha?* | How? |
| *Haisha' anit'j?* | Who are you? |
| *Hozhooniish, hani baa?* | Is it good news? |
| *Na.* | For you. |
| *Nisin doo.* | I do not want it. |
| *Ooshdla.* | I believe it. |
| *T'aadoo shaa nanit'ini.* | Do not bother me. |
| *Yinishye* ———. | My name is ———. |
| *Nizah haa?* | How far is it? |
| *Naninahi, t'aadoo l baa.* | Leave it alone. |

ZUÑI:

| | |
|---|---|
| *Thluwal'emaku.* | Get up, move on. |
| *Hop tona'wakia?* | Where are you? |
| *Ti'nawe.* | Tell him to come. |
| *Te'wunau' sona.* | All right. |
| *Ma'imati?* | What do you wish? |

DAKOTA:

| | |
|---|---|
| *Hou Koda or Hou Kola.* | Greeting, friend. |
| *Echa.* | Well done. |
| *Henala.* | I have spoken. |
| *Chinto.* | Certainly. |
| *Hin yanka po.* | Wait. Hold on. |
| *Hi Hi.* | Thank you. |

| | |
|---|---|
| *Ho hetcetu.* | It is well. |
| *Kuwa.* | Come. |
| *Waste.* | Good, well. |
| *Yekiya wo.* | Let's go. |
| *Ye sin yo.* | Don't go. |
| *Inahkani.* | Hurry. |
| *Kechuwa.* | Dear one/Darling. |
| *Wanunchchun.* | Sorry. |
| *Mah.* | Look here. |
| *Naka'es.* | Of course. |
| *Tu'we hca.* | Who indeed. |
| *Tu la.* | Shame on you. |
| *Toka ce ecanon sni he?* | Why have you not done it? |
| *Toketu he?* | How are you? or How is it? |
| *To'na?* | How many? |
| *Tona ee he?* | Which are they? |
| *Nito nakapi?* | How many are there of you? |
| *He.* | Look here. |
| *Ece. Tuwe kakesa?* | Who would believe it? |
| *E pce'ca.* | I think so. |
| *Han waste.* | Good night. |
| *Hou ke che wa?* | How are you? |
| *Tnau wau an.* | Very well. |
| *Won ne tuo ka?* | Are you tired? |
| *Wi a ka.* | Look there. |
| *Ta ha na dah pe.* | Come here. |
| *Ena ka nee.* | Hurry. |
| *To ke ya nun ka ho wo?* | Where are you? |
| *Wakta ya unpo.* | Watch out. |
| *Hinapa non we.* | Let it be so. |
| *Anpe'tu wi tanyan'hina'pe njnwe'.* | May the sun rise well. |
| *Maka' ozan'zan tanyan.* | May the earth appear. |
| *Hlihe'iciya po.* | Take courage. |
| *Nama'hon ye.* | Hear me. |
| *Epelo.* | I have said it. I have spoken. |
| *O'wakiyin kte.* | I intend to help. |
| *Iho' lena' eanyan'ka yo.* | Behold all these things. |
| *He'camon we?* | Who did it? |
| *Ehan'na.* | A long time ago. |
| *Ta'ku yaka'pelo.* | What you are saying is true. |

| | |
|---|---|
| *Kowa'kipe sni.* | I fear not. |
| *He' conon so?* | Did you do that? |
| *Ini'la.* | Be still. |
| *Tanyan.* | All is well. |
| *Ta'ku ote'hika.* | With all manner of difficulties. |
| *Naya'honpi huwo'?* | Do you hear? |
| *Wanla'ka so?* | Did you see it? |
| *He'camon we?* | Who did it? |
| *Nunwe'.* | So be it. |

# NUMBERS

| NUMBER | TRIBE OJIBWA | TRIBE WINNEBAGO | TRIBE CHEROKEE | TRIBE CHOCTAW |
|---|---|---|---|---|
| One | Ba shik | He Zun ko ra | Sar quoh | Chuffa |
| Two | Neensh | Noomp | Tar lee | Tuk lo |
| Three | Nis we | Taun | Chaw ie | Tu chi na |
| Four | Ne win | Jope | Ner kee | Ush ta |
| Five | Na nun | Sarch | His skee | Tath la pi |
| Six | Nin god was we | Ha ka wa | Su tah lee | Han a li |
| Seven | Nish was we | Sha ko we | Gar le quoh | Un tuk lo |
| Eight | Shous we | Ha roo wunk | Choo na lah | Un ru xhi na |
| Nine | Shang as we | He zun ke choo ne | Law na lah | Chak ka li |
| Ten | Me das we | Ka ra pa ne za | Lar too | Po ko li |

| NUMBER | TRIBE MANDAN | TRIBE ARAPAHOE | TRIBE ASSINIBOIN | TRIBE COMANCHE |
|---|---|---|---|---|
| One | Mayena | Chas sa | Wash ee nah | Sem-mus |
| Two | Nanpash nonpe | Neis | Noompah | Wa-ha |
| Three | Naamene | Nos | Yam min nee | Pa-hu |
| Four | Tobash | Yeane | To pah | Ha-yar ooh wa |
| Five | Guiyyun | Yar thun | Zap tah | Mo wa ka |
| Six | Guima | Nee toh ter | Shak pah | Nah-wa |
| Seven | Kuupa | Nee sor ter | Shak ko wee | Toh a chote |
| Eight | Tottogge | Noh sor te | Shak kan do ghah | Nah wa wa cho te |
| Nine | Moyybe | See au toh | Noom'p chee won kah | Sem mo man ce |
| Ten | Pirogue | Mah toh toh | Wix chem nee nah | Shur mun |

| NUMBER | DAKOTA | CHEYENNE | CADDO | WICHITA |
|---|---|---|---|---|
| One | Wan chah | Nuke | Whis'te | Cherche |
| Two | Nom pah | Ne guth | Bit | Mitch |
| Three | Yah mo nee | Nohe | Dow'o | Daub |
| Four | Ta pah | Nove | He a'weh | Daw'quats |
| Five | Zah pe tah | Noane | Dis'sick kah | Es'quats |
| Six | Shack coope | Nah sa to | Dunk' kee | Ke'hass |
| Seven | Shack o | See so to | Bis'sick ah | Ke' o pits |
| Eight | Shah en do | Noh no to | Dow sick'ah | Ke o tope |
| Nine | Nep e chu wink ah | Soto | He we sick ah | Sherche kui'te |
| Ten | Wick o chimen ee | Moh toto | Bir'neh | Skid'a rash |

| NUMBER | APACHE | NAVAHO | PUEBLO | ZUÑI |
|---|---|---|---|---|
| One | Tah'se tas | Tiah ee | Guih | To pin tai |
| Two | Nah'kee | Nah kee | Guih yet | Quee lee |
| Three | Tai | Tanh | Poh yeh | Hah ee |
| Four | To | Tee | Io nouh | Ah wee tai |
| Five | Astle | Es t'lah | Poh noub | Ahp tsi |
| Six | Kostan | Hsu tah | Sih | To pah lik keeah |
| Seven | Gastede | Soos tsle | Choe | Quil lah lik keeah |
| Eight | Zapee | Tsai pee | Keeh beh | Hi ah lik keeah |
| Nine | Gastai | Nastai | Kual nouh | Ten ah lik keeah |
| Ten | Sesara | Nez nah | Tah eh | Ah'tem hlah |

# MONTHS OF THE YEAR

## WINNEBAGO:

The Winnebagoes had twelve moons for a year. They did not keep an account of the days in a year. The year was divided into summer and winter, and they subdivided the summer into spring and winter into fall. When snow was on the ground it was winter. The season between the time of the melting of the snow and the starting of hot weather was called spring. During the continuance of hot weather they called it summer; and from the appearance of frost to the falling of snow was called fall. Spring was the starting of the year.

They differ somewhat in their names for the moons, but these are the ones generally known:

| | | |
|---|---|---|
| 1st Moon | *Me-two-zhe-raw* | Drying the earth. |
| 2nd Moon | *Maw-ka-wee-raw* | Digging the ground, or planting corn moon |
| 3rd Moon | *Maw-o-a-naw* | Hoeing corn |
| 4th Moon | *Maw-hoch-ra-wee-daw* | Corn tasseling |
| 5th Moon | *Wu-toch-aw-he-raw* | Corn popping, or harvest moon |
| 6th Moon | *Ho-waw-zho-ze-raw* | Elk whistling |
| 7th Moon | *Cha-ka-wo-ka-raw* | Deer running |
| 8th Moon | *Cha-ka-wak-cho-naw* | Deer's horns dripping |
| 9th Moon | *Honch-wu-ho-no-nik* | Little Bear's time |
| 10th Moon | *Honch-wee-hutta-raw* | Big Bear's time |
| 11th Moon | *Mah-hu-e-kee-ro-kok* | Coon running |
| 12th Moon | *Ho-a-do-ku-noo-nuk* | Fish running time |

## CREEK:

The new year of the Creeks commenced immediately after the celebration of the busk ceremony, the ripening of the new corn, in August. The year was divided into two seasons only, winter and summer, and subdivided into successive moons, beginning the winter with the moon of . . .

| August | *Heyothlucco* | The big ripening moon |
|---|---|---|
| September | *Otauwooskochee* | Little chestnut moon |
| October | *Otauwooskolucco* | Big chestnut moon |
| November | *Heewoolee* | Falling leaf moon |
| December | *Thlaffolucco* | Big winter moon |
| January | *Thlaffochosse* | Little winter moon |
| | | Starts the summer moon |
| February | *Hootahlahassee* | Windy moon |
| March | *Tausauthoosee* | Little spring moon |
| April | *Tausutcheelucco* | Big spring moon |
| May | *Kechassee* | Mulberry moon |
| June | *Kocholassee* | Blackberry moon |
| July | *Hoyeuchee* | Little ripening moon |

## DAKOTA:

As with all things in Indian life there were many variations. By the time the white man would write down what he heard, it didn't always agree with all the other things that may have been put down. This is true about the months. Other Dakota or Sioux may have had other names for their months, but again this in one of the more accepted ones:

| January | *Citchi* | Hard moon |
|---|---|---|
| February | *Wicate wi* | Raccoon moon |
| March | *Istawicayazan wi* | Sore eye moon |
| April | *Magaokada* | Moon in which the geese lay eggs |
| May | *Wozupiwi* | Planting moon |
| June | *Wazustecasa wi* | Moon when strawberries are ripe |
| July | *Wasunja wi* | Moon when geese shed their feathers |
| August | *Wasutonwi* | Harvest moon |
| September | *Canwapegi wi* | Moon when the leaves turn brown |
| October | *Wayuksapi wi* | Corn harvest moon |
| November | *Waniyetu wi* | Winter moon |
| December | *Tahecapsun wi* | Moon when the deer sheds its horns |

# INDIAN PRAYERS

**CHIPPEWA PRAYER**

| | |
|---|---|
| *Kaugig ahnahmeauwin* | Ever let piety or prayer |
| *We tebiegadau* | Be the rule of our lives |
| *Gitchy Monedo atau* | The Great Spirit alone |
| *Songee sauge au dan* | Alone let us love |
| *Matche pemaudezewin* | All evil living of mankind |
| *Kaukinna, Kaukinna* | All, all, that's bad or weak |
| *Matche pemaudezdwin* | All evil living as a tainted wind . |
| *Kaukinna wabenundau* | All, let us all forsake. |
| | (literal translation) |

**CHEYENNE PRAYER**

| | |
|---|---|
| *Ehani nah-hiwatam* | He our father |
| *Napave vihnivo* | He hath shown his mercy unto me |
| | In peace I walk the straight road. |

**PAWNEE PRAYER**

| | |
|---|---|
| *Atius* | Father thou |
| *Ha, is-tewat* | Look upon us |
| *Askururit* | Now partake we |
| *Weta tsihakawatsista* | Of the corn with thee. |
| *Nawa Atius* | Now Father |
| *iri ta-titska* | Our thanks be unto thee |
| *iri asuta hawa* | Our thanks renew our plenty |
| *iri rurahe* | Our thanks |
| | Renew these thy gifts to us. |

**OJIBWA PRAYER**

| | |
|---|---|
| *Mish e mon dau kwuh* | I am the Great Spirit of the day |
| *Mis e mon dau kwuh* | The overshadowing power |
| *Ne maun was sa hah kee* | I illuminate the earth |
| *Ne maun was sa hah kee* | I illuminate the heaven |
| *Way, ho' ho ho ho* | |
| *In ah wau how mon e do* | Look thou at the Spirit |

390

| | |
|---|---|
| *In ah wau how mon e do* | It is he that is spoken of who |
| *I au au jim ind* | stays our lives |
| *Gee zhik oong a bid* | Who abides in the sky. |

| | |
|---|---|
| *Ate lena tawa makiye* | Father, all these he has |
| *can makohaza majin hiyeye cin* | made me own, |
| | The trees and the forests |
| | standing in their places. |
| *Le anpetu waste* | This day is good |
| *Aneptu mitawa kon letu nenwe* | May this be the day I consider |
| | mine. |
| *Ateuapi kin* | Thus the father saith, |
| *Maka owancaya* | Lo, he now commandeth |
| *Lowan nisipe-lo* | All on earth to sing |
| *Heya-po* | To sing now |
| *Heya-po* | Thus he has spoken |
| *Oyakapo-he* | Thus he has spoken |
| *Oyakapo-he* | Tell afar his message |
| | Tell afar his message. |

ARAPAHO LULLABY
| | |
|---|---|
| *Cheda-e* | Go to sleep |
| *Nakhu kahu* | Baby dear, slumber, |
| *be be* | Baby. |

## *INDIAN SIGN LANGUAGE*

The Indian sign language is closely related to picture writing. Sign language is believed to have originated in the buffalo country when the tribes came to hunt. They indicated if they were friendly or hostile by gestures. It became so popular that even tribes living close to one another, but speaking a different tongue, would use sign language to communicate with each other, instead of learning the other's language.

One or both hands are used; Indians seldom used facial expressions when using sign language. It must be remembered that one sign could mean several things. The list here is just a sampling of the many signs and terms in this silent speech.

ACROSS—Place the left hand, with back up, about 12 inches out from the body. Pass the partially closed right hand over the left, making a slight curve.

ADD—Place the right hand flat on the palm of the left hand, in front of the body. Lift them both upward several times, up and down about 3 inches, to indicate piling up.

AFRAID—Bring both hands out in front of the body, from chest level. Use only the index finger of each hand, and bring them back a few inches, then slightly downward, having the finger somewhat curved.

AFTERNOON—Form an incomplete circle with the thumb and index of the right hand, then raise it toward a point directly overhead, and sweep down toward the horizon.

ALL—Move the right hand, held flat, in a horizontal circle from right to left. Hold the hand chest-high.

ALL GONE—Point both hands, extended, at each other in front of the chest. Then wipe ends of fingers of right hand across palm and fingers of the left hand the same way.

ALONE—Hold the right hand, using the first finger, upward in front of the neck, then move it outward in sinuous motion.

ANGRY—Place closed right hand near the forehead, with back of thumb at the forehead. Move hand slightly outward and, by wrist action, give a small twisting motion.

ASTONISH—Hold the palm of the left hand over the mouth. Sometimes the right hand is also raised. This denotes great surprise, but at times can mean pleasure or disappointment.

BELOW—With the backs of both hands in front of the body, the left resting on the right, drop the right hand below the left, to indicate distance.

BE STILL (silent)—Put tips of fingers of right hand over lips, and incline head slightly to the front.

BLESS YOU—Raise both hands, palms outward, and the hands pointing front and upward. Lower hands several inches, then push them slightly toward the person indicated.

BRAVE—Hold the left fist about 8 inches from the center of the body, then bring right fist 6 inches above, and a little in front. Strike downward with right fist, using elbow action. Press second joints of the right hand passing close to knuckles of the left.

CALLED (what is your name?)—Use right hand with thumb touching the index finger; snap out index finger toward the person.

CANNOT—Hold left hand flat and edgewise, out in front of the body. Point right index finger at center of left finger. Then move right index finger forward until it strikes left palm, then bounces off and down to right.

CENTER—Make a horizontal circle, with the index finger and thumb of left hand. Then place the tip of right index in circle just formed.

CLOUD—Hold hands, extended horizontally, backs up, and above head. Touch the index fingers, then swing hands downward in a curve to each side. This signifies the sky.

COLD—With both hands closed, and held in front of the body, in front of the shoulder, bend the body slightly, then give a motion of the hands and arms as though shivering from the cold.

COME—Extend first finger of right hand, then move the finger toward the face.

COUNTRY—Point to the ground with the first finger of the right hand, then spread both hands low, and to the right, and left.

CRAZY—Bring closed right hand to forehead, pointing upward. Turn the hand so as to make a small horizontal circle, turning upward toward the sun, and to the left. (To make the word for "medicine," do the same but turn the hand to the right.)

CRY—With first finger of each hand close to eyes, indicate tears by tracing them down the face.

CUT—Bring right hand, held flat, near the chest to right. With an elbow action strike downward to left, then reverse and do the same.

DAYBREAK—Place both hands extended with backs out on a horizontal plane, right hand above, with little finger touching the left index finger. Raise the right hand a few inches.

DEFY—Place thumb between index and second finger of right hand, point it sharply toward the person.

DIRT—Point to ground with one finger.

DOWN—Point downward with right index finger.

DRAW NEAR—With right hand slightly curved, and in front of

393

right shoulder, draw hand downward, then in toward the body. Hold the hand flat and upright.

EARTH—Point with right index finger to the ground, reach down and rub thumb and tip of finger together.

EAT—With right hand almost closed, pass tips of fingers in a curve downward past the mouth two or three times.

FACE—Bring right fist down across the face.

FOLLOW—Palms of the hands facing each other, with left hand a bit ahead, thrust both hands forward in a zigzag motion.

FOREVER—Place the open right hand, palm toward the right side of the head, but just clear of the head, then move it forward and backward twice, past the front and rear of the head.

FRIEND—Hold right hand in front of the neck, palm outward. The index and second finger are extended upward, until the tips of the fingers are as high as the head.

GIVE—Hold right hand flat, pointing to front, palm upward in front of body at about shoulder height. Move hand in and out a few times.

GO—Hold right hand flat in front of body, then extend it quickly, palm upward. Repeat this about three times.

GOOD—Hold the flat right hand, back upward in front of and close to chest, close to left side. Then move hand out quickly to front and right, keeping in a horizontal plane.

GRAB (seize)—Move open hands out in front of the body, then close them quickly and draw them toward the body as if seizing something.

GREAT—Put palms toward each other, then bring extended hands out in front of chest. Separate the hands and repeat.

GREAT HUNGER—Hold the little finger of the right hand edge-wise against the center of the body, then move the finger from right to left as if cutting something in two.

HAIR—Touch the head to denote hair.

HARD—Hold out the left hand with palm upward, strike it with the right fist two or three times.

HEAR—Hold right hand cupped behind right ear.

HEART—Bring closed right hand over the heart, with hand pointing downward.

HEAVY—Hold hands flat in front of body with palms upward. Raise the hands slightly and let them drop a few inches.

HIDE—Hold out left hand pointing obliquely to right. Hold right hand in same relative position pointing at left hand, then pass right down under left.

HIGH—Hold right hand flat with back upward in front of right shoulder. Raise or lower hand to the heights desired to be shown.

HONEST—Hold one finger of the right hand, back up, under the chin and close to the neck. Move the finger straight to the front. This also means straight from the heart or straight from the tongue.

HUSH—Hold hands flat, back upward and in front of body, almost as high as the shoulder. Point fingers to the front, then lower the hand slowly. (This also means quiet down or be quiet.)

I, ME, MYSELF—Extend thumb to touch center of chest.

INCREASE—Hold hand out in front of body, palms facing each other a few inches apart and fingers pointing to front. Separate hands and move them out and apart by gentle jerks.

INFERIOR (in rank)—Index fingers side by side and extended and pointing upward. The finger to represent the inferior is lowered a little. If there are several persons of inferior rank, the right index finger is held a little higher than the extended left finger.

JEALOUS—Hold the hands close and near the chest on each side. Move the right elbow a little to the right and rear, then the left elbow a little to the left and rear. Repeat three times.

JOKE—Hold right hand, back downward, in front of mouth, separate the fingers slightly, keeping them curved and pointing forward. Move the hand to front and upward.

JOY—Hold both hands, fingers partly closed, in front of chest. Keep the palms upward, then move them up and down a few times.

JUMP—Hold the closed right hand near to right shoulder. Then point fingers, with thumbs touching the other fingers, and move hand to front upward and then over and down in a vertical curve.

KEEP—Grasp the left index finger with right hand and move hand slightly to right and left.

KNOW—Hold right hand back up and close to the left side of chest. Sweep hand outward and slightly upward, turning

395

hand by wrist action until the palm is nearly upward, thumb and index finger extended and other fingers closed, move thumb and index fingers horizontal, index pointing nearly left, thumb pointing to front.

LIES (to speak with a forked tongue)—Bring two fingers of the right hand to the right side of the mouth, fingers pointing to the left, then move the hand to the left and past the mouth.

LIGHT—Hold extended hands flat, and back downward, at the height of the chest, and a few inches in front of the body. Put fingers apart, and pointing to front, raise the hands briskly by wrist action a few times.

LOVE—Cross wrists a little in front of the heart, the right nearest the body. The hands should be closed, with backs upward and outward. Press right forearm against the body and left wrist against the right.

MANY—Hold the hands well to the front, fingers curved and pointing to the front; move hands toward each other on a vertical curve downward, then move them slightly upward, as though grasping hands; finish full movement with hands opposite and a few inches apart.

MEET—Hold one finger on each hand opposite each other and pointing upward and toward each other until tips of index fingers meet.

MIRROR—Hold up right hand, with palm flat and facing face, about twelve inches away. (This indicates a hand mirror.)

NIGHT—Hands are extended flat in front of the body, about ten inches apart, the back of the right hand a little higher than the left hand. Move the right hand to the left, and the left hand to the right, then turn the hand just a little.

NO—Hold flat right hand extended, and in front of body, palm upward, fingers pointing to the front and a bit to the left. Swing the hand to the right and front while turning hand, so that thumb is up and the back downward.

PEACE—Clasp the hands in front of the body, with back of left hand down, and right hand placed in palm of left hand.

PEOPLE—Hold up all five fingers of one hand in front of chest.

PLENTY—Hold extended five fingers of both hands well out to right and left, then bring them together, as if gathering up something.

PUSH—Place both fists near the chest, holding arms rigid, then move them a few inches forward.

QUESTION (what, where, when, why, and who)—Hold the five fingers of the right hand palm outward at about shoulder height, fingers and thumb extended and separated, pointing upward. Turn the hand slightly, by wrist action, two or three times. If the person is at a distance, hold the hand higher, and move it from right to left.

RAIN (falling from clouds)—Hold closed hands in front of head, close to each other and to head. With backs up, lower hands a little by wrist action, and while doing so open hands; repeat twice.

RECOVER (from illness or danger)—Place one finger of right hand over chest, back upward, forearm horizontal. Raise the hand until forearm is straight, then turn hand until back is to the front.

RED (face paint)—With fingers pointing upward, rub the right cheek with inside first joint of index finger of right hand. Do this in a circular motion.

SCOLDING (fight or quarrel)—Bring index fingers of both hands pointing upward several inches apart and opposite each other in front of body, level with shoulder. Move right tip of finger toward left tip, then move the left tip of finger toward the right, and repeat several times.

SEIZING HOLD OF—Hold left fist, back to left shoulder, then seize left wrist with right hand, and pull it to the right. Cross wrists in front of body, right on top, with hand closed.

SICK (ache)—Hold all five fingers of right hand in front of body, wave them in and out two or three times to denote throbbing.

SMELL (odor)—Bring two fingers of the right hand, separate, to the chin, backs outward, then by wrist action move the hand upward so that the nose is passed between the tips of the fingers.

STOP—Hold flat right hand, palm outward, in front of body at shoulder height. Move hand sharply to the front and downward, stopping suddenly.

SUN RAYS (hot)—Hold flat hands above head, a few inches

apart, then bring the hands downward, and slightly toward the head.

TAKE—Push the index finger of the right hand well out in front, and to the right of the body. Then pull the hand quickly toward the body, while curving the index finger into a hook.

TASTE—Touch the tip of the tongue with the right index finger.

TELL ME—Open the right hand, placed palm upward, in front of the mouth, then draw it toward the hips in a quick jerk.

THANK YOU—Extend both hands flat, with backs upward, in a sweeping curve, outward and downward toward the person.

THROW AWAY—With both hands closed and held at the side near the chest, drop them downward and to the rear, at the same time opening them, as though expelling something.

TIRED—Hold one finger of each hand together with backs upward, then lower the hands a few inches while drawing them slightly toward the body.

TRADE—Hold up one finger of each hand, then in a semicircle strike them past each other.

UP—Point upward with the index finger of the right hand.

UPRIGHT (stand)—Bring one finger of the right hand to the right and front, and higher than the right shoulder; point the finger upward.

WITH—Hold the left hand flat, with back to left in front, then bring the side of the extended right index finger against the center of the left palm, the index finger pointing to the front.

WIPE OUT—Hold right hand flat in front of body, then wipe flat right hand across body.

WORK—Bring flat hands in front of body, edgewise, a few inches apart. The right hand is higher and to the back of the left hand. Raise and lower the hands by wrist action, to indicate working.

WOUND—Hold one finger of the right hand in front of body, then move the hand briskly toward the body; turn the index finger of the left hand, so that it grazes the surface of the body.

YES—Hold the right hand, with the back to the right, in front of the right breast, about the height of the shoulder. With the index finger, point upward with the other fingers closed and the thumb resting on the second finger. Move the hand a little to the left, and downward, at the same time closing the index finger over the thumb.

YOU—Point one finger of the right hand at the person addressed.

## INDIAN PICTURE WRITING

Records were kept of time and important events by drawing or painting simple pictures or symbols on skin, bark, or stone. This was, in a way, a permanent record of the Indian sign language, for the drawings were made in a way that brought to mind the idea of the thing the Indian was trying to express. Often the picture writing was artistic, and the pictures became symbols. Eventually a few lines came to convey an idea that had formerly required a more complete picture.

Color stood for ideas, and tattooing, in some tribes, was a form of picture writing by marks on the persons face or body. Some persons were tattooed with complete stories as to their exploits and bravery.

The Indian called the white man's writing, "painted speech," because he considered his picture writing as speech also.

Picture writing was used on shields, drum heads, tipis, and tipi linings, and in the records of the Plains Indians called the "Winter Count."

## WINTER COUNT SHOWING OLD METHOD OF STARTING IN CENTER

Winter Count is an Indian calendar or record by picture writing, painted or drawn on a buffalo robe, telling a story of events covering a certain period, person, or family.

This Winter Count tells a story of one family. The story begins in the center at the black tipi showing a bird flying over it. At that time a son was born and as an eagle had flown over the tipi, the baby boy was named Eagle. This is shown by the drawing of a cradle board with the eagle attached to it. Read to the left of the tipi and continue the circle around, until Eagle is shown in full headdress.

This was made on heavy chamois-colored material; the drawings or picture writing were made with black wax crayon

399

# INDIAN PICTURE WRITING

 Ancient bird

 Antelope

 Arrows

 Bad

 Bear tracks

Beaver trail

 Talk

 Bird tracks

 Deer

 Blanket

 Bow and arrow

 Boy

 Brothers

Buffalo

Camp

Boat

 Come

Day

Discovery

Eagle

Evening

Girl

Hear

 Hungry

Hunt

Island

Lightning

Man

Wise man

Medicine man

Morning

Mountains

Night

Three nights

Noon or midday

Peace pipe

Power

Rain cloud

River

Deep snow

Spirit

Star

Sun

Tree

Treaty

Three years

Sunrise

Sunset

Talk or trading

Trade

Top or head man

Wind

Winter weather

Strong

Bright
(Moon and Sun)

Time
(Each circle represents
a year)

War

Clear day

Whirlwind

Woman

Earth lodge

Geese

Hidden

Many buffalo

Eagle

Travois

Turtle

War

Cold and snow  Directions  Camp fire

Peace flag  Pipe  River fight

Sky  Spirit above

Great Spirit above  Singing  Stormy

and then a hot iron was run over the underside to set the crayon. Fur-look fabric was cut in the shape of a skin, including a rolled piece for a tail. The two pieces were then stitched together, or they could be glued. To save expense, a bit of fur-fabric could be stitched along the edge here and there and then put on heavy felt, or an old fur coat or fur piece could be used. India ink could be used for the drawing if a small Winter Count is made. These could be made in miniature for baby announcements, or make a large one as a wall hanging. Use your own symbols and pictures to tell the story of your marriage, your children, or just a summer vacation.

*Interpretation by Spotted Elk of*
*Red Horse Owner's Winter Count*
(Painted in black on a 40"-long deer hide)
(Covers Dates 1786–1953)

1786   First time they saw pine and got the limbs. They brought it back to the camp victorious.
1787   The man hit the game. (A man bet all his possessions except his wife and he lost.)
1788   They killed each other's horses.
1789   First time they rode horseback against the enemy.
1790   They killed a woman (Sioux).
1791   Bear Ear got killed.
1792   Black Stone got killed.
1793   A good white man came.
1794   Little Beaver came.
1795   Same man, second time he came, he got burned.
1796   Tent Stakes came home victorious.
1797   People from here went on a war. A man brought a scalp back with long hair.
1798   A man had smallpox and shot himself.
1799   Measles or some kind of rash.
1800   Crows died and rolled on tipis (because of the cold).
1801   Snow blew into tipis.
1802   Indian artichoke dug out of snowbanks, all they had to eat.
1803   They killed a man with one leg called Lame Duck.

Winter Count
Read left to right, top to bottom
(*See opposite page for explanation*)

1804     Glue froze to death.

1805     Stabber froze to death.

1806     Enemy killed last of the Badgers (man).

1807     They (enemy) came and killed Black Stone.

1808     Many pregnant women died (cold).

1809     The son of Man Big in the Middle died.

1810     Many bands of Indians got together. All had the flags (Rosebud and Standing Rock).

1811     The enemy met and killed a man before he came to them. He was wearing a red coat.

1812     The first time they hunt for wild horses. (Rope them for their own.)

1813     They killed Wita Pahatu with a hatchet.

1814     Indians or chiefs went to Washington, D. C. They all died over there.

1815     War with enemy. They fight with dirt.

1816     There was plenty of meat (buffalo) on the ribs that winter.

1817     First time they saw that kind of blanket. (A blanket with a stripe, popularly called a skunk blanket.)

1818     They fight with the Skutani (another tribe).

1819     They took some prisoners. The Skutani took Sioux prisoners and they went after them angry.

1820     Eight white men came.

1821     First time they saw guns.

1822     They went with white men to attack the enemy.

1823     Little Dog stole horses and brought them back.

1824     Bear Cloud killed a man using the magic power of the bear medicine.

1825     Some died in the flood.

1826     Kaiwa came back sick from spoiled meat. (Three went out, found meat, two died.)

1827     They hunted the buffalo on snowshoes.

1828     They killed the Crow Indians.

1829     Marked Face would not let them (people) go.

1830     Blestan (a white man) came.

1831     He came again and got burned.

1832     They killed some Skutani.

1833     Meteor shower.

1834     They had a fight with the Cheyennes.

| | |
|---|---|
| 1835 | He Wanji Ca fought with a buffalo. |
| 1836 | They fought against a different tribe. |
| 1837 | A man whose name was Part of His Face Painted Red was killed. They took everything. |
| 1838 | Mad Dog prayed. |
| 1839 | We attacked the Pawnee. |
| 1840 | They brought many horses. |
| 1841 | There was drunken fighting. |
| 1842 | Feather Earring prayed. |
| 1843 | They brought something sacred. |
| 1844 | He Crow got killed. |
| 1845 | White Buffalo got killed. |
| 1846 | There were chokecherries that winter. |
| 1847 | Many broke their legs that winter. |
| 1848 | They killed a transvestite. |
| 1849 | Many people had the cramps in the winter. |
| 1850 | Smallpox epidemic. |
| 1851 | They gave them many things. |
| 1852 | The snow was deep. A man sneaked in and they killed him. |
| 1853 | Deer Dung broke his neck. |
| 1854 | They killed thirty white men. |
| 1855 | They went on the warpath and came back victorious but with frozen feet. |
| 1856 | White Beard would not give up his things. |
| 1857 | Good Honor Woman had a child without a father. First time this happened. |
| 1858 | We killed fifteen Pawnee. |
| 1859 | They killed a man carrying a knife. |
| 1860 | Big Crow prayed. |
| 1861 | They stole a big herd of horses. |
| 1862 | They scalped a boy near the camp. |
| 1863 | They killed a man and a woman. |
| 1864 | They were fighting with the white man. |
| 1865 | Many Deers made peace because many died. |
| 1866 | They left the tipi and ran away. |
| 1867 | A writer spent the winter. (Francis Parkman.) |
| 1868 | They killed a man wearing a spotted war bonnet. |
| 1869 | An Omaha Indian was killed. |
| 1870 | The women went after wood and got killed. |

1871 They crossed it with Broken Foot.

1872 They killed one Pawnee.

1873 Red Fish danced the Sun Dance alone.

1874 Utes stole horses.

1875 They made peace with Utes.

1876 They fought with Three Stars. General George Crook (called 3 Stars by Indians). (June month of Custer battle.)

1877 They climbed the sacred hill.

1878 The Cheyennes climbed the hill and they made them stay up there.

1879 Spotted Coyote was killed.

1880 First time they lived in a white man's house.

1881 Chief Spotted Tail died.

1882 They went to look for buffalo.

1883 Last time they went to look for buffalo. Red Kettle broke his neck.

1884 White Buffalo shot a woman.

1885 They shook hands with the train engineer.

1886 Turned Over was shot.

1887 Flat Ground shot somebody by accident.

1888 The issuing of clothes (dishes, blankets, etc.) ended here.

1889 Three Stars came to buy land. (Angelique Fire Thunder was born.) (Crook again.)

1890 Big Foot was killed. (Wounded Knee Massacre.)

1891 The soldiers who walked came (artillery).

1892 Covered Face was run over by a wagon and was killed.

1893 First boarding school at Pine Ridge burned down.

1894 Two Sticks' neck was cut off. (He was hanged.)

1895 They held the first big meeting (Tribal Council).

1896 White Bird died.

1897 Slaughter house burned down.

1898 First time many babies born without a father.

1899 First time the government took the hides back.

1900 Many horses were killed in a storm (May 5).

1901 They had smallpox.

1902 First time they dig in the ground.

1903 Black Kettle went hunting and got killed (It happened

in Wyoming. One woman and her husband, Charlie Smith, killed by officers.)

1904    They started allotting the lands.
1905    Allotment of land.
1906    Allotment of land. Woman had smallpox and died. (Lena Standing Bear, Luther's mother.)
1907    Allotment of land.
1908    Allotment of land. (Red Horse Owner died.)
1909    Allotment of land. Bishop Hare died.
1910    Allotment of land.
1911    Allotment of land. Some cousins killed a deer.
1912    Allotment of land.
1913    Allotment of land.
1914    Allotment of land.
1915    End of allotments. The snow was deep and very cold, much sickness. Bishop Biller died of a heart attack at Rosebud.
1916
1917    World War I. U. S. against Germany.
1918    March 29. William Fire Thunder came back from war.
1919    Victory Dance.
1920    Victory Dance.
1921    Victory Dance.
1922
1923    Horse Dance at Allen. (Red Horse Owner's wife died.)
1924
1925
1926
1927
1928    Sun Dance at Rosebud. Airplane flew over.
1929    Pine Ridge Sun Dance.
1930    Pine Ridge Sun Dance. Meat cooked in tripe with hot stones.
1931    They issue out blankets.
1932    Vaccination.
1933    Civilian Conservation Corps at Allen.
1934    First time they brought buffalo to the CCC camp.
1935    WPA

1936 New Deal.
1937 Vaccination.
1938
1939 Lung X-rays.
1940 John White Wolf killed in auto accident.
1941 Jan. 26. Stella Even Galligo died. U. S. declared war on Japan. Germany and Italy declared war on U. S. Trachoma.
1942 Jan. 4. Charles Dubray froze to death.
1943
1944
1945 Germany surrendered. Roosevelt died. Japanese surrendered.
1946 Victory Dance.
1947 Chest X-ray.
1948
1949 Timothy Iron Bear electrocuted in Lincoln, Nebr. 34 below zero, much snow. Many Indians ride in airplane. Airplane brought relief for Indians.
1950
1951
1952
1953

# INDEX

411

414

415

416